DEVELOPING SUPERVISORS AND TEAM LEADERS

IMPROVING HUMAN PERFORMANCE SERIES

Series Editor: Jack J. Phillips, Ph.D.

DEVELOPING SUPERVISORS AND TEAM LEADERS

DONALD L. KIRKPATRICK

BUTTERWORTH
HEINEMANN

Boston   Oxford   Auckland   Johannesburg   Melbourne   New Delhi

Library of Congress Cataloging-in-Publication Data

Kirkpatrick, Donald L.
  Developing supervisors and team leaders / Donald Kirkpatrick
     p. cm.—(Improving human performance series)
  Includes bibliographical references and index.
  ISBN 0-87719-382-7 (alk. paper)
    1. Supervisors—Training of. 2. Supervision of employees—Study and teaching. 3. Supervisors—Training of—Case studies. 4. Supervision of employees—Study and teaching—Case studies. 5. Teams in the workplace—Management—Study and teaching. I. Title. II. Series.

HF5549.12 .K568 2000
658.4'07124—dc21

                                                                                    00-064047

British Library Cataloguing-in-Publication Data
A catalogue record for this book is available from the British Library.

The publisher offers special discounts on bulk orders of this book.
For information, please contact:
Manager of Special Sales
Butterworth–Heinemann
225 Wildwood Avenue
Woburn, MA 01801–2041
Tel: 781-904-2500
Fax: 781-904-2620

For information on all Butterworth–Heinemann publications available, contact our World Wide Web home page at: http://www.bh.com

10 9 8 7 6 5 4 3 2 1

Printed in the United States of America

5/23/04

CONTENTS

3

PHILOSOPHY, STRATEGY, AND GUIDING PRINCIPLES 14

4

CONDITIONS FOR MAXIMUM LEARNING BY SUPERVISORS 30

5

DETERMINING TRAINING NEEDS AND SETTING OBJECTIVES 47

10

ON-THE-JOB PERFORMANCE APPRAISALS

11

COACHING FOR IMPROVED PERFORMANCE

12

Selecting and Training New Supervisors 212

Part II
Case Studies of Specific Programs 239

13

A Comprehensive In-House Program 241

14

Coaching to Win: A Management Training Program 252

15

A 10-Day Certificate Program for Supervisors

Management Institute, University of Wisconsin,
   Milwaukee, Wisconsin, 271
Summary, 277

16

An Evaluation of a Training Program

Management Institute, University of Wisconsin,
   Milwaukee, Wisconsin, 279
Summary, 299

17

A Front-Line Leadership Development Program

GE Medical Systems, Milwaukee, Wisconsin, 302

18

A Leadership Development Program

First Indiana Bank, Indianapolis, Indiana, 315
Shipboard Rules for Smooth Sailing, 318
Course Overview, 318
Before the Next Lab, 321
Cruise to Leadership Evaluation Form, 322
Cruise to Leadership Final Evaluation Form, 323

FOREWORD

I can't think of anyone better equipped to take us through the ins and outs of supervisory training and development than Donald L. Kirkpatrick. His many hats as a training manager, author, consultant, professor emeritus, and past president of the American Society for Training and Development (ASTD) have provided Don with a wealth of experience in how to train supervisors. Given the fact that 86 percent of organizations with 1,000 to 10,000 employees offer supervisory skills training, this book should be a vital addition to your HRD reading shelf.

Don sees training not as an expense but as an investment. When the need is properly researched and the training sessions are designed to produce improved performance, the return on investment will greatly exceed the cost of training. Throughout the book, numerous case studies, forms, checklists, and assessments serve to document the process of designing and delivering high-impact supervisory training programs.

I'm particularly impressed by Don's infinitely readable writing style. It's crisp. To the point. No wasted words. It's as if I were inside his head as we traversed each train of thought. Or, perhaps more accurately, he was inside *my* head, anticipating my need to know and giving me just the right amount of information and illustration to meet that need.

It gives me great pleasure to commend another book from the hand of Donald L. Kirkpatrick.

Scott Parry
Chairman, Training House
Princeton, N.J.

PREFACE

Supervisory training and development continues to be a major concern in organizations of all types and sizes. Training and human resources professionals consider this to be one of their top priorities. Changes of all kinds necessitate continuous updating of knowledge and skills, as well as changes in attitudes. The situation is common, not only to industry but also to government, hospitals, and retail organizations. The question is "how to do it effectively" and not "whether it should be done."

The term *supervisor* has been used throughout this book to describe the first level of management, whether in an office or in a factory. In some organizations, it would be synonymous with the term *foreman*. Emphasis has been placed on "how to do it" by describing practical principles, techniques, and examples. In the last section of the book, 10 case studies describe what a variety of organizations are doing to train and develop their supervisors.

The terms *training* and *development* are usually used together. I have not tried to distinguish between the two. In general, the term *training* refers to the teaching of specific knowledge and skills required on the supervisor's present job. The term *development* is broader and contributes to the growth of the individual and preparation for higher-level jobs.

The principles and techniques described in this book are designed to meet the challenges that face supervisors in the new millennium. Four of the most common ones are: diversity in the work force; the need for quality improvement; employee empowerment, with emphasis on self-directed work teams; and teamwork.

All organizations have had and always will have diversity in the work force. Not only are there differences in race and gender, but also in attitudes, education, emotional stability, skills, and many more physical and personality traits. I have been conducting training classes since 1949, and I have always emphasized the need to understand employees and respect their differences. The same need exists today and will exist in the future. The current emphasis reflects the increasing percentage of the work force made up of women, minorities, immigrants, and the disabled—which makes training in this area particularly important.

The principles of training, however, remain the same. The whole concept of "determining needs" is based on the challenge to help supervisors be more effective by giving them the knowledge and skills they need. This certainly includes the importance of understanding their employees. Programs on such issues as human relations and leadership are designed to change attitudes, as well as to teach important knowledge and skills.

There is also nothing new about the need for quality improvement. Organizations have always had an objective of producing products that meet the quality standards their customers require. They have had to balance quality with quantity, cost, and the schedule requirements of their customers. With increased competition from Japan and other nations, they have had to upgrade their quality standards or else go out of business.

One of the first concerted efforts to achieve a quality standard was to adopt the "Quality Circle" concept, which had been so successful in Japan. Getting employees to participate in improving quality (as well as reducing cost, improving productivity, and making other improvements) was the basic approach. Many organizations then realized that even more needed to be done, so they implemented "statistical process control" (SPC) as recommended by W. Edwards Deming. Currently, "total quality improvement" and "Total Quality Management" have been widely accepted as a philosophy and implemented in many organizations. Because of these changes, "quality" has received a high priority in determining the training needs of supervisors.

The terms *leadership, empowerment,* and *self-directed work teams* have become buzzwords in books, articles, and the language of business and industry. Warren G. Bennis has expounded the philosophy that *manager* and *leader* are separate and distinct terms. In doing so, he has obviously used the term *manager* to describe a certain type of manager who is not a leader. This simply emphasizes what we training professionals have always tried to do: develop and improve leadership qualities in supervisors and in higher-level managers. As for the term *empowerment*, this has simply added another dimension to the ideas of "participation" and "involvement," which have been emphasized for many years.

There are four basic approaches a supervisor can use in making decisions. The following approaches should consider the quality of the decision, as well as acceptance by those who will implement it:

1. Decide without getting any input from subordinates.
2. Ask subordinates for input, consider it, and then decide.
3. Conduct a problem-solving meeting with subordinates and lead them in reaching a consensus.
4. Give subordinates the power/authority to make decisions without the leadership/influence of the supervisor.

The last of these approaches is "empowerment" with the formation of "self-directed work teams." In his 1981 book, *The Change Resistors,* George S. Odiorne stated, "The best option for change is one created by the people who must implement it, or one for which the implementers can claim ownership." In 1963, Norman R. F. Maier emphasized the need for involvement. He stated that the greater the need for acceptance on the part of those implementing a decision, the more the need for participation. "Quality Circles" are built on involvement. The only thing new about empowerment is the degree to which employees participate.

Some organizations have found involvement to be very effective in terms of improving quality, increasing productivity, reducing costs, and otherwise benefiting the organization. They have also found that it has improved morale and the quality of work life (QWL). Other organizations, however, have found that using empowerment has *not* been successful. I think it is a mistake to describe empowerment as the answer to all productivity and morale problems or to recommend it without reservations. In some cases, a stated objective is to eliminate a level of management.

I strongly urge top management to be very cautious in implementing a "self-directed work team" approach. They should consider the following factors in deciding how much of the "empowerment" approach to adopt and force on their supervisors:

- The culture of the organization
- The urgency of the decision
- The scope of the decision
- The need for acceptance by those who will implement the decision

■ The attitudes of the employees toward the idea of helping the organization

■ The qualifications of the subordinates in terms of knowledge and experience

■ The desire of the employees to participate

I like the words used in a policy statement by Honeywell, which encourages supervisors/managers to delegate decision making to the lowest *appropriate* level. This encourages involvement and possibly empowerment, but still gives supervisors/managers the authority to decide what is appropriate.

In addition to diversity in the work force, total quality improvement, and empowerment, much emphasis is being placed on the need for teamwork. This requires special attention, especially by top management. Supervisors are under pressure to build teamwork among their employees, while top management frequently does not practice it. The following example illustrates the point. In my "Management Inventory on Managing Change" test, I include the following item to be answered "agree" or "disagree" by supervisors:

Most managers in my organization would welcome ideas and suggestions from people in other departments.

I have been surprised and disappointed to find that 89 percent of the supervisors who answered this question, marked "disagree"—and these supervisors were from organizations that send supervisors to management training programs. It is a terrible indictment of top management that most of them won't even listen to ideas and suggestions from others. The discussion of the item revealed that most managers put up a barrier with such attitudes as: "If I want your advice, I'll ask for it," "Don't tell me how to run my department," or "What makes you think you are qualified to offer me advice on how to run my department?" These same managers were also instructing their supervisors to build teamwork!

It is also interesting that all of the supervisors who completed the "Management Inventory on Managing Change" test answerd "agree" to the following item:

Managers should welcome ideas and suggestions from all sources.

The difference between this item and the previous one is the substitution of the word *should* (theoretical) for *would* (actual).

Upper-level managers must exemplify teamwork if they expect their supervisors to build it in their departments. Training managers must impress this upon their upper-level managers, in addition to training supervisors, in principles and techniques for building teamwork.

The title of this book, *Developing Supervisors and Team Leaders*, was chosen because most of the concepts, principles, and techniques apply to team leaders, whether or not they are supervisors.

This book was written especially for human resources and training professionals, as well as for executives and middle-level managers. It describes classroom programs as well as on-the-job approaches, including performance appraisal and coaching. Many references have been included. A number of them are from years past, but they have been included because the concepts, principles, and techniques are not out of date. Of special interest will be the description of the comprehensive books listed in the Bibliography.

ACKNOWLEDGMENTS

I am grateful to the late Dr. Russell Moberly, who hired me right out of college to teach supervisory training courses at the Management Institute, University of Wisconsin in Madison. I am also indebted to Brad Boyd, Earl Wyman, Ron Bula, and the late Norm Allhiser, with whom I worked at the Management Institute, both in Madison and in Milwaukee. In addition, I'd like to thank my many friends and colleagues associated with the American Society for Training and Development who have contributed to my knowledge and growth.

I am also grateful for the support given me by my wife, Fern, and by two of my children, Sue Muehlbach, senior training manager at Hartford Life Insurance Company in Minneapolis, and Jim Kirkpatrick, Organizational Effectiveness manager at First Indiana Bank in Indianapolis.

Finally, I'd like to thank the good Lord for giving me the gifts and talents to teach and write.

Donald L. Kirkpatrick
2000

PART I

PLANNING, IMPLEMENTATION, AND EVALUATION

1

THE IMPORTANCE OF SUPERVISORY TRAINING AND DEVELOPMENT

Very few organizations are satisfied with the performance of their first-level supervisors and foremen. Research conducted at the University of Wisconsin's Management Institute indicates that supervisors are 50 to 65% effective—as evaluated by mid- and top-level managers. The main reasons cited for such limited effectiveness are that they lack:

- A clear understanding of what is expected of them.
- The proper attitude and motivation to do their best.
- The knowledge and skills that are necessary to do the job.

Which of these causes for inadequate performance can be corrected by effective training and development? The first one—not understanding what is expected—is a communication, not a training, problem. It can be corrected by clear and complete communication between supervisor and boss. The second condition—poor attitude or lack of motivation—can be improved through training and development. And the third—lack of knowledge and skills—clearly can be corrected by effective training.

IMPROVING PERFORMANCE OF CURRENT DUTIES

Training and development can be important in improving the performance of supervisors in their jobs as they now exist. Attitudes, knowledge, and skills can all be improved. Such improvement can change the job behavior of supervisors, thus producing better performance and results.

Recently, I conducted a short training course for supervisors at a small Wisconsin shoe manufacturer. The objective of the program was to reduce turnover, and the main focus was on effective induction and training of new employees. At the end of the program, we evaluated it by asking the participants for their reactions. They were less than enthusiastic. Typical comments indicated that "the ideas that Kirkpatrick expressed were good, but they don't agree with the way things are done here."

These reactions prompted a research study in which I was asked to interview supervisors to determine their attitudes toward the company as well as to extract their recommendations. In the personal interviews, I asked four questions:

1. How do you feel about your job?
2. How do you feel about the company?
3. What are your main problems in doing your job?
4. What suggestions do you have for improvement in the company?

The earful of complaints I received about many aspects of the company reflected a general feeling of frustration and low morale on the part of the supervisors—negative attitudes that were probably reflected in the attitudes and performance of their subordinates. Clearly, the attitudes of these supervisors, as well as their knowledge and skills, had to be improved if the morale and productivity of the workers were to be improved.

After I completed the interviews, I gave the company executives a report. They began to take steps to correct the policies, procedures, and practices that were causing poor supervisory attitudes.

This foregoing example illustrates three points about supervisory training and development:

- The attitudes of supervisors can have a significant impact on the effectiveness of the program. I'm sure that my ideas and recommendations were not accepted by the supervisors of the shoe manufacturing company because of existing management policies and practices that had created low morale.
- Negative attitudes of supervisors must be changed if the workers are expected to improve performance and increase productivity.
- Negative supervisory attitudes can't be corrected in the classroom if they reflect unsatisfactory job conditions such as low pay, inadequate work forces, poor management policies, delays in getting raw materials, and excessive pressures for production.

The main thrust of supervisory training and development should be to improve the performance of a supervisor on the current job. Attitudes, knowledge, and skills can be improved and immediate payoff obtained in improved performance and productivity of the workers they supervise.

Improving Performance of Future Duties

A second need for training and development exists if the job of the supervisor is changing along with changes in the organization. The content of this training should include both the technical and managerial aspects of the supervisor's job. In the technical area, a supervisor may need to learn more about computers, automatic equipment, quality control, the labor agreement, raw materials, manufacturing processes, and other technical subjects related to the job and the department. The managerial aspects may focus on the latest and best approaches in such areas as leadership, motivation, decision making, performance appraisal, quality improvement, and teamwork, as well as employee involvement and empowerment.

New training needs emerge if the current supervisor is being considered for a higher level position. These, of course, are related to the job of middle-management instead of first-level management. The technical needs may include an increased understanding of computers, automation, statistical process control (SPC), and just-in-time (JIT) management.

Managerial training topics might include organization development, personnel planning, delegation, styles of leadership, decision making, and strategic planning. These are in addition to a better understanding of motivation, communication, the development of subordinates, and the quality of work life (QWL). The higher the level of the manager, the more emphasis should be placed on managerial skills as opposed to technical knowledge.

SUMMARY

Supervisory training and development are needed for three main reasons. First, training can improve attitudes, knowledge, and skills, as well as increase personal effectiveness and that of the department. Second, the jobs of most supervisors will be different in the future. Therefore, new knowledge—technical and managerial—must be acquired in order to perform effectively the first-level management job.

Finally, as some supervisors are promoted to middle-management jobs, training and development can prepare them for an effective performance on the new job when the promotion occurs.

Time and money spent on supervisory training and development are not an expense. They are an investment in the future of the organization in the recognition that people are an organization's most important asset. Benefits should be viewed as a return on the investment. The extent of the benefits will depend on many of the factors that are covered in this book.

Benefits to the supervisor can include improved attitudes, knowledge, skill, performance, and rewards. Benefits to the organization can include increased productivity, improved quality, reduced costs, improved morale, and greater profitability.

It must be mentioned that training may not be the answer to improving supervisory performance. The well-known Peter Principle[1] (that every employee tends to rise to his or her level of incompetence) must be considered. The term *incompetent* implies that no amount of training or coaching will help. In these cases, the supervisor must be removed from the job, or the job must be modified to fit the supervisor.

---

[1]Laurence Peter and Raymond Hull, *The Peter Principle* (New York: Morrow Publishing Co., 1969).

2

RESPONSIBILITY AND AUTHORITY FOR SUPERVISORY TRAINING

Four different people in an organization can be held responsible for the training and development of a supervisor: the supervisor, his or her boss, top management, and the training professional.

The supervisor. It is generally agreed that each supervisor is responsible for his or her own development. While some supervisors accept the entire responsibility and lay out their own program for self-development, the majority do not. Therefore, it is not advisable for organizations to adopt the philosophy that development is the sole responsibility of the supervisor.

The boss. It is a well-accepted principle that every boss is responsible for the development of subordinates. This seems logical because the boss is responsible for the performance of subordinates, and that performance depends largely on their training and development. Most job descriptions for a department head, superintendent, or other middle-management job spell out the responsibility for training and developing subordinates, with particular emphasis on improving performance on the current job.

Top management. Policymaking executives in an organization have a special responsibility for the training and development of first-line supervisors. They must also provide the proper climate for growth and development, as well as provide time and money. If the organization is large enough, professional staff should be added to the payroll to plan and implement effective training programs. Professional staff may be full-time training and development specialists. In smaller organizations, the personnel or human resources manager may be assigned this responsibility along with employment, salary administration, and other duties.

The training professionals. Training professionals are paid to see that effective training is carried out. They, too, are responsible for seeing that supervisors are properly trained to do their jobs. As "experts," they should understand how supervisors learn and realize the type of training that will help them reach their maximum potential. Their success depends on their ability to work effectively with managers without the power to force their ideas and programs on line management. Influence, not power, is their key to success.

If supervisors, bosses, policymaking executives, and training professionals all carry out their responsibilities, chances are great that supervisors will be effectively trained and developed. In accomplishing these results, it is important to recognize the amount of authority that accompanies the responsibilities.

The Supervisor

The fact that supervisors have much of the responsibility for their own personal development does not necessarily mean that they also have the authority for it. On personal time, of course, they can attend seminars, read books, or take correspondence courses. They probably would not have the authority, however, to spend the company's money or take off a workday to attend a seminar.

THE BOSS

Bosses, on the other hand, usually have much authority. Most of them can send supervisors away for a day or a week to attend a seminar on company time. They can also assign supervisors books to read and give them special job assignments in order to improve knowledge and skills. In other words, bosses have the authority to tell their subordinates what to do and when to do it, and they can usually commit company money and time.

TOP MANAGEMENT

Top executives also have the additional authority to establish policy and approve budgets. They must make it clear that they support supervisory training and development and establish a written policy that explains their philosophy. Budgets for training and development should reflect their support, and these budgets should not be trimmed indiscriminately when business becomes slow. Some organizations clearly demonstrate their lack of commitment to training and development when training professionals are the first to be terminated when profits or budgets are reduced. Top executives must recognize and support the idea that training is an investment, not an expense.

In addition to a written policy and adequate budgets, top executives must provide company time for supervisors to attend training classes. This shows that supervisory training will benefit the organization, as well as the supervisors who receive it. Such a commitment to training creates positive attitudes on the part of supervisors. These positive attitudes are necessary if maximum benefit is going to be realized from the time and money spent.

Tuition refund plans should be established to pay all, or nearly all, of the expenses for training courses that supervisors complete on their own time. Three possible approaches are:

1. The organization pays all fees if the course is completed with a passing grade. The supervisor pays for and keeps all books that are required.

2. The organization reimburses tuition costs as follows:

  - If the supervisor gets an A: 100%
  - If the supervisor gets a B: 90%
  - If the supervisor gets a C: 80%
  - If the supervisor gets a D or F: 0%

  The supervisor pays for and keeps books that are required.
3. The organization reimburses 75 percent of the tuition cost if the supervisor passes the course. The supervisor pays for and keeps books that are required.

Many modifications of these approaches are used by various organizations. Examples are described in Chapter 6 under "Educational Assistance Programs."

In all of these approaches, the organization pays most of the costs, while the supervisor spends some of his or her own money and time. The organization strongly supports training and development but expects the supervisor to contribute something because both parties benefit from the training.

TRAINING PROFESSIONALS

Training professionals have no authority over the training and development of supervisors. They must sell ideas to the boss as well as to the supervisors themselves. Influence must substitute for authority.

Four possible approaches that training professionals can use are to: (1) provide whatever help the line manager requests; (2) help the line manager determine the training needs of the department and help develop a program to meet these needs; (3) develop an effective training program and sell it so that the line manager will want it; and (4) develop an effective training program and sell it to top management so that line management will not dare disapprove.

Let's look at these four possibilities, one at a time:

1. **Provide help as requested.** This is a desirable approach, especially if line managers are sold on training. If enough line managers are desirous of help, the staff professionals do not need to do any selling—they will be kept busy providing training help as requested. The professionals must be sure that the training is effective. When other line managers learn about the effective program, they will also request training help. At some point, the training department may be

expanded to meet the needs. Line managers who are being served will be most supportive of such staff additions. This is an in-house consulting approach.

2. **Assist in determining and meeting needs.** This approach, part selling and part providing help as asked, can be very successful. The professional should stimulate the line manager to think about problems and help determine which problems can be solved, in whole or in part, by training activities. The professional is helping the line manager solve problems. In so doing, he must communicate and sell training know-how and capabilities to the line manager. The line manager will use training professionals if it will help meet objectives without costing too much time or money.

Three strong qualities needed to implement this approach are

- A thorough knowledge of training principles, approaches, and available resources
- Skill in selling ideas
- The ability to deliver a quality program

A professional with these qualifications can be very successful. Line managers are usually willing to give this kind of a staff person a try. If the results are good, they will probably ask more supervisors to go through the program. And one line manager will tell another that it is a good training program. As long as line managers are convinced that the professional is providing a service that is worth the time and money, they will continue to ask for help. This is also a consulting approach.

3. **Develop a training program and sell it.** The success of this approach depends on the training professional's ability to develop or purchase a training program and to sell it to line management. The staff person should be sure that the program meets the needs of the supervisor. One of the best ways is to involve line managers (and perhaps the supervisors themselves) in the decisions related to the program.

For example, several alternative proposals can be made to line managers, and the final decision can be left to them. Or the professional can recommend and sell a specific program that he or she is confident will meet the needs. Obviously, a history of successful programs will make it much easier to sell programs to line supervisors.

Therefore, the professional should do a thorough job in planning programs that will be effective.

4. Develop a training program and force acceptance. Some professionals are able to carry out their training responsibility by enjoying the status and power that make line managers reluctant to refuse help. Under this approach, the training professional develops a program, sells it to the top executive, and then puts it into operation. Line managers will participate whether they think it's effective or not.

The initial program may get started because managers don't dare refuse to participate. If it is successful, the situation can change into one of the three that have been described. Power and status may become irrelevant, and the professional will be effective because of the acceptance and enthusiasm of line management. If the initial program is ineffective, however, the status and power of the professional will disappear, and one of the other approaches must be used.

SUMMARY

The responsibility for the training and development of first-line supervisors should be shared among supervisors, bosses, top management, and training professionals. Supervisors should be responsible for wanting to improve and for requesting assistance. They should also be willing to contribute some time and money for personal growth.

The boss has the responsibility and the authority to stimulate, encourage, assist, and follow up to see that proper training is given. The boss has the responsibility and the authority to stimulate, encourage, assist, and follow up to see that proper training is given. The boss should be held accountable for the on-the-job development of subordinates.

Top management must provide the climate, philosophy, policies, time, and money for supervisory training and development. If the organization is large enough, professionals should be hired to plan and implement effective training programs. The training professionals must also have the responsibility (usually without authority) to see that effective training is accomplished.

3

PHILOSOPHY, STRATEGY, AND GUIDING PRINCIPLES

To be effective in training and developing supervisors, it is important to have and communicate philosophy, strategy, and policies related to the development of employees. This chapter offers examples from five well-known and respected organizations.

DANA CORPORATION, TOLEDO, OHIO

Following are some of the policies of the Dana Corporation that relate to the selection and training of supervisors as presented by Larry Lottier, the dean of Dana University's Business School.

People

We are dedicated to the belief that our people are our most important asset. Wherever possible, we encourage all Dana people within the entire world organization to become shareholders or, by some other means, to own a part of their company.

We believe that people respond to recognition, freedom to participate, and the opportunity to develop. We also believe that people should be involved in setting their own goals and judging their own performance. The people who know best how the job should be done are the ones doing it.

People at Dana should accept only total quality in all tasks they perform, and endorse productivity plans that allow people to share in the rewards of productivity gains. All Dana people should identify with the company, and this identity should carry on after they have left active employment. Facilities with people who have demonstrated a commitment to Dana will be competitive and thus warrant our support.

Wages and benefits are the concern and responsibility of managers. The Management Resource Program is a worldwide matter—it is a tool that should be used in the development of qualified Dana people. We encourage income protection, health programs, and education. On-the-job training is an effective method of learning. A Dana manager must prove proficiency in at least one line of our company's work, such as in marketing, engineering, manufacturing, or financial services. Additionally, these people must prove their ability as supervisors and be able to get work done through other people. We recognize the importance of gaining experience both internationally and domestically.

Our people should move across product, discipline, and organizational lines. These moves should not conflict with operating efficiency. We believe in promoting from within. Dana people interested in other positions are encouraged to discuss job opportunities with their supervisor.

Managers are responsible for the selection, education, and training of all people. All Dana people should have their job performance reviewed at least once a year by their supervisors.

Ultimately, we provide programs to support the Dana Style, and we encourage the professional and personal development of all Dana people.

Organization

We discourage conformity, uniformity, and centralization. At Dana, there is a minimum number of management levels.

Responsibility is, therefore, pushed as far into the organization as possible. Organizational structure must not conflict with doing what is best for all of Dana.

We stress an organizational structure that allows the individual maximum freedom to perform and participate. This is intended to stimulate initiative, innovation, and the entrepreneurial spirit that is the cornerstone of our success. We also offer small, highly effective, support groups to service the specialized needs of the Policy Committee and the world organization at large, as requested. At Dana, there are task forces rather than permanent staff functions. We don't have company-wide procedures. If an organization requires procedures, it is the responsibility of the manager to create them.

Communication

We communicate regularly with shareholders, customers, Dana people, the general public, and financial communities. It is the job of all managers to keep Dana people informed. Each manager must decide on the best method of communication. Direct communication with all of our people eliminates the need for a third-party involvement. All managers shall periodically inform their people about the performance and plans of their operation.

FLORIDA POWER CORPORATION, ST. PETERSBURG, FLORIDA

According to V. W. Thurn, Manager of Employee Development at Florida Power Corporation, effective training could be defined as a process that enables persons to do something they could not do before they were subjected to that process.

Properly designed training is job-related and changes on-the-job behavior if the immediate supervisor stimulates the employee's interest. The training must be reinforced by line management.

The modern concept of training is therefore seen to be performance-oriented and is based on sound principles of learning. It is aimed at achieving behavioral change in order to meet clearly defined organizational job needs.

Performance Orientation

To be effective, training must have supervisory involvement in order to improve job performance. It is essential, when preparing any training program, that the job be analyzed carefully. This analysis will determine what the learners must do and what they need to know to be able to perform effectively.

Principles of Learning

Educational and industrial psychologists have, as a result of their extensive research, been able to establish that learning depends mainly upon three factors: the learner, the learning resources, and the learning technique.[1]

1. *The learner.* The learner decides if he or she will learn. It is therefore essential to provide a learning situation that motivates the learner. This is best achieved by satisfying the learner's needs for accomplishment, responsibility, and recognition during the learning process.
2. *The learning material/resources.* To ensure that learning is effective, the learning material/resources must be meaningful, presented in logical sequence, and in optimum-size steps (not too big or too small).
3. *The learning technique.* The following points are important when selecting a learning technique:

   - Learning is most effective when it is applied in practice. Passive learning should be avoided and active participation encouraged.
   - A feedback system should be built into any program.
   - Feedback must be an ongoing process and should enable learners to identify and correct their own errors.
   - Learning is reinforced by practice, and controls should be reduced as performance improves.
   - Those in control of the learning environment should provide direction during the learning process and should not attempt to control it.
   - The learner should be encouraged to practice what he or she has learned in as many different situations as needed.

---

[1]Carl Rogers, *Freedom to Learn: A View of What Education Might Become* (Columbus, Ohio: Charles E. Merrell, 1969).

Learning Objectives

If learning is to be effective, it is important that the learner and the trainer should know precisely what is required on the job. Clearly defined objectives stating the performance/action required, the conditions, and the required standards are essential. The Criterion-Referenced Instruction (CRI) approach developed by Mager and Pipe has been the basis of the process we used.[2]

Systematic Approach

A systematic approach is shown in Figure 3-1. The terms are used as follows:

- **Diagnosis**—An analysis of a performance problem in order to determine whether training is the most economic and effective method of improving performance.
- **Preparation**—What takes place after training has been selected as the best solution. Course developers determine the objectives using analysis data and performance standards, measure existing skills, and select the method of measuring when competence has been achieved by each learner.

Figure 3-1. *A systematic approach to training programs*

---

[2]P. Pipe, *Objectives—Tool for Change* (Belmont, Calif.: Pitman Learning, 1975).

- *Development*—Selection of the best learning materials, techniques, and strategies. The feedback system is considered during this state and is an integral part of any well-designed training program.
- *Implementation*—Testing the training program or system on members of the targeted population.
- *Evaluation*—The final step, which consists of evaluating the training so that the efficiency and effectiveness can be determined and the program improved as needed.

IBM,
Armonk, New York

IBM, according to management development consultant Robert G. MacGregor, has shifted to become a market-driven quality company. This change has directed IBM's attention to responding to the customer's needs with total solutions. With this focus, IBM has undertaken a major restructuring of the business and has changed the role of all managers in IBM.

With this change, management education focuses on four areas:

1. New emphasis has been placed on the importance of the basic beliefs and values of IBM. John Akers has been quoted a number of times that "everything about IBM can change except the basic beliefs and values."

2. IBM has increased its focus on leadership with a series of course offerings that were introduced in 1990 and will continue. These offerings include "Transformational Leadership," an awareness-level course; "The Journey Continues," a skills development course; and "The Leadership Commitment," a series of offerings in the areas of empowerment, teams, risk taking, and change management.

3. The area of general business management has been given increased attention. Managers are being asked to manage their areas as if it were their own business. Courses have been developed to provide managers with the necessary skills to be general managers and entrepreneurs.

4. A continued emphasis is placed on skills in managing people. Managers in IBM are expected to continue to demonstrate the strong people management skills that have been required in the past. The focus in this area has not changed.

The new role of the first-line manager is described in the following excerpt from a white paper, "The Changing Role of the First-Line Manager," prepared by the corporate management development staff with input from IBM managers around the world:

> The first-line manager continues to be responsible for preserving and implementing our Basic Beliefs; recognizing employees' contributions, performance planning, counseling, and evaluation in our human resource programs; and interacting day-to-day with employees regarding various issues, and offering support, guidance, coaching, and nurturing. This has not changed.
>
> What has changed is the delegation of many management prerogatives to the individual closest to the customer. For that person to make good business decisions in managing customer relationships, management must share some of its responsibilities—controlling, communicating, and understanding business directions —with employees who are not managers.

Empowerment

In today's IBM, the manager should motivate and guide employees to address customer needs effectively and to ensure customer satisfaction. The customer must come first. This is nothing new. What is new, or at least different, is that the responsibility for satisfying and delighting the customer now belongs to every IBM employee, regardless of position or job title.

We are moving toward this goal worldwide by removing excessive or inappropriate levels of approval and increasing delegation to the person closest to the customer. Information must be shared freely, so that individuals have the knowledge to make and implement IBM decisions, and people must be held responsible for the quality of their decisions.

In this environment, the first-line manager is more like a coach. Rather than calling all the plays, the manager must empower employees by giving them a clear understanding of their responsibility and authority and knowledge of how best to respond to customer needs, both internal and external. Managers must ensure a free and open flow of up-and-down communication and information. They must make certain that their people are well trained, highly motivated, and have the tools to do their jobs.

Managers must also ensure that every individual is encouraged to take appropriate risks to achieve breakthroughs, according to the former director of education and management development. In this free and open management system, managers and employees must trust one another and work together as partners to achieve mutual goals.

Managers should have documented plans, developed jointly with employees, showing how they and their teams are implementing IBM's overall commitment to market-driven quality.

With a shared purpose, common objectives, and commitment to the plans, all employees will be able to carry out their own responsibilities and be accountable for their actions.

Teamwork

In transforming IBM, more and more work is being accomplished by teams. While task forces, teams, and teamwork have long been a way of life in IBM, departmental, organizational, and hierarchical relationships have traditionally constituted the primary structure. In a market-driven quality organization, work may best be done through the creation of teams in which individuals come together and synergistically develop a result greater than the sum of their individual achievements.

This emphasis on teams does not mean that IBM has forsaken its commitment to individual accomplishment or recognition. Individuals continue to be encouraged to perform to the best of their abilities. Only when the team succeeds, however, will all individual team members succeed, and only when all team members succeed individually will the team succeed. Trust is essential in teamwork.

Managing Teams

What is the role of the first-line manager in managing teams? On a specific project, people for whom the manager is responsible may be working in areas outside the manager's organizational responsibility, presenting new challenges. Managers must, therefore, develop and nurture an atmosphere that encourages open communication—the free flow of ideas and views.

To make certain that teams work smoothly together, managers must find ways to motivate groups to achieve agreed-upon goals and must promote progress without intervening unnecessarily. When needed, the manager must support the team with ideas, resources, and other forms of assistance. Finally, the manager must evaluate the team's work products and give feedback in order to ensure positive business results.

A manager's responsibility in managing teams is distinguished from that of a team leader because the manager retains all the people-management responsibilities for an employee. We have adapted our practices to incorporate team initiatives and will continue to do so.

Management of Change

The role of the first-line manager in managing change is more critical in today's environment than ever before. There is no question that IBM must continue to change if it is to compete successfully globally. First-line managers must create a climate in which their employees understand the reasons for change and "buy into" the process. There is a concurrent requirement to determine and decide what should remain the same. For example, every manager must have a commitment to the principles, values, and beliefs of IBM and, at the same time, show a willingness to change everything else.

KIMBERLY-CLARK CORPORATION, NEENAH, WISCONSIN

To encourage and facilitate the development of supervisors and other salaried employees, Kimberly-Clark has initiated an organized program called the Educational Opportunities Plan. According to Kimberly-Clark training and development manager Kenneth D. Peterson II, this plan consists of three parts: Employee Self-Development ("KimEd"), Family Education ("FamEd"), and Extended Education Leaves.

The KimEd portion of the plan is an annual program (funds do not accumulate from year to year) for employee self-development. The purpose of KimEd is to offer employees the chance to explore activities that will help them become more knowledgeable, more skilled, and better able to realize their full potential.

With KimEd funds, employees can maintain and improve knowledge and skills that relate directly to their jobs. They may also broaden and acquire knowledge and skills not directly related to the job. With KimEd funds, employees may even pursue a cultural interest.

While the employee self-development part of the plan (KimEd) is an annual program, the family education savings portion (FamEd) is a long-range program under which funds can accumulate from year to year. The purpose of FamEd is to help employees set aside funds for employee education and the education of members of the family. FamEd is made up of three types of accounts: a basic account, an employee savings account, and a savings incentive account. All three accounts earn interest and grow from year to year.

KimEd: Eligibility

Salaried employees become eligible for plan benefits after completing six months of continuous service. The plan year is July 1 through June 30. Except during the first year of eligibility, KimEd allotments are made on July 1. For exempt salaried employees, the KimEd allotment will be $650. For nonexempt salaried employees, the KimEd allotment will be $525. On June 30 (the last day of the plan year), any portion of the KimEd allotment that has not been used or authorized for use will lapse. In other words, the KimEd allotments do not accumulate, but new allotments are made every July 1.

KimEd funds may be used to help meet the cost of academic, cultural, or job-related vocational courses. All courses of instruction must be offered by an institution or organization accredited by an approved accrediting association—or by an institution, organization, or individual approved by the Educational Opportunities Plan Committee. For employees within two years of eligibility for unreduced retirement benefits, KimEd funds may also be used to cover nonjob-related vocational courses and avocational courses, such as hobbies and crafts.

KimEd funds can also be used to cover the cost of other job-related activities such as job-related educational seminars. In addition, KimEd funds can be used for special books and tapes that are job-related.

FamEd

FamEd, which provides educational funds for employees and their families, consists of three types of accounts:

1. *FamEd Company Basic Amount Account.* Except in the first year of eligibility, $150 will automatically be credited to a FamEd Company Basic Amount Account in the employee's name each time he or she receives a new KimEd allotment. In the first year of eligibility, the amount credited depends upon the date the employee becomes eligible.

2. *FamEd Employee Savings Account.* This is an optional savings account in which employees may set aside from $50 to $200 per plan year through payroll deduction.
3. *FamEd Company Savings Incentive Account.* If employees choose to contribute to their FamEd Employee Savings Account, Kimberly-Clark will credit their FamEd Company Savings Incentive Account with an amount equal to 20 percent of the employee's contribution.

Unlike the KimEd funds, which lapse at the end of each plan year, the FamEd accounts continue to accumulate from year to year. The money saved in the FamEd Employee Savings Account goes into a trust fund and earns income. FamEd money credited to the Basic Amount Account and Savings Incentive Account does not go into the trust fund but is credited to the employee's account on the plan's books and earns interest at the rate earned by the fund.

In other words, the combined FamEd funds earn income to help pay for future education expenses for employees and their families. While the amount credited to the FamEd Basic Amount Account will be less if an employee first becomes eligible during the second half of the plan year, the employee may still contribute up to $200 to the FamEd Employee Savings Account and receive the 20-percent Savings Incentive Credit. FamEd funds are available for the employee and spouse as well as children or other dependents under age 25, who have either earned a high school diploma or reached age 18.

FamEd funds may be used to help pay the cost of all recognized educational courses of instruction. As with KimEd, these courses of instruction must be offered by an institution or organization accredited by an approved accrediting association—or by an institution, organization, or individual approved by the Educational Opportunities Plan Committee. Primary and secondary school courses, however, are covered only for the employee's spouse.

If employees choose to make savings contributions to the FamEd account, they may withdraw the savings (and any earnings on those savings) at any time by simply completing an authorization/payment request form and submitting it to the Education Plan Unit Coordinator. In other words, employees can use the optional savings portion of the FamEd account as they would a regular savings account. When withdrawing any savings from the FamEd account for other than a FamEd or KimEd activity, however, the Company Savings Incentive Account balance will be reduced by 20 percent of the amount withdrawn.

Extended Education Leaves

In some cases, extended education leaves of as much as one year with pay may be granted to employees who have shown a high level of performance and ability. These special leaves are granted to provide an opportunity for individuals to pursue special activities that could not otherwise be pursued or that would require a long period of time and serious inconvenience.

Administration

A Plan Committee is established to act on behalf of the company in certain matters regarding the plan. As part of their duties, the committee interprets the plan, adopts rules and procedures for operating the plan and handling claims, decides questions of eligibility for participation, and provides the plan administrator and trustee with facts and directions for making proper payments under the plan. A separate committee is established to act on behalf of the company in certain matters regarding extended education leaves.

SERVICEMASTER, DOWNERS GROVE, ILLINOIS

The objective of the ServiceMaster Supervisory Development approach is much broader than simply improving on-the-job skills. As discussed by William Newell, ServiceMaster's director of training, the emphasis and determination of this process is to have each unit or section of development for supervisors have application in the many aspects of their own personal life, as well. Instructors are encouraged to emphasize that leadership is a quality that will enhance a person's relationship with his or her family and increase his or her effectiveness in civic and possibly religious activities.

More specific objectives of supervisory training at ServiceMaster are to:

- Teach the basic elements of planning, which will provide a platform for both obtaining results and developing people.
- Demonstrate the necessity for follow-through on plans—to teach supervisors to act on and review plans in order to provide the best possible leadership to the people they lead.

- Demonstrate both the need for delegation and the basic techniques involved.
- Establish that giving good orders is one of the most crucial tasks a leader must accomplish to get things done through other people.
- Teach leaders (supervisors) to provide specific, measurable, challengeable, but achievable performance expectations for the people they lead (designing effective job descriptions and standards of performance).
- Teach the supervisor to communicate and implement performance expectations that will provide consistency and direction, as well as improve productivity.
- Teach supervisors how to develop a successful communication climate of openness and trust.
- Teach supervisors the job skill training process for improving employee performance.

The specific content in the training and development of supervisors centers on the following concepts:

- Understanding the benefits of planning and the associated critical steps involved in the process.
- Incorporating project management by breaking projects down to small objectives and priorities.
- Providing effective delegation by using proven guidelines and understanding how to use them.
- Teaching how to give good written and verbal orders.
- Teaching the basic skills of designing effective job descriptions and standards of performance.
- Demonstrating how to use standards to improve employee performance.
- Teaching supervisors the "how to's" for planning effective communications, such as how to eliminate communication killers and how to clarify their communications process.
- Helping supervisors learn the process to identify initiative in those they lead and how to nurture it.
- Helping supervisors understand their role and their responsibility to understand the positive aspects of effective training, along with the basic ways people learn.

Supervisors are trained by managers and then placed at the facilities ServiceMaster serves in the health care, education, and industrial markets. The time frame for this development to occur varies by market and facility. The most effective way to teach, train, and develop supervisors would involve monthly meetings with a time duration of 1½ – 2 hours.

The participants learn through a variety of teaching methods, such as

- Overhead visuals
- Case studies
- Videos
- Role playing
- Small group discussion
- Written assignments
- Accountability sessions
- Team assignments
- Review of recent articles

Participants receive a manual for each unit taught. They are asked to put their own names on their workbooks and encouraged to write in them, which gives them ownership of not only the workbooks but of the session.

Instructors for supervisory training and development are often ServiceMaster personnel with the job title of "people development managers" who are trained and certified in this process. Many of ServiceMaster's account managers and area operations managers are also qualified to teach this program. General information on ways to facilitate group discussion—such as classroom set-up/seating arrangements, encouraging participants to jot down key words and phrases in answer to questions throughout each unit, and having participants break into small groups of three to four people to answer case study questions—are in an instructor's manual for each unit to be taught.

A common practice of instructors is to send general information to participants well in advance to include the following:

- Advance assignment direction
- Session overview
- Type of format to meeting
- Materials they need to bring
- List of supplemental readings

A one-week course for middle and upper-level managers was also designed and implemented at ServiceMaster. Why is this case study included in a book on supervisory training and development? Three reasons stand out:

1. Middle- and upper-level managers must set an example for their subordinate supervisors. They must be leaders to emulate and to inspire the supervisors to be leaders.

2. When supervisors return to their jobs after attending a training program, their bosses (managers) must provide a positive climate for changes in behavior. In order to do this, their managers should receive the same kind of training that the supervisors do so that they are in a good position to be mentors and coaches.

3. By attending a management training program, middle- and upper-level managers can participate in developing subject content for courses for the supervisors who report to them.

In summary, at ServiceMaster there are essential aspects that must be developed with supervisors. These aspects or tasks, include *inspecting, motivating, training,* and *directing. To inspect,* a supervisor must know what to look for and how to interpret what is observed in terms of performance. Motivation calls for skills in people handling. Motivation skills can be learned in order to turn "negatives" into "positives."

One-on-one training is a great teacher/learner experience that fosters trust and confidence. The supervisor must be trained properly to train those who report to him or her. As in any other leadership position, a supervisor must have the capability to direct and "use" the work force as a team. The supervisor directs the how, the where, the when, and with what tools a job must be accomplished.

Summary

These five examples illustrate the philosophy, strategy, and guiding principles that underlie the training and development of these companies' supervisors. In each of these examples, emphasis has been placed on concern for people and the belief that each one is important. Also, these companies consistently provide opportunity for people to grow and develop. A continuous emphasis is placed on managers as "leaders" who involve their subordinates in the decision-making process.

"Empowerment" and "teamwork" are mentioned as means of getting maximum motivation and productivity from all employees.

Differences, as well as similarities, are evident in comparing these five organizations. Each has tailored philosophy, strategy, and guiding principles to coincide with corporate culture. Every organization should do the same.

4

CONDITIONS FOR MAXIMUM LEARNING BY SUPERVISORS

If training efforts are to be successful, consideration must be given to supervisors as learners. Some of the theories and principles of adult learning are described below. The 11 authors represented here are only examples of the many who have written articles and books on the subject. Even though some of them were written a number of years ago, they still apply in today's business world.

Stephen D. Brookfield

In his book, *Understanding and Facilitating Adult Learning,* Brookfield refered to much research that has been done on "learning." He quoted W. B. James who in 1983, devised the following set of basic principles of adult learning after a team of researchers had undertaken a search of articles, research reports, dissertations, and textbooks on adult learning:

1. Adults maintain the ability to learn.
2. Adults are a highly diversified group of individuals with widely differing preferences, needs, backgrounds, and skills.
3. Adults experience a gradual decline in physical/sensory capabilities.
4. Experience of the learner is a major resource in learning situations.
5. Self-concept moves from dependency to independency as individuals grow in responsibility, experience, and confidence.
6. Adults tend to be life-centered in their orientation to learning.
7. Adults are motivated to learn by a variety of factors.
8. Active learner participation in the learning process contributes to learning.
9. A comfortable, supportive climate, is a key to successful learning.[1]

Nathaniel Cantor

In his book *The Learning Process for Managers,* Cantor stated that "the average adult has learned how not to learn. He has learned how to avoid genuine, positive learning. His learning has come from anxiety, apprehensiveness, and fear of disapproval."

Genuine learning, according to Cantor, requires a change in behavior. Learners organize their attitudes, feelings, and understanding. No one ordinarily enjoys such experiences. Most of us have developed an involved system of defenses against the inevitable conflict between outward conformity and the independent need for self-expression. The ambivalence and conflict we experience over denying that at times our needs are different from the needs of others will not evaporate.

---

[1]Stephen D. Brookfield, *Understanding and Facilitating Adult Learning* (San Francisco: Jossey-Bass Publishers, 1990).

Individuals struggle to create their own syntheses or to resist creating anything of their own. The most important contribution that can be made by anyone close to the learner is to remove the threat of recrimination, reprisal, or disapproval.

The popular idea that learning is a process of storing data and that the more data one has the more learning one possesses is false. Facts are integrated in relation to the ongoing experience of the learner. Seeing interrelationships and readjusting and modifying behavior is the essence of learning. To learn is to reshape, reform, and remake one's experience.[2]

ANDREW HENDRICKSON

In an article in *Adult Leadership*, Hendrickson stated nine principles for consideration by those who are called on to teach adults:

1. Good teaching takes into account past negative school experiences, remoteness of past schooling, and the self-doubts of adults, and provides (at the earliest possible time in the class) for encouragement and an experience of success.
2. Good teaching takes into account the relation between a pleasant social atmosphere and a satisfying educational experience.
3. Good training takes into account not only the need for an early experience of success but the need for frequently recurring experiences of success.
4. Good teaching takes into account the learning speed of learners.
5. Good teaching recognizes the validity of the principle of involvement.
6. Good teaching recognizes the adults themselves as a prime teaching resource.
7. Good teaching recognizes the concreteness and immediacy of most adult goals.
8. Good teaching takes into account the key place that motivation holds in the learning process.
9. Good teaching recognizes physical and mental fatigue as a deferring factor in adult learning.[3]

---

[2]Nathaniel Cantor, *The Learning Process for Managers* (New York: Harper and Brothers, 1958).

[3]Andrew Hendrickson, "Adult Learning and the Adult Learner," *Adult Leadership* (February, 1966). Copyright © 1965. The Sunday School Board of the Southern Baptist Convention. All rights reserved. Used by permission.

J.R. KIDD

In his book *How Adults Learn,* Kidd discussed theories of learning, as well as their application in the teaching situation. Some of his theories include the following:

- The physical and sensory equipment of people of all ages is ample for most kinds of learning if it is used efficiently.
- There is nothing about aging itself that prevents or seriously hampers learning.
- A constellation of feelings associated with love (such as respect, admiration, generosity, sympathy, friendliness, encouragement) has much more "efficiency" for learning than do feelings associated with anger or fear.
- Of all the factors pertaining to success in learning, the most critical are those of motivation—how a person deeply engages himself or herself in the learning transaction. Subject matter, environmental factors, methods, and techniques are also important, but they must be seen in the light of the key word *engagement.*

There is no hierarchy of values in learning; every factor can be of critical importance—on occasion, fresh air may be as important as fresh ideas. Environment—the place, shape, and character of the facility—affects the amount and quality of learning.

An astonishing variety of forms, methods, techniques, and devices is available to the agent in adult learning. One of the chief skills of the teacher of adults includes the ability to select. For example, it is possible to convey facts to large groups of adults, but the sound pattern of languages is best learned in groups of no larger than six people. Where skills are being taught, ample opportunity and facilities must be provided for practice.

The choice of participants, such as those who have had similar or very different previous experience, markedly affects the educational outcome. For some tasks, the best results are achieved when the participants are self-selected.

In every activity, arrangements must be made for the expression of a number of factors—for example, anticipating and dealing with apprehension or resistance to learning; gaining and holding attention, and providing for clear exposition; allowing for a two-way flow of communication; and ensuring that there is testing, application, and appraisal of the knowledge, skill, or attitude.

Among the most important developments in recent years have been many new applications of the "reality" principle—planning a learning experience that is concrete, vivid, and relevant. Examples of this are the use of actual machines, devices, or mockups in training; role playing; and utilizing the "exercise," the case method, and the "T" (training) group found in sensitivity training programs.

Another noteworthy gain has been in the application and use of learning devices, such as motion picture films. Devices do not replace the teacher, but they can be an effective and economical means to good learning.

The key to learning is engagement: a relationship between the learner, the task or subject matter, the environment, and the teacher. Some of the factors within this relationship are already established by the nature and experience of the learner, but many of the factors are not fixed in any way; they can be modified and improved with planning and practice.[4]

Malcolm S. Knowles

One of the best-known authors concerning learning theory is the late Malcolm Knowles. Here, from *The Training and Development Handbook*, are some assumptions that he described as the *andragological model*:

- Adults have a need to know why they should learn something.
- Adults have a deep need to be self-directing.
- Adults have a greater volume and different quality of experience than youth.
- Adults become ready to learn when they experience in their life situation a need to know or be able to do in order to perform more effectively and satisfyingly.
- Adults enter into a learning experience with a task-centered (or problem-centered or life-centered) orientation to learning.
- Adults are motivated to learn by both extrinsic and intrinsic motivators.

Based on these assumptions, Knowles draws the following implications for practice:

---

[4]J.R. Kidd, *How Adults Learn* (New York: Associated Press, 1959).

1. Establish a climate that is conducive for learning. Two broad aspects of climate must be considered: institutional climate and the climate of the training situation.
2. Create a climate for mutual planning. It is critical that a planning committee or task force be used which is representative of all the constituencies that the program is designed to serve.
3. Diagnose the participants' learning needs.
4. Translate learning needs into objectives.
5. Design and manage a pattern of learning experiences. Involve the participants in developing the plan.
6. Evaluate the extent to which the objectives have been accomplished. Develop procedures for involving the participants in the evaluation.[5]

GORDON LIPPITT

In an issue of *Journal of ASTD*, the late Gordon Lippitt reminded training and development people of the following principles of learning:

All human beings learn. Even older adults can learn. The old adage that "you can't teach an old dog new tricks" is wrong. It is just more difficult because the elderly have learned some wrong attitudes and skills.

Learning is an active process. People learn best when they are actively involved and interact with the teacher, boss, fellow students, environment, and learning stimulus. One does not learn by being passive. For learning to be effective, there must be an active process of synthesis and usually requires proper environmental conditions.

Learning is individualistic. Each person learns in accordance with his own personality, perception, expectation, and readiness. Persons attending a learning experience will go away with different things that they have learned.

Learning takes place at various levels. Learning experiences must be planned to fit the student's level of:

---

[5]Malcolm S. Knowles, "Adult Learning," in *The Training and Development Handbook*, 3rd ed. (New York: McGraw-Hill, Inc., 1987).

- *Knowledge*—This level of learning may be achieved through managing, conditioning, one-way communication, or similar approaches. It should not be confused with application of the knowledge.
- *Skill*—This level of learning requires adaptation and practice. Being able to convert intentions and knowledge into practical results requires learning in the "action" context and will utilize role playing, skill practices, videotape feedback, along with practice, and other action-oriented methods of learning.
- *Attitude*—At this level of learning, we are dealing with perceptions, past experiences, and values. Learning which produces changes in attitude is much harder to achieve and it will require more sophisticated methods, such as confrontation learning, laboratory training, or sensory experiencing.

These three levels of learning must be considered if we are to achieve and maintain *performance change* as a result of training and development activity. Those of us involved in the educational process should have performance improvement as a goal, rather than the mere acquisition of new words, gimmicks, or temporary responses that slip back into the same routine because change was not "fully" learned or reinforced. This is the challenge for all of us as we assess the needs of our organizations, design learning experiences, and evaluate the effect of our efforts.[6]

ROBERT MAGER

In his book *Developing Attitudes Toward Learning*, Robert Mager described a number of factors that should be considered:

- Learning is for the future; that is, the object of instruction is to facilitate some form of behavior at a point after the instruction has been completed.
- The likelihood of the students putting their knowledge to use is influenced by their attitude for or against the subjects; things disliked have a way of being forgotten.

---

[6]Gordon Lippitt, "Concepts of Learning and the Development Process," *Journal of the American Society for Training and Development* (May 1969).

■ People influence people. Teachers, and others, do influence attitudes toward subject matter—and toward learning itself.

■ One objective toward which to strive is that of having the students leave your influence with as favorable an attitude toward your subject as possible. In this way, you will help to maximize the possibility that they will remember what they have been taught, and will willingly learn more about what they have been taught.[7]

Garry Mitchell

According to Mitchell, there are 10 recognized principles of adult learning that should be considered in developing a training program. These include the theories that people:

1. Learn only when they are ready to learn.
2. Learn best what they actually perform.
3. Learn from their mistakes.
4. Learn easiest what is familiar to them.
5. Favor different senses for learning.
6. Learn methodically and, in our culture, systematically.
7. Cannot learn what they cannot understand.
8. Learn through practice.
9. Learn better when they can see their own progress.
10. Respond best when what they are to learn is presented uniquely to them. Each of us is different.

Robert W. Pike

In his *Creative Training Techniques Handbook*, Robert Pike set out seven laws of learning:

1. **The Law of the Teacher.** The teacher must know what is to be taught. You can't teach what you haven't learned. And you must teach from a prepared life as well as from a prepared lesson. The most

---

[7]Robert Mager, *Developing Attitudes Toward Learning* (Belmont, Calif.: Lake Publishing Co., 1984). Copyright © 1984 by Lake Publishing Compant, Belmont, Calif. 94002.

effective instructors on any topic generally are those who have experienced what they are teaching.

2. **The Law of the Learner**. The learner must attend with interest to the material being presented. If you are teaching, you can create a motivational environment. You can do that by answering the learner's question: "What's in it for me?" The learner has to see the benefits for himself or herself. What will they get out of it? How can they apply it? How can they use it?

3. **The Law of the Language**. The language you use must be comprehensible to the learner. Nobody likes experts; we want to knock them off their pedestals. Everybody, however, loves the learner. Start where people are, and take them where they need to be. Go from the known to the unknown. When you use words or terms unfamiliar to the learners, define them immediately. Language should be a stepping stone, not a stumbling block.

4. **The Law of the Lesson**. The truth or content taught must be learned through the truth or the content already known. Again, go from where the learners are. Build on what they already know.

5. **The Law of the Teaching Process**. You must excite and direct your learners' self-motivation. People often learn best through self-discovery. There are basically three ways people learn, and the first two don't work, so don't use them:

- You can tell people things.
- You can use statistics.
- We can put people in situations where they discover for themselves how effective or ineffective they are. People learn most effectively when they are actively involved in the learning process, not passively observing it.

6. **The Law of the Learning Process**. The learner must reproduce in his or her own life the content to be learned. Learning does not take place until behavior has changed. We're talking about being able to apply—not simply to know but also to do. Just because the instructor has rapport with the learners doesn't automatically guarantee that learning is going to occur. You want to involve as many senses as pos-

sible and use as many approaches as you can so that people grasp and apply the material you want them to learn.

7. **The Law of Review and Application**. You must confirm the completion of the content taught. And you do that by emphasizing practical application. Ask, "How can you use this in real life?" and "What do you expect if you apply what you've been learning?"

RON ZEMKE AND SUSAN ZEMKE

Based on extensive research, Ron Zemke, president of Performance Research Associates, and his wife, Sue Zemke, offer a number of ideas and recommendations.

Adult learners can't be threatened, coerced, or tricked into learning something new. Birch rods and gold stars have minimum impact. Adults can be ordered into a classroom and prodded into a seat, but they cannot be forced to learn. Though trainers are often faced with adults who have been sent to training, there are some insights to be gathered from the research on adults who seek out a structural learning experience on their own. It's something we all do at least twice a year, the research says. We begin our running tally from this base camp. Following are 30 things our research has taught us:

1. Adults seek out learning experiences in order to cope with specific life-changing events, such as marriage, divorce, a new job, a promotion, being fired, retiring, losing a loved one, and moving to a new city.

2. The more life-changing events an adult encounters, the more likely he or she is to seek out learning opportunities. Just as stress increases as life-changing events accumulate, the motivation to cope with change through engagement in a learning experience increases. Since the people who most frequently seek out learning opportunities are people who have the most years of education, it is reasonable to guess that, for many of us, learning is a coping response to significant change.

3. The learning experiences adults seek out on their own are directly related—at least in their own perceptions—to the life-changing events that triggered the seeking. Therefore, if 80 percent of the change being encountered is work-related, then 80 percent of the learning experiences should be work-related.

4. Adults are generally willing to engage in learning experiences before, after, or during the actual life-changing event. Once convinced that the

change is a certainty, adults will engage in any learning that promises to help them cope with the transition.

5. Although adults have been found to engage in learning for a variety of reasons—job advancement, pleasure, love of learning, and so on—it is equally true that, for most adults, learning is not its own reward. Adults who are motivated to seek out a learning experience do so primarily because they have a use for the knowledge or skill being sought. Learning is a means to an end, not an end in itself.

6. Increasing or maintaining one's sense of self-esteem and pleasure are strong secondary motivators for engaging in learning experiences. Having a new skill or extending and enriching current knowledge can be both, depending on the individual's personal perceptions.

7. Adult learners tend to be less interested in, and enthralled by, survey courses. They tend to prefer single-concept, single-theory courses that focus heavily on the application of the concept to relevant problems. This tendency increases with age.

8. Adults need to be able to integrate new ideas with what they already know if they are going to keep—and use—the new information.

9. Information that conflicts sharply with what is already held to be true, and thus forces a re-evaluation of the old material, is integrated more slowly.

10. Information that has little "conceptual overlap" with what is already known is acquired slowly.

11. Fast-paced, complex, or unusual learning tasks interfere with the learning of the concepts of data they are intended to teach or illustrate.

12. Adults tend to compensate for being slower in some psychomotor learning tasks by being more accurate and by making fewer trial-and-error ventures.

13. Adults tend to take errors personally and are more likely to let them affect their self-esteem. Therefore, they tend to apply tried-and-true solutions and take fewer risks. There is even evidence that adults will misinterpret feedback and "mistake" errors for positive confirmation.

14. The curriculum designer must know whether the concepts and ideas will be in concert or in conflict with learner and organizational values. As trainers at AT&T have learned, moving from a service to a sales philosophy requires more than a change in words and titles. It requires a change in the way people think and value.

15. Programs need to be designed to accept viewpoints from people in different life stages and with different value "sets."

16. A concept needs to be "anchored" or explained from more than one value set and appeal to more than one developmental life stage.

17. Adults prefer self-directed and self-designed learning projects seven to one over group-learning experiences led by a professional. Furthermore, the adult learner often selects more than one medium for the design. Reading and talking to a qualified peer are frequently cited as good resources. The desire to control pace and start/stop time strongly affects the self-directed preference.

18. Nonhuman media such as books, programmed instruction, and television have become popular in recent years. One piece of research found them very influential in the way adults plan self-directed learning projects.

19. Regardless of media, straightforward how-to is the preferred content orientation. As many as 80 percent of the polled adults in one study cited the need for applications and how-to information as the primary motivation for undertaking a learning project.

20. Self-direction does not mean isolation. In fact, studies of self-directed learning show self-directed projects involve an average of 10 other people as resources, guides, encouragers, and the like. The incompetence or inadequacy of these same people is often rated as a primary frustration. But even for the self-professed self-directed learner, lectures and short seminars receive positive ratings, especially when these events give the learner face-to-face, one-to-one access to an expert. Apparently, the adult learner is a very efficiency-minded individual. Allen Tough suggests that the typical adult learner asks, "What is the cheapest, easiest, fastest way for me to learn to do that?" and then proceeds independently along this self-determined route. An obvious tip for the trainer is that the adult trainee has to have a hand in shaping the curriculum of the program.

21. The learning environment must be physically and psychologically comfortable. Adults report that long lectures, periods of interminable sitting, and the absence of practice opportunities are high on the irritation scale.

22. Adults have something real to lose in a classroom situation. Self-esteem and ego are on the line when they are asked to risk trying a new behavior in front of peers and cohorts. Bad experiences in traditional education, feelings about authority, and the preoccupation with events outside the classroom all affect in-class experience. These and other influencing factors are carried into class with the learners as surely as are their gold Cross pens and lined yellow pads.

23. Adults have expectations, and it is critical to take time up front to clarify and articulate all expectations before getting into content. Both trainees and the instructor/facilitator need to state their expectations. When they are at variance, the problem should be acknowledged and a resolution negotiated. In any case, the instructor can assume responsibility only for his or her expectations, not for those of trainees.

24. Adults bring a great deal of life experience into the classroom, an invaluable asset to be acknowledged, tapped, and used. Adults can learn well—and much—from dialogue with respected peers.

25. Instructors who have a tendency to hold forth rather than facilitate can hold that tendency in check—or compensate for it—by concentration on the use of open-ended questions to draw out relevant trainee knowledge and experience.

26. New knowledge has to be integrated with previous knowledge—that means active learner participation. Since only the learners can tell us how the new fits, or fails to fit, with the old, we have to ask them. Just as the learner is dependent on us for confirming feedback on skill practice, we are dependent on the learner for feedback about our curriculum and in-class performance.

27. The key to the instructor role is control. The instructor must balance the presentation of new material, the debate and discussion, the sharing of relevant training experience, and the clock. Ironically, we seem best able to establish control when we risk giving it up. When we shelve our egos and stifle the tendency to be threatened by challenge to our plans and methods, we gain the kind of facilitative control we seem to need to effect adult learning.

28. The instructor has to protect minority opinion, keep disagreements civil and unheated, make connections between various opinions and ideas, and keep reminding the group of the variety of potential solutions to the problem. Just as in a good problem-solving meeting, the instructor is less an advocate than an orchestrator.

29. Integration of new knowledge and skill requires transition time and focused effort. Working on applications to specific back-on-the-job problems helps with the transfer. Action plans, accountability strategies, and follow-up after training all increase the likelihood of that transfer. Involving the trainees' supervisor in pre- and post-course activities helps with both in-class focus and transfer.

30. Learning and teaching theories function better as a resource than as a key to understanding. The four currently influential theories—humanis-

tic, behavioral, cognitive, and developmental—all offer valuable guidance when matched with an appropriate learning task. A skill-training task can draw much from the behavioral approach, for example, while personal growth-centered subjects seem to draw gainfully from humanistic concepts. The trainer of adults needs to take an eclectic rather than a single theory-base approach to developing strategies and procedures.

SUMMARY

An analysis of the ideas of these 11 authors reveals some common threads, as well as some differences of opinion as to the most significant aspects of the learning process. To look at learning from the standpoint of supervisory training and development, it is important to consider the factors noted in Figure 4-1.

One of the most important factors is the attitudes that supervisors bring to the training and development situation. These attitudes have an impact on the learning that will take place in the program. Supervisors may have negative attitudes toward the training program for a number of reasons:

■ A poor attitude toward the job and toward the company in general—perhaps related to salary, pressures, or frustrations.

■ A training schedule that may be inconvenient or that may require supervisors and learners to take training on their own time.

■ A subject content that has been determined by training and personnel people or even by top management instead of by supervisors and middle-management people.

■ Inappropriate instructors. Perhaps a young college graduate is teaching mature, experienced supervisors how to do the job better, or an outside psychologist has been called in to act as a teacher. The instructor may lack the respect of the supervisors who will be attending the meeting.

■ A reaction to what they have heard about the training program. Perhaps they have been given insufficient information on the purpose of the training program and how it will help them, and they view the program as a complete waste of time and effort.

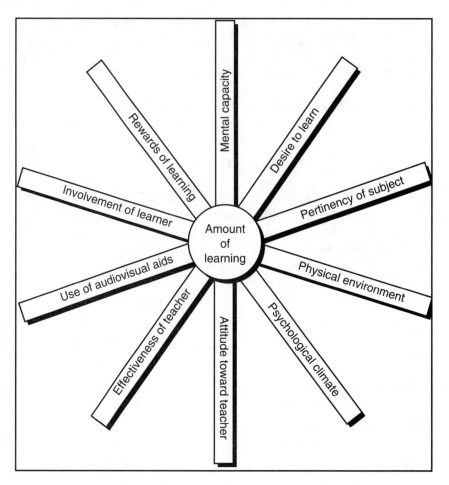

Figure 4-1. *Factors affecting learning*

It is easy to see that a negative attitude on the part of the learner can have a detrimental effect on the effectiveness of the program. A learner who comes to the program with one or more of these negative attitudes is not going to put forth very much effort to learn. The teaching will probably be quite ineffective unless the attitude of the learner can be changed.

On the other hand, supervisors may come to a training program with a great deal of enthusiasm. They may be looking forward to it and recognize an opportunity for personal growth and development that will help them, as well as the company. This is the kind of attitude that can result in maximum learning. Those who plan supervisory and training programs should try to plan them and promote them in such a way that supervisors will come to the program with enthusiasm.

Consideration should be given to other classroom and on-the-job factors that affect learning. First, it must be recognized that learning is a process of change. The desired outcomes of a typical training program are changes in attitudes, knowledge, skill, and on-the-job behavior. Problems arise if supervisors resist the changes that are being encouraged by those who are teaching the programs. Perhaps they worry that their boss will not support the changes; perhaps they do not feel comfortable with the new ways; or, if their old attitudes, habits, and behavior have proved to be successful, they may be reluctant to change because of the insecurity that would come with a new approach.

Another important factor related to the effectiveness of the teaching has to do with the anxieties and fears created in the classroom itself. If the climate is one in which participants do not feel free to speak up, they will not participate in the learning process. This kind of negative climate can be created by the instructor or by a top management person who may be in the meeting, either observing or as part of the group. The instructor can create a positive climate, and the presence of open-minded top management can encourage supervisors to say what they think.

One of the principles of learning that has been highlighted by several of the people who have been quoted in this chapter has to do with the learners' involvement and participation. All agree that active participation in the training sessions can improve the learning that takes place—not necessarily on the part of the one who participates but on the part of others in the group who can learn from the person who makes a contribution.

Another important principle that must be considered when planning and implementing a program is that it must be practical. As Knowles said, it should be "problem centered," and the people in the group should be able to apply it immediately. The closer the content is to this ideal, the more the participants will learn.

The facilities themselves should be conducive to effective learning. The comfort and relaxation of participants is important to effective learning. Consideration should be given to the room setup—including the ventilation, schedule, breaks, and even the chairs and tables.

A final important factor is that learning should be a series of successes. People should like what they're learning; they should feel that it is beneficial to them and that they can use it on the job. If skills are being taught, opportunities must be provided for practice, because people do not learn skills just by listening and discussing.

As Mager put it, "If we are to look for changes in on-the-job behavior, we should have the student leave the classroom with as favorable an attitude toward the subject as possible. In this way, you will help to maximize the possibility that he or she will remember what has been taught and will willingly learn more about what has been taught."[8]

The planners and implementers of supervisory training and development must maximize the learning possibilities on the part of the supervisors. They must:

- Create enthusiasm for the training activities in which they are engaged.
- Plan and implement training and development programs and activities so that supervisors maintain a high degree of enthusiasm and desire for them and thereby maximize the learning that takes place.
- Recognize that supervisors are adults who have feelings and emotions that must be considered. These supervisors probably want to be involved in the planning of the training program, perhaps to identify the subjects of greatest help to them and to participate in the training process itself.

All of these principles and theories in learning can be put to good use in a carefully planned and conducted training and development program.

---

[8] Ibid.

5

DETERMINING TRAINING NEEDS AND SETTING OBJECTIVES

Effective training programs are based on the needs of the supervisors to be trained—that is, the attitudes, knowledge, and skills the supervisors need in order to do their job effectively. The following questions must be answered in order to determine these needs: Who should determine the needs? Should the program focus on current needs or future needs?

There are at least six different kinds of people who can help determine the needs for supervisory and development program:

1. top-level managers;
2. bosses of the supervisors to be trained;
3. staff personnel in the organization, such as human resource managers and training and development professionals;
4. the supervisors themselves;
5. subordinates of the supervisors to be trained; and
6. outsiders, such as consultants, psychologists, and research specialists.

Top-level managers. A common approach is for an organization's managers to decide what their supervisors need in the way of training and development. They base their recommendations on personal opinions, what other organizations are doing, the most pressing problems in the organization, among other subjective and objective criteria.

Bosses. The immediate bosses of the supervisors to be trained are in a good position to help determine the needs of their subordinates. They would base it on their direct contact.

Staff personnel. Another common approach is for someone in the human resources or training department to determine the supervisory training needs. This, too, can be done subjectively or objectively. The staff may look at what other companies are doing, see what kind of training is being offered by universities and professional or trade associates, analyze the jobs and performance of the supervisors, or simply decide what they think is best for the supervisors.

Supervisors themselves. Supervisors probably would like to establish their own needs. They feel they are in the best position to judge what will be helpful to them in the performance of their job. Some companies use this approach by interviewing the supervisors or by using a questionnaire to ask them what they need.

Subordinates of the supervisors. Even though the subordinates may be in the position to know the weaknesses and needs of their supervisors, they are not often asked to express those opinions. Many supervisors would not like the idea of their subordinates being asked for such information. And in many organizations, neither the top management nor the staff personnel feel that it's appropriate to ask hourly and clerical workers for the training needs of their bosses. An indirect approach is to use attitude surveys. Organizations that use 360 degree "feedback" to evaluate performance will probably also use it to determine needs.

Outsiders. Larger companies, in particular, make use of outside consultants and psychologists to help them determine training needs for the supervisors in the organization. These consultants may use a very elaborate system of questionnaires and interviews to determine needs. They may also suggest personal experiences and ideas from other organizations and possibly sell them to the company for which they work at the moment.

It is difficult to judge which of these six approaches is the best. The more important question, however, is, which is most practical? Information from several of these sources would be better than the information from any one source alone. For example, the supervisors themselves could be asked to express their own needs. They understand their jobs, and they know what their current and future problems are likely to be. They also understand some of their own personal weaknesses and what might help them do their jobs most effectively. Another important reason for asking them is that they are more likely to have a positive attitude toward learning the material if they have helped to develop it.

In addition to soliciting the opinions of the supervisors themselves, it is a good idea to ask managers for their opinions and recommendations on the needs of the supervisors who report to them. The immediate bosses of supervisors are in a good position to see the problems that have occurred and may have in mind ways to improve efficiency, productivity, and general performance. Also, they will probably support the training program if they have helped determine it.

Organizations with specialists in the field of training and development should certainly involve them in determining supervisory needs. Perhaps they can provide the most help by setting up questionnaires, interviews, or approaches by which the opinions of supervisors, as well as upper-level managers, can be obtained and quantified. They also should have derived ideas from the techniques used by other organizations to determine needs. Where the climate is right, subordinates can provide some helpful information about supervisory training needs. Great care should be taken in obtaining this information, however; subordinates should not be asked for their opinions unless their supervisors have given their permission.

Whether outsiders are used depends largely on the ability of—and time available for—the organization to determine its own supervisors' needs. Small companies, as well as large, can benefit from the use of outside consultants.

Should the Program Focus on Current or Future Needs?

The answer to this question of current versus future needs is that, in general, the focus should be on the current jobs. Improved knowledge, skills, and attitudes in this area result in the greatest payoff. Supervisors learn best when they can immediately use what they learn, and because most supervisors remain in their current job for many years, the main thrust of a training program should be on the present. As certain supervisors move into higher-level jobs or jobs that become more complicated, many of the approaches and techniques that they use on their current jobs will have direct application there.

Yet, sometimes training programs regarding future needs are very important. For example, if a new computer or a new tape-controlled machine is being introduced into a company, supervisors should understand the basic principles and features of such equipment so that they may do their jobs better. Similarly, new management skills or knowledge should be taught to the supervisors as the need for them is anticipated—before they are actually needed on the job. For example, if a large number of employees are going to be hired in a department, supervisors should receive advanced training in how to induct and train these new employees to work effectively in that department.

Some organizations identify a few people as candidates for higher-level jobs. Special attention should be given to these people in training to prepare them for their future positions. In most cases, they will be sent to outside programs to receive training sponsored by organizations, such as universities. Sometimes, however, they may be trained in certain operations of the company by the department heads and other supervisors.

How Should Needs Be Determined?

There are many ways of determining the training needs of supervisors. Some of the more common and more effective methods are described as follows:

Job Analysis. One approach for determining training needs is to analyze the jobs of the supervisors. William Stewart made such an analysis of the tasks performed by industrial supervisors. His goal was to eliminate the "erroneous guessing in training needs, opportunities, or current whim on the part of those who control training [that] often underlies the weakness of many supervisory training programs."

Stewart surveyed 717 supervisors representing 100 industrial organizations in Ohio. He gave them a questionnaire listing 120 tasks that they might perform and asked them to select one of three categories to indicate their opinion of the importance attached to each task as representing an area of first–line supervisory training needs:

Important—Of considerable value for training purposes. It is desirable that training be conducted in the area relating to the task.

Average—Of moderate value for training. Some consideration should be given to conducting training areas related to the task.

Not important—Of little or no value for training purposes.

The second group of questions asked of these supervisors concerned the performance frequency of each task. They were required to indicate how often they actually performed the task. Possible responses to these questions were:

Often—The task is usually performed one or more times a week.

Occasionally—The task is usually performed less than once a week but more than five times a year.

Seldom—The task is performed fewer than five times a year.

Never—The task is never performed.

After collecting, tabulating, and analyzing the data to determine training needs of the supervisors in the study, Stewart concluded that tasks concerned with human involvement and understanding were significant first-line supervisory training needs regardless of the type of work done in the department and that common needs existed in the personnel aspects of problem solving.[1] Stewart's approach can be used in other organizations. The results, however, could be entirely different.

Another approach to determining needs is to look at descriptions of the jobs of a supervisor. The job description sketches the outlines and high spots of the job, but it isn't complete enough to be used to determine

---

[1]William Stewart, "Determining First-Line Supervisory Training Needs," *Training and Development Journal* (April 1970).

needs or develop a course, so the second step is to conduct a task analysis dealing with the specific tasks that might be included on the job.

The job description and task analysis provide a picture of the kinds of knowledge, skills, and attitudes the supervisor must have to perform the job. These, then, could be considered training needs, particularly those of new supervisors, but they also could be considered the starting point for determining the needs of current supervisors. Obviously, the current knowledge, attitudes, and skills have to be considered in relationship to what those supervisors need to have in order to do their job.

Analysis of the Problems. A look at records may reveal certain training needs. For example, an excessive turnover rate of new employees may pinpoint a supervisory training need. Or an excess amount of scrap in a certain department may indicate a need for training supervisors in quality control or other aspects of their job. Other indications of supervisory training needs may be the accident record or the absentee record of employees, or an analysis of recent grievances.

Exit Interviews. Exit interviews, conducted with employees who are leaving the organization, are another technique for locating problem areas and possible supervisory training needs. The purpose of such interviews is to determine why the employee is leaving and any possible problem areas on the job that can be solved by supervisory training. To be objective, these interviews should be conducted by someone in the human resources department or by someone other than the immediate supervisor.

Attitude Surveys. A common way of pinpointing training needs is to survey the attitudes of employees. Attitude surveys are usually prepared by outside organizations to measure employee attitudes toward working conditions, pay, supervisory practices, management policies, and other job-related items. The results of these surveys indicate some of the supervisory training needs that can help to improve attitudes of employees. These surveys should be conducted on a regular basis—perhaps once a year—to identify new needs, as well as to see what improvement has taken place.

Following are case studies of approaches used by two organizations.

Wisconsin Gas Company

With the assistance of Jerry Kluza, an independent consultant, Wisconsin Gas Company (Milwaukee, Wisconsin) developed and implemented a program called "Supervisor Review: Improving Our Working Relationships." Here are details on the program:

- **What is the main purpose of the supervisor review?** The purpose of the review is to help us develop the best possible management skills and working relationships to make us stronger as a company. The management style team looked at various ways to increase management effectiveness. The team recommended using the supervisor review as a way to get people talking to one another. Those channels of communication may already be open. If they're not, this is a tool to begin a dialogue. It's also another way for managers to get an answer to the question, "How am I doing?"
- **When will it start?** The review will be conducted this year on a division-by-division basis depending on each division's work load. Prior to the review, each division head will conduct meetings to discuss management practices and the supervisor review process.
- **Who will be reviewed?** Everyone with supervisory responsibilities, from the president on down, will be reviewed. Right now there are approximately 200 people with supervisory responsibility.
- **How does the supervisor review work?** You will be asked to review your supervisor by filling out a questionnaire organized around the four key characteristics—competence, integrity, participative leadership skills, and communication skills. The questionnaire will contain about 35 questions and will include room for comments. The responses will be anonymous.
- **Who will see the survey results?** An outside company will tabulate the results and prepare the feedback report. The company that is working with us to prepare the questionnaire and will be tabulating the responses is Kluza Associates. A feedback report will be provided to the supervisor being reviewed. A one-page

feedback summary will be provided to the supervisor's boss and the division vice-president. The one-page summary will also be added to the supervisor's personnel file. The person being reviewed and his or her supervisor will go over the feedback report and look for ways to build on strengths and work on areas that need improvement. The person being reviewed will also go over the results with the work group that filled out the question-naire.

■ *What happens after the review is completed?* After the feedback report has been returned to the supervisor being reviewed, the supervisor and the supervisor's boss will work together to come up with a development plan that might include such things as additional training, and so on. Supervisors and managers are also expected to share results and seek out feedback from the people in their work group who filled out the questionnaire.

■ *Will this replace the performance review process that management uses now?* No. The supervisor review is an additional tool we can use to improve performance by strengthening our management skills and improving our working relationships. It is intended to give managers and supervisors more information about how they are doing. It is another way for us to build on individual strengths and focus on areas that need improvement.

■ *Is this an ongoing effort?* Yes. We are committed to improving management practices. Change won't occur overnight; improvement will happen with time and teamwork. The survey is an important first step, but an ongoing effort and commitment on everyone's part is required to make sure that the results of the survey lead to improved management practices.

■ *Will it affect pay?* Yes, but not until you have had the opportunity to adjust to the process and work on achieving results. The pay tie-in will occur over three years. The first year, we will find out where we are today as managers and supervisors. The second year, we will implement individual development plans and work toward personal improvement. The third year, we will use the results along with other factors to evaluate employees on pay and promotion.

■ *What other resources are available to develop management skills?* The corporate library has reference materials (books, periodicals, and audio programs) and many independent-study courses that can help develop interpersonal skills. Many of these

are described in the Professional Development and Training Catalog.
- ■ *Where do I go if I have questions?* If you have questions about how the supervisor review works or how it is administered, the human resources department can help (see Figure 5-1).

Supervisor Review

All employees were asked to react to each item concerning their supervisor according to the following key:

A. My supervisor almost never does this.
B. My supervisor seldom does this.
C. My supervisor sometimes does this.
D. My supervisor usually does this.
E. My supervisor does this most of the time.

Competence

_____ 1. Is knowledgeable about his/her job.

_____ 2. Makes changes that result in improvements.

_____ 3. Plans and organizes work with clear properties.

_____ 4. Makes appropriate and timely decisions.

_____ 5. Effectively deals with poor performance.

_____ 6. Is customer focused—with both inside and outside "customers."

_____ 7. Is company minded and takes pride in doing his/her work.

_____ 8. Is helpful in working with me to develop measurable goals and objectives.

_____ 9. Encourages me to learn from my mistakes, develop, and grow.

_____ 10. Tries to keep me engaged and challenged by my responsibilities.

_____ 11. Measures results and progress toward goals.

_____ 12. Give good guidance and advice.

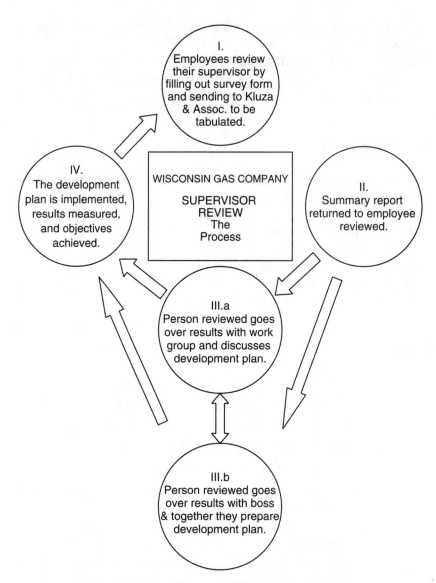

Figure 5-1. *The Process of the Supervisor Review*

Comments on this supervisor's competence:

_____

_____

Communication

_____13. Keeps me informed of things I need to know to do my job effectively.

_____14. Encourages me to share ideas and concerns by being accessible and approachable.

_____15. Puts ideas across clearly.

_____16. Listens and considers what I have to say.

_____17. Is tactful when interacting with others.

_____18. Keeps me informed of how I'm doing.

Comments on this supervisor's communication skills:

_____

_____

Integrity and Fairness

_____19. Demonstrates openness and honesty in dealing with me.

_____20. Can be trusted to keep a confidence.

_____21. Treats all workers equally.

_____22. Is trustworthy.

_____23. Shows concern and respect for individuals.

_____24. Has work rules but knows when to exercise flexibility.

_____25. Is fair in dealing with people.

Comments on this supervisor's integrity and fairness:

_____

_____

Participative Leadership

_____26. Encourages innovation.

_____27. Involves others in decisions that affect them.

_____28. Sets guidelines that allow me to do my work independently.

_____29. Actively promotes cooperation between individuals, departments, and divisions.

_____30. Gives credit when credit is due others.

_____31. Delegates authority clearly and appropriately.

_____32. Encourages participation by asking for my opinions and ideas.

_____33. Allows for disagreement without becoming irritated.

_____34. Encourages me to uncover and solve problems.

_____35. Resolves conflicts constructively.

Comments on this supervisor's participative leadership:

_____

_____

According to Jody Zanton, coordinator of personnel and employee development, the feedback form of this survey has been well accepted by the supervisors and helpful in determining training needs.

Advisory Committee

One of the best approaches to determining needs is to work with a carefully selected advisory committee of six to ten managers who are interested in supervisory development. They can represent different functions and levels in the organization. The committee can advise on subjects, schedules, group size, and composition, as well as other aspects of the program. They can also be involved in implementing the program (introducing conference leaders, teaching certain topics) and can be good salespersons for it.

To get maximum use from the advisory committee, the training professional should provide them with data to be discussed. For example, the results of questionnaires should be given to the committee so that their interpretations and decisions can be based on data instead of on off-the-cuff opinions.

ALLEN-BRADLEY, MILWAUKEE, WISCONSIN

John Flagge, Program Supervisor, Technical Training, Human Resources of Allen-Bradley, provides the following description of how Allen-Bradley uses an advisory committee.

The objective is to:

1. Serve in an advisory capacity for the training and development function. Committee members will represent functional areas throughout the company. The committee will provide feedback and evaluation of present and proposed training efforts. The evaluation will be based on constructive criticism and results evaluation.

The functions are to:

1. Recommend changes in existing training programs to meet the challenging needs.
2. Evaluate the need for new training programs based upon changes in technology, management theory, etc.
3. Recommend changes consistent with long-range strategies.
4. Make recommendations relative to course format, timing, facilities, content.
5. Communicate with department management within their function so as to represent a broad cross-section of viewpoints.
6. Serve as a communications link between the training and development function and all functions to improve and encourage two-way communications.

Organization

1. The advisory training committee will meet on a semiannual basis to evaluate progress and discuss mutual problems and suggestions.
2. The training advisory committee will consist of subcommittees whose focus will be dependent on current and strategic issues.

    a. Committee 1 will consist of at least two members from each functional area. These members will address current and strategic issues as they pertain to the company. Each member of this cross-functional committee will be a permanent member of the training advisory committee.
    b. Committees 2–7 will consist of at least six members of their specific functional area. The members of each of the functional committees will address current and strategic issues

as they pertain to their functional area. Each committee will appoint a chairperson and that chairperson will be a permanent member of the training advisory committee.

3. The Program Supervisory, Technical Training, will appoint a co-chairperson on an annual basis to assist in scheduling committee meetings and establishing an agenda.

Performance Review

In organizations with a formal performance review program, the complete forms can be analyzed to determine supervisory training needs. Performance reviews usually identify the weaknesses and the areas of improvement needed. These can be analyzed and quantified to determine which subject areas and which kinds of training activities can best help supervisors perform their jobs better. (Chapter 10 describes this approach in detail.)

Questionnaires

Probably the simplest method of determining needs is to prepare a questionnaire that can be administered to supervisors themselves and/or to higher-level managers. Figure 5-2 contains a sample form that any organization can use, although it should be adapted to include all possible topics for supervisory training that might apply to a par-

Please put an "X" after each topic to indicate your need for that topic:

	Great Need	Some Need	Little Need
1. The job of supervisor (objectives, functions, authority, responsibility)			
2. Leadership styles			
3. Interpersonal communication principles, barriers, approaches, methods			
4. Written communication			
5. Oral communication			
6. Listening			

Figure 5-2. *Questionnaire for determining subject content for training*

	Great Need	Some Need	Little Need
7. Conducting productive meetings			
8. Interviewing			
9. Speed reading			
10. Understanding and motivating employees			
11. Orienting and training employees			
12. Supervising minority employees— diversity in the work force			
13. Appraising employee performance			
14. Preventing and handling complaints/grievances			
15. Planning			
16. Discipline			
17. Decision making			
18. Empowerment—self-directed work teams			
19. Managing change			
20. Delegation			
21. Managing time			
22. Building teamwork			
23. Improving quality			
24. Resolving conflict			
25. Building morale among subordinates			

Other suggested topics:

Figure 5-2. *Cont'd*

ticular organization. The use of three columns makes it easy to tabulate and quantify the needs as determined by the supervisors themselves.

Figure 5-3 shows a tabulation of the results of surveying 21 supervisors. In order to use the data in planning, a weight of "2" has been given to Column 1 ("Great Need"), "1" to Column 2 ("Some Need"), and "0" to the Column 3. The weighted score—Column 1 plus Column 2—has been calculated and then converted to the rank order shown on the left side of the form.

Please put an "X" after each topic to indicate your need for that topic:

Rank Order		Weighted Score	(Weight) 2 Great Need	1 Some Need	0 Little Need
10	1. The job of supervisor (objectives, functions, authority, responsibility)	29	10	9	2
3	2. Leadership styles	34	13	8	0
17	3. Interpersonal communication principles, barriers, approaches, methods	25	7	11	3
15	4. Written communication	26	9	8	4
13	5. Oral communication	27	8	11	2
23	6. Listening	16	5	6	10
21	7. Conducting productive meetings	19	4	11	6
20	8. Interviewing	20	6	8	7
24	9. Speed reading	14	2	10	9
3	10. Understanding and motivating employees	34	13	8	0
2	11. Orienting and training employees	35	15	5	1
7	12. Supervising minority employees—diversity in the work force	32	12	8	1
18	13. Appraising employee performance	24	8	8	5
15	14. Preventing and handling complaints/grievances	26	10	6	5
25	15. Planning	10	2	6	13
7	16. Discipline	32	12	8	1
3	17. Decision making	34	13	8	0
13	18. Empowerment— self-directed work teams	27	9	9	3

Figure 5-3.
A completed questionnaire

Please put an "X" after each topic to indicate your need for that topic:

Rank Order		Weighted Score	(Weight) 2 Great Need	1 Some Need	0 Little Need
3	19. Managing change	34	14	6	1
22	20. Delegation	18	6	6	9
10	21. Managing time	29	11	7	3
1	22. Building teamwork	40	19	2	0
7	23. Improving quality	32	11	10	0
12	24. Resolving conflict	28	9	10	2
18	25. Building morale among subordinates	24	8	10	3

Other suggested topics:

Figure 5-3. *Cont'd*

The same process can be followed to get input from bosses. The topics would be the same, but the instructions at the top of the form would read instead, "Please put a check in the appropriate column after each topic to indicate your opinion of the need of supervisors who report to you." A comparison could then be made of the rank order of topics determined by the bosses with the rank order determined by the supervisors themselves. Other data should also be considered in deciding which needs are most important and urgent.

Interviews

A common way of determining supervisory training needs is to interview the supervisors themselves, their bosses, or both. To be an effective technique, a patterned interview should be used. This means that the same questions should be asked of different people so that responses can be quantified.

Following is a guide for a **patterned interview with supervisors:**

We are planning a training program to help you do your job better. You can help us determine subject content by answering the following questions:

1. What problems exist in your department?
2. What problems do you foresee in the near future?
3. What subjects should be included in a training program to help solve these problems?
4. What other topics should be included in order to help you do your job better?
5. When would be the best time for you to attend a classroom training program?
6. When is the worst time?

A checklist of possible topics described in Figure 5-2 can be used in Question 3 so that the tabulations can be quantified. The same type of approach can be used in conducting interviews with the bosses of the supervisors to be trained. These interviews are more personal and can provide more detailed information than questionnaires, but they are much more time-consuming.

Tests and Inventories

Another way of determining supervisory training needs is to test the supervisors on their attitudes, knowledge, and skills that are important in doing their job. (This testing could be a supplement to the job analysis described previously.)

Tests and inventories can be developed and tailored to the organization, or appropriate standardized tests can be used to assist in determining needs. I've developed standardized tests on the subjects of communications, human relations, managing change, time management, performance appraisal and coaching, along with leadership, motivation, and decision making.[2] Items are to be answered "agree" or "disagree." Samples of each of these inventories follow.

---

[2]Donald L. Kirkpatrick, *Supervisory/Management Inventories* (Elm Grove, Wis.: Donald L. Kirkpatrick, 1992).

Supervisory Inventory on Communication

_____ 1. A good definition of communication is the sending of information from one person to another.

_____ 2. The misunderstanding of an order or instruction can have serious results on safety, production, and cost.

_____ 3. A sender has failed to communicate unless the receiver understands the message the way the sender intended it.

_____ 4. When it is important that a new policy be understood by all employees, the best way to communicate is through channels of authority in the organization.

_____ 5. If employees do not understand, they will usually indicate lack of understanding by asking questions or by saying that they don't understand.

_____ 6. If a supervisor is busy, it is best to tell an employee who wants to talk, "I'm busy right now, contact me later."

_____ 7. The shorter a memo, the more clear it is likely to be.

_____ 8. "Verbal" means the same as "oral."

_____ 9. Oral communication is more effective than written.

_____10. A supervisor has failed to communicate unless the employee understands, accepts, and carries out the instruction.

Supervisory Inventory on Human Relations

_____ 1. Anyone is able to do most any job if he or she tries hard enough.

_____ 2. Intelligence consists of what we've learned since we were born.

_____ 3. Everyone is either an introvert or an extrovert.

_____ 4. An employee's attitude has little effect on his production.

_____ 5. People will work faster and longer if they always have a little more work ahead of them than they can possibly do.

_____ 6. A good supervisor must be able to perform all the jobs in the department.

_____ 7. In training an employee, the first thing the supervisor should do is show in detail how the job is performed.

_____ 8. To correct a worker who has made a mistake, a good supervisor will begin by pointing out the mistake.

_____ 9. The supervisor is closer to management than to subordinates.

_____10. It is a good idea to praise an employee in front of other employees.

Management Inventory on Managing Change

_____ 1. Managers should constantly be looking for changes that will improve department efficiency.

_____ 2. Suggestion systems are good because the suggestion goes to a neutral party instead of to the person who is in a position to implement it.

_____ 3. Managers should freely suggest changes to managers in other departments.

_____ 4. People who don't understand the reasons for a change will always resist it.

_____ 5. If subordinates participate in the decision to make a change, they are usually more enthusiastic in carrying it out.

_____ 6. "You can't make a silk purse out of a sow's ear."

_____ 7. "Ne Stupefaciamus" is good advice.

_____ 8. If you were promoted to a management job, you should make the job different than it was under your predecessor.

_____ 9. Bosses and subordinates should have an understanding regarding the kinds of changes that can be implemented by the subordinate without getting prior approval from the boss.

_____10. You've decided on a change and announced it. You then receive more data and now know it's a mistake. You should retract the decision and apologize for the mistake.

Management Inventory on Time Management

_____ 1. A manager should maintain a proper balance between time spent on the job, with the family, on personal hobbies, and for outside church, professional, and community organizations.

_____ 2. More discretionary time should be the goal of a manager.

_____ 3. Managers should be judged and rewarded on the basis of the amount of time they devote to the organization.

_____ 4. It is desirable for every manager to spend some time doing jobs under his or her supervision in order to keep a hand on the pulse of the organization.

_____ 5. A manager should always do the most important things first.

_____ 6. Unwanted visitors should be treated "coolly" so they won't stay long.

_____ 7. All managers should know how to say "no" to bosses, subordinates, and all other members of management.

_____ 8. The best way to control a meeting is to prevent it from getting out of control.

_____ 9. Delegation means the same as job assignment.

_____10. Delegation always saves time for a manager.

Management Inventory on Performance Appraisal and Coaching

_____ 1. The same performance appraisal program (forms, procedures, interview) should be used for performance improvement, as well as for salary adjustments.

_____ 2. An understanding by the subordinates of "what's expected by the boss" is an important prerequisite to the appraisal of performance.

_____ 3. A standard of performance should be challenging (requiring a stretch but reachable).

_____ 4. A standard of performance must be specific and measurable (dollars, percentages, numbers, etc.)

_____ 5. In the appraisal interview, a specific Performance Improvement Plan (identifying who will do what and when) should be jointly developed to improve the performance that needs improvement.

_____ 6. An important part of the Performance Improvement Plan is to determine what the boss can do to help the subordinate improve performance.

_____ 7. Managers as well as coaches should treat everyone equally.

_____ 8. Getting the job done (winning) is more important than building good attitudes and high morale.

_____ 9. When subordinates have been trained to do a job a certain way, they should be given the freedom to do it differently if they wish.

_____10. Action should be taken to remove players/employees who can't meet the standards of performance.

Management Inventory on Leadership, Motivation, and Decision Making

_____ 1. There is a clear distinction between a "leader" and a "manager."

_____ 2. A person with leadership qualities can be successful as a manager in any kind of organization or department.

_____ 3. In order to be effective, a manager must be able to perform all the jobs in the department he/she supervises.

_____ 4. The popular saying, "If it ain't broke, don't fix it" is good advice for managers.

_____ 5. It is possible for a manager to "motivate" employees.

_____ 6. Employees will do what their manager *inspects* rather than what the manager *expects*.

_____ 7. Managing by walking/wandering around (MBWA) is a sure way to improve employee attitudes and increase productivity.

_____ 8. Employees who are asked for their opinions regarding a decision to be made are usually more enthusiastic in implementing the decision than those who were not asked.

_____ 9. A group decision usually ends up with a "camel" while trying to create a "horse."

_____10. A manager who supervises an employee who is not able to do a job should remove him/her from the job or modify the job so that it can be performed effectively.

The last inventory also includes a question on the amount of participation and empowerment that should be given to subordinates when

Please circle the ones you answered incorrectly according to the scoring key.

1	2	3	4	5	6	7	8	9
10	11	12	13	14	15	16	17	18
19	20	21	22	23	24	25	26	27
28	29	30	31	32	33	34	35	36
37	38	39	40	41	42	43	44	45
46	47	48	49	50	51	52	53	54
55	56	57	58	59	60	61	62	63
64	65	66	67	68	69	70	71	72
73	74	75	76	77	78	79	80	

My score = 80 − _____ =
(# wrong)

Figure 5-4.
Form for tabulating inventory responses

making a decision. It asks for past practices, as well as what should be done in the future.

A tabulation of responses to these inventories will reveal attitudes and knowledge. Figure 5-4 is an example of a form that can be used to obtain this data. After scoring the test/inventory, individuals are asked to circle those items they answered incorrectly and to tabulate their score. These forms are then collected and tabulated. The participants keep their tests. Training program objectives and content can be based on these data. The inventories can also be used to stimulate lively and practical discussions (see Chapter 7) and to evaluate the effectiveness of the program (see Chapter 8).

The eight inventories are concerned with concepts, principles, and techniques that relate to supervision in all organizations. Some content of the supervisory training programs should be added that relates to specific technical knowledge that is important for supervisors in that organization.

MGIC,
MILWAUKEE, WISCONSIN

Sample Questions, Product Knowledge Test. Training professionals at MGIC (Mortgage Guarantee Insurance Company) in Milwaukee developed a Product Knowledge Test consisting of 40 questions. It is given to supervisors as a pretest at the beginning of a training program to determine needs and then administered again at the end of a program as a posttest to evaluate the learning that has taken place. Following are some of the questions from that test:

_____ 1. MGIC is the only private MI company to offer . . .

    A. Condo status and loan progress reports

    B. Underwriting guidelines and premium rate bulletin boards

    C. Auto-delegated and auto-premium payments

_____ 2. How many times will MGIC/FAX retry a document delivery, if a lender's FAX machine is busy?

    A. Once

    B. Twice

    C. Five Times

    D. Ten Times

    E. Indefinitely

_____ 3. RDS III currently offers delivery of two basic documents other than commitments. What are they?

    A. Loan sale notices and endorsements

    B. Premium acknowledgments and endorsements

    C. Loan sale notices and premium acknowledgments

    D. Endorsements and loan sale notices

_____ 4. Which of the following is NOT an RDS III bulletin board?

    A. The MGIC Resource Directory

    B. MGIC Premium Rates

    C. The MGIC Underwriting Guideline Summary

    D. The MGIC Mortgage Market Summary

_____ 5. Which of the following is NOT a category in the Loan Progress Report?

A. Loans approved

B. Loans-in-suspense

C. Loans denied

D. Loans received

_____ 6. MGIC/FAX offers high speed delivery for . . .

A. Commitments

B. Premium acknowledgements

C. A + B

_____ 7. RDS III can be offered on a "sometimes" basis. True or False?

_____ 8. When selling in RDS III, it is best to target:

A. Managers

B. Processors

C. Technical support people

D. A + B

E. All of the above

_____ 9. To receive the underwriting guideline bulletin board that is appropriate for his area of the country, a lender must enter a five-digit zip code. True or false?

_____ 10. Which private mortgage insurers are able to provide electronic loan status?

A. MGIC and GE

B. MGIC, GE, and PMI

C. MGIC, GE, and CMAC

MGIC PLUS

_____ 11. In addition to enhancing MGIC's investment income opportunities, single premiums benefit the company because they are earned at a more accelerated pace than annual premiums. True or false?

_____ 12. The size of the ceding commission that MGIC receives from the reinsurers is determined by loan amount, not premium dollars. True or false?

_____ 13. Which of the following do not affect the MGIC PLUS buying decision?

A. Consumer

B. Realtor

C. MGIC Underwriter

D. Secondary Market Manager

E. Servicing Manager

F. All of the above

G. None of the above

H. Both B + C

I. Both C + E

_____ 14. When preparing a truth-in-lending disclosure for a loan with a financed single premium, mortgage insurance should always be disclosed for the life of the loan. True or false?

_____ 15. FNMA will allow a "no cash out" refinance loan to exceed 90% LTV by the amount of a financed mortgage insurance premium as long as the combined loan-to-value does not exceed 95%. True or false?

_____ 16. FNMA will allow a 4% seller contribution on a fixed rate lean with a financed annual premium. The base LTV is 90% with a combined LTV of 91%. True or false?

_____ 17. The following is not a benefit of MGIC PLUS for the lender:

    A. Conventional program to compete with FHA

    B. Decreased servicing costs on single premium loans

    C. Increased investment income

    D. Increased origination and servicing fee income

    E. None of the above

    F. Both A + C

_____ 18. MGIC is the only mortgage insurer offering special single premium pricing on liens with temporary buy-downs. True or false?

_____ 19. MGIC, GE, and PMI are the only mortgage insurers offering a nonrefundable single premium. True or false?

_____ 20. GE and MGIC have the same refund policy for refundable single premiums. True or false?

_____ 21. Effective December 7, 1989, savings associations are required to maintain minimum risk-based capital of _____%.

    A. 3%

    B. 1.5%

    C. 8%

    D. 6.4%

    E. None of the above

_____ 22. The new "risk-based capital" regulations for S&Ls have caused many of them to:

    A. Convert whole loans into securities

    B. Begin originating home equity loans

    C. Put MI on their uninsured 90s

    D. All of the above

    E. A + C

    F. B + C

_____ 23. A healthy institution is acquiring a troubled S&L. Which MGIC Capital Markets Service are they most likely to need in order to successfully complete the acquisition?

    A. Portfolio analysis

    B. Quality control services

    C. Contract underwriting

    D. Conduit services

Assessing Performance Effectiveness

According to Dane Gaines and James C. Robinson, needs can be determined by collecting information to determine gaps between desired and actual performance, as well as by identifying the relationship between desired operational results and the skills or knowledge required to accomplish them.[3] Either questionnaires or interviews (or both) can be used. Figure 5-5 lists the advantages and disadvantages of each.

Advantages	Disadvantages
Questionnaires	
• More people can be included in study, to meet considerations of time and cost.	• It is difficult to create good questions and requires a high degree of knowledge regarding the situation to do so; potential answers must also be created.
• Respondents can be in several locations and still be included in the study.	
• Confidentiality is more protected.	
• Each question is consistently presented to the respondent.	• You cannot ensure that the individual receiving the questionnaire will be the one responding to it.
• Results are easy to tabulate (if closed questions are used).	• Response rate may be poor.
• Cost per instrument is less than with other data collection methods.	• Instrument must be piloted to ensure clarity, which requires additional time.
	• Respondent may not understand the survey (even though it was piloted), and a certain percentage of returned surveys may need to be discarded due to responding errors (such as marking two answers to the same question).

Figure 5-5.

Advantages and disadvantages of data collection methods

[3]Dana Gaines Robinson and James C. Robinson, *Training for Impact* (San Francisco: Jossey-Bass, 1989).

Advantages	Disadvantages
Interviews	

Advantages	Disadvantages
• Respondents have opportunity to give information openly and freely.	• They are labor intensive, requiring more time to include enough respondents.
• If question is unclear, interviewer can restate.	• If more than one person conducts interviews, each person must present each question in a similar manner.
• If response is unclear, interviewer can probe for clarity.	
• They are easier to create than questionnaires, because only questions need to be created (not potential answers).	• Confidentiality of respondents cannot be ensured.
• They provide increased control over high response rate.	• Cost per interview is higher than cost per questionnaire.
• As new information is obtained, the interview process can be adapted so that additional information, other than what was initially considered, can be collected.	• Tabulation is time-consuming (must be done manually); if more than one individual analyzes data, inter-rater reliability must be ensured.

Figure 5-5. *Cont'd*

Comparing Methods for Determining Needs

In his chapter in The Training and Development Handbook, Geary Rummler compared four methods for determining training needs: training needs survey, competency study, task analysis, and performance analysis. Figure 5-6 outlines the approaches and sets out the advantages and disadvantages of each one. Rummler believes that a professional trainer is likely to use all four approaches at some time.[4]

In Figure 5-7, S.V. Steadham describes the advantages and disadvantages of nine basic needs assessment techniques.[5]

(text continued on page 84)

[4]Geary A. Rummler, "Determining Needs," in *The Training and Development Handbook*, 3rd ed. (New York: McGraw-Hill, 1987).

[5]S.V. Steadham, "Learning to Select a Needs Assessment Strategy," *Training and Development Journal* (January 1980). Copyright 1980, the American Society for Training and Development. Reprinted with permission. All rights reserved.

	Training Needs Survey	Competency Study	Task Analysis	Performance Analysis
Starting Point	What knowledge and skill is required?	What competencies are required?	What tasks are required?	What job performance is required?
General Approach	• Ask key people what knowledge and skills they think or feel the trainee-performers require to do their job (or "X" portion of their job). • Prioritize the knowledge and skills recommended and summarize as a topical list, a training agenda, curriculum, etc.	• Ask key people what competencies they think the trainee-performer requires to do the job (or "X" portion of the job.) • Determine the knowledge and skills required to attain the stated competencies. • Prioritize the knowledge and skills recommended and summarize as a training agenda or curriculum.	• Determine what tasks are required of the trainee-performer in order for the job to be performed correctly and successfully. • Determine the knowledge and skills required to correctly perform the tasks identified. • Prioritize the tasks, and thereby the knowledge and skills, and summarize as a training design document, training agenda, or a curriculum	• Determine what performance is required • Determine the critical job outputs or "accomplishments." • Determine what tasks are required of the trainee-performer to produce the job outputs or "accomplishments." • Determine the knowledge and skills required to correctly perform the tasks identified. • Determine what other factors (in addition to knowledge and skills) influence job performance (such as job design, resources, consequences and feedback).

Figure 5-6.

Comparison of four approaches to determining training needs

	Training Needs Survey	Competency Study	Task Analysis	Performance Analysis
Starting Point	What knowledge and skill is required?	What competencies are required?	What tasks are required?	What job performance is required?
General Approach				• Prioritize the knowledge and skills required based on impact on job performance and summarize as a training design document, training agenda, or curriculum. • Summarize recommendations and modify negative influences identified above.
Advantages of This Approach	• Fast, inexpensive. • Broad involvement. • Low risk. • Low visibility.	• Relatively fast, inexpensive. • Broad involvement. • Consensus. • In addition to training needs, articulation and agreement on a success "profile" for the performer.	• Precise identification of tasks and required knowledge and skills. • Is a form of output and can be measured. • Broad involvement. • Objective, validated by observation.	• Links knowledge and skill requirements to job performance. • Can validate, evaluate. • Addresses other factors affecting performance.

Figure 5-6. *Cont'd*

	Training Needs Survey	Competency Study	Task Analysis	Performance Analysis
Starting Point	What knowledge and skill is required?	What competencies are required?	What tasks are required?	What job performance is required?
Advantages of This Approach		• Identify generic training needs covering a broad population (e.g., supervisors, first-time managers).		• Impact of job output is established and therefore can prioritize prioritize input.
Disadvantages of This Approach	• Not precise or specific. • Based on opinion, albeit "expert." • Difficult to validate. • Difficult to set priorities. • Difficult to relate to output, to evaluate importance of training. • Once you ask people what training they feel is important, there is an implicit expectation that you will deliver it.	• Difficult to relate to output, to evaluate training. • Difficult to assess relative importance of competencies and therefore difficult to set priorities for knowledge and skills input. • Consensus will not necessarily identify the critical difference between exemplary and average performance. • Does not address other factors influencing performance. • Can be highly visible.	• Takes time and skill. • Visible. • Difficult to assess relative importance of tasks and therefore difficult to set priorities for knowledge and skills input. • Does not address other factors affecting performance.	• Takes time and skill. • Visible.

Figure 5-6. Cont'd

Source: Reprinted with permission from McGraw-Hill from Geary A. Rummler, "Determining Needs," in The Training and Development Handbook, 3rd ed. (New York: McGraw-Hill, 1987).

Technique	Advantages	Disadvantages
Observation		
• Can be as technical as time-motion studies or as functionally or behaviorally specific as observing a new board or staff member interacting during a meeting. • May be as unstructured as walking through an agency's offices on the lookout for evidence of communication barriers. • Can be used normatively to distinguish between effective and ineffective behaviors, organizational structures, and/or processes.	• Minimizes interruption or routine work flow or group activity. • Generates in data, highly relevant to the situation where response to identified training needs/interests will impact. • (When combined with a feedback step) provides for important comparison checks between inferences of the observer and the respondent.	• Requires a highly skilled observer with both process and content knowledge (unlike an interviewer who needs, for the most part, only process skill). • Carries limitations that derive from being able to collect data only within the work setting (the other side of the first advantage listed in the preceding column). • Holds potential for resondents to perceive the observation activity as "spying."
Questionnaires		
• May be in the form of surveys or polls of a random or stratified sample of respondents, or an enumeration of an entire "population." • Can use a variety of question formats: open-ended, projective, forced-choice, priority-ranking. • Can take alternative forms such as Q-sorts, or slip-sorts, rating scales, either predesigned or self-generated by respondent(s).	• Can reach a large number of people in a short time. • Are relatively inexpensive. • Give opportunity of expression without fear of embarrassment. • Yield data easily summarized and reported.	• Make little provision for free expression of unanticipated responses. • Require substantial time (and technical skills, especially in survey model) for development of effective instruments. • Are of limited utility in getting at causes of problems or possible solutions. • Suffer low return rates (mailed), grudging responses, or unintended and/or inappropriate respondents.

Figure 5-7.

Advantages and disadvantages of nine basic needs assessment techniques

Technique	Advantages	Disadvantages
Questionnaires		
• May be self-administered (by mail) under controlled or uncontrolled conditions, or may require the presence of an interpreter or assistant.		
Key Consultation		
• Secures information from those persons who, by virtue of their formal or informal standing, are in a good position to know what the training needs of a particular group are: a. Board chairman b. related service providers c. Members of professional associations d. Individuals from the service population • Once identified, data can be gathered from these consultants by using techniques such as interviews, group discussions, questionnaires.	• Is relatively simple and inexpensive to conduct. • Permits input and interaction of a number of individuals, each with his or her own perspectives of the needs of the area discipline, group, etc. • Establishes and strengthens lines of communication between participants in the process.	• Carries a built-in bias, since it is based on views of those who tend to see training needs from their own individual or organizational perspective. • May result in only a partial picture of training needs due to the typically nonrepresentative nature (in a statistical sense) of a key informant group.

Figure 5-7. Cont'd

Technique	Advantages	Disadvantages
Print Media		
• Can include professional journals, legislative news/notes, industry trade magazine, in-house publications.	• Is an excellent source of information for uncovering and clarifying normative needs. • Provides information that is current, if not forward looking. • Is readily available and is apt to have already been reviewed by the client group.	• Can be a problem when it comes to the data analysis and synthesis into a usable form (use of clipping service or key consultants can make this type of data more usable).
Interviews		
• Can be formal or casual, structured or unstructured, or somewhere in between. • May be used with a sample of a particular group (board, staff, committee) or conducted with everyone concerned. • Can be done in person, by phone, at the work site, or away from it.	• Are adept at revealing feelings, causes of and possible solutions to problems the client is facing (or anticipates); provide maximum opportunity for the client to represent himself or herself spontaneously on his or her own terms (especially when conducted in an open-ended, nondirective manner).	• Are usually time-consuming. • Can be difficult to analyze and quantify results (especially from unstructured formats). • Unless the interviewer is skilled, the client(s) can easily be made to feel self-conscious. • Rely for success on a skillful interviewer who can generate data without making client(s) feel self-conscious, suspicious, etc.

Figure 5-7. *Cont'd*

Technique	Advantages	Disadvantages
Group Discussion		
• Resembles face-to-face interview technique, e.g., structured or unstructured, formal or informal, or somewhere in between. • Can be focused on job (role) analysis, group problem analysis, group goal setting, or any number of group tasks or themes, e.g., leadership training needs of the board. • Uses one or several of the familiar group facilitating techniques: brainstorming, nominal group process, forcefields, consensus rankings, organizational mirroring, simulation, and sculpting.	• Permits on-the-spot synthesis of different viewpoints. • Builds support for the particular service response that is ultimately decided on. • Decrease client's "dependence response" toward the service provider since data analysis is (or can be) a shared function. • Helps participants to become better problem analysts, better listeners, etc.	• Is time-consuming (therefore initially expensive) both for the consultant and the agency. • Can produce data that are difficult to synthesize and quantify (more a problem with the less structured techniques).
Tests		
• Are a hybridized form of questionnaire. • Can be very functionally oriented (like observations) to test board, staff, or committee member's proficiency. • May be used to sample learned ideas and facts. • Can be administered with or without the presence of an assistant.	• Can be especially helpful in determining whether the cause of a recognized problem is a deficiency in knowledge or skill or, by elimination, attitude. • Results are easily quantifiable and comparable.	• The availability of a relatively small number of tests that are validated for a specific situation. • Do not indicate if measured knowledge and skills are actually being used in the on-the-job or "back home group" situation.

Figure 5-7. Cont'd

Technique	Advantages	Disadvantages
Records, Reports		
• Can consist of organizational charts, planning documents, policy manuals, audits, and budget reports. • Employee records (grievance, turnover, accidents, etc.). • Includes minutes of meetings, weekly, monthly program reports, memoranda, agency service records, program evaluation studies.	• Provide excellent clues to trouble spots. • Provide objective evidence of the results of problems within the agency or group. • Can be collected with a minimum of effort and interruption of work flow since it already exists at the work site.	• Causes problems, or possible solutions often do not show up. • Carries perspective that generally reflects the past situation rather than the current one (or recent changes). • Need a skilled data analyst if clear patterns and trends are to emerge from such technical and diffuse raw data.
Work Samples		
• Are similar to observation but in written form. • Can be products generated in the course of the organization's work, e.g., ad layouts, program proposals, market analyses, letters, training designs • Written responses to a hypothetical but relevant case study provided by the consultant.	• Carry most of the advantages of records and reports data. • Are the organization's data (its own output).	• Case study method will take time away from actual work of the organization. • Need specialized content analysts. • Analyst's assessment of strengths/weaknesses disclosed by samples can be challenged as "too subjective."

Source: S.V. Steadham, "Learning to Select a Needs Assessment Strategy," in *Training and Development Journal*, January 1980, 30, pp. 56–61. Copyright 1980 by the American Society for Training and Development, Inc. Reprinted with permission. All rights reserved.

Converting Needs to Objectives. According to Martin Broadwell, "The most important single consideration in the teaching-learning process is the setting of objectives. Taken in proper perspective, the entire course from beginning to end should revolve around objectives. These statements should be readily accepted by any instructor who is trying to produce a specific quantity and quality of learning."[6] In other words, before we plan program content, select leaders, and determine techniques or aids, we should be sure that we have carefully determined and stated the objectives that we are going to try to accomplish.

Robert Mager has done much to encourage the setting of proper objectives. In his book *Preparing Instructional Objectives,* he has outlined not only the need for objectives but also specific techniques for setting them. According to Mager, "Course objectives represent a clear statement of instructional intent, and are written in any form necessary to clarify that intent." Mager describes the characteristics that objectives should have, among them the following:

- An objective says something about the student. It does not describe subject content, instructor, or the kinds of classroom experience to which the student will be exposed.
- An objective is about ends rather than means. It describes a product rather than a process. As such, it describes what students are expected to be like at the end of instruction rather than the means that will be used to get them there.[7]

The setting of objectives is an important part of the training process. Time and care should be used to be sure that the objectives are carefully determined before course content is developed.

Kinds of Objectives

There are five kinds of objectives that can be determined and stated. They are concerned with attitudes, knowledge, skills, job behavior, and results that are expected to be accomplished. The first three can be accomplished in the classroom. The last two must be accomplished on the job. Following are some examples of each:

---

[6]Martin Broadwell, *The Supervisor and On-the-Job Training,* 2nd ed. (Reading, - Mass.: Addison-Wesley, 1977).

[7]Robert Mager, *Preparing Instructional Objectives* (San Francisco: The Center for Effective Performance, 1997).

Attitude Objectives

- Supervisors feel that most workers want to take pride in the work they do.
- Supervisors realize that the time they spend in inducting and training new employees is well spent.
- Supervisors realize that upward communication is important to the morale and performance of workers.
- Supervisors feel that they are an important part of management.

Knowledge Objectives

- Supervisors can list and describe Abraham Maslow's Hierarchy of Needs.
- Supervisors understand the new contract provisions that have been negotiated into the union labor agreement.
- Supervisors understand the new personnel policy on vacations.
- Supervisors can list in sequence the following four steps to use in training employees.

  1. Prepare the worker.
  2. Present the operation.
  3. Try out performance.
  4. Follow up.

Skill Objectives

- Supervisors know how to use the four-step method for training new employees.
- Supervisors know how to use the checklist when inducting new employees.
- Supervisor know how to conduct problem-solving conferences.
- Supervisors know how to complete a flow-process chart.
- Supervisors know how to conduct an effective performance appraisal interview.
- Supervisors can write effective memos and reports.
- Supervisors know how to present information effectively in front of a group.

Job Behavior Objectives

- Supervisors use the four-step method for training whenever they train a new employee.
- Supervisors handle 90 percent of grievances at the first level.
- Supervisors listen actively when subordinates come to them with problems.
- Supervisors use the induction checklist whenever a new employee comes into their department.
- Supervisors conduct effective problem-solving conferences.

Results Objectives

- Turnover of new employees will be reduced to 5% per month by June 1.
- Grievances will be reduced to three per month by May 1.
- Morale will be improved from a year ago as measured by the attitude survey to be conducted in September.
- Accident frequency will be reduced to 2% by September 1.
- Absenteeism will be reduced to 1% by July 1.

Characteristics of Objectives

Classroom objectives of knowledge and skills should be stated from the standpoint of the learner, not the trainer and, whenever possible, all objectives should be stated in specific and measurable terms.

Summary

The many principles and techniques for determining needs and setting objectives outlined in this chapter are important prerequisites for selecting subject content for in-house program and approaches for meeting the needs and reaching the objectives. Other chapters will discuss the approaches that should be considered.

6

An Overview of Training and Development Techniques

A variety of methods are available to improve the knowledge, attitudes, and skills of supervisors. Selection of the appropriate technique or techniques depends on objectives, subject content, costs, availability of materials and instructors, and time considerations. Some of the most common methods include on-the-job development (as discussed in Chapters 10 and 11); internal classroom training (Chapters 7 and 8); and outside institutes, conferences, and seminars (Chapter 9). This chapter briefly describes several other popular methods and provides references for obtaining more information (see Figure 6-1).

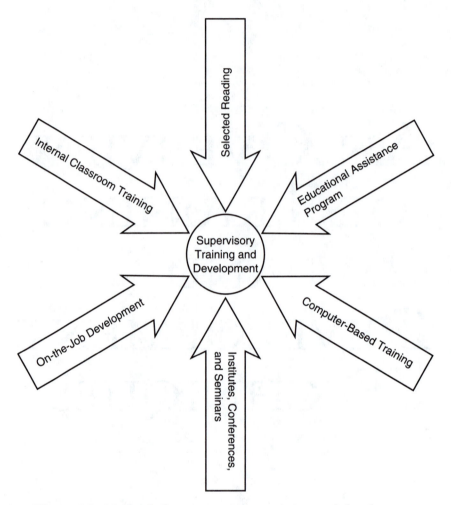

Figure 6-1. *Methods for surpervisory training and development*

Educational Assistance Programs

When supervisors attend outside management development programs held during business hours, the organization nearly always pays all of the costs and provides company time. When supervisors attend evening programs on their own personal time, educational assistance programs usually apply. Following are descriptions of the educational assistance programs of three organizations.

A Large Oil Company

The purpose of the Educational Assistance Program is to provide substantial financial assistance to eligible employees who take, on their own time from an approved educational institution, approved courses of an educational or vocational nature which will benefit both them and the Company.

The Company will reimburse a participating employee for 85 percent of certain costs incurred in connection with the courses taken. There is no limit to the total reimbursement allowable for any one employee.

Participation in the program will not constitute a guarantee of advancement in earnings or job level.

Eligibility

A regular employee who (a) is not on a leave of absence or layoff and (b) is not receiving educational assistance from some other agency which would duplicate aid received under this program is eligible to participate. The educational assistance allowance which is payable under the Veteran's Readjustment Act, however, will not disqualify an employee for participation.

Temporary, casual, part-time, or dual-status employees are not eligible to participate.

Approved Courses

Courses may be approved if they (a) add to the employee's effectiveness in his or her present assignment or (b) contribute to the individual's overall development in such a manner as to be beneficial to both the employee and the Company. Courses may also be approved which do not meet the requirements of (a) or (b) but which are required in a curriculum that leads to a degree which does.

Correspondence courses may be approved when no classroom course is available locally in the particular subject desired, when the employee's work schedule interferes with enrollment in local educational institutions, or when such a course for some special reason would be more suitable for the employee.

Review courses may be approved when taken for the purpose of passing an examination to be licensed or certified, e.g., to be admitted to the practice of law or to qualify as a certified public accountant (CPA), certified life insurance underwriter (CLU), or a

Fellow of the American Actuarial Society. Another type of review course which may also be approved is one taken for the purpose of achieving improved scores on enrollment tests such as the Graduate Management Admission Test or the Law School Admission Test. One course of each type may be approved for reimbursement.

Approved Educational Institutions

Educational institutions which will be approved are accredited schools, colleges, universities, trade schools, associations, professional societies, and organizations of a similar nature which may sponsor after-hours educational courses.

Reimbursement

An employee participating in the program will receive payment for 85 percent of the cost of reimbursable items provided the following conditions are met:

- The recipient is an employee of the Company at the time the courses are completed.
- The courses are completed with at least a passing grade as evidenced by a certification from the school on the refund application or a grade report.
- Receipted bills for all reimbursable items are submitted.
- Application for a refund is made within a reasonable time after completion of course work.

In the event an employee does not complete a course because of military service or as a result of a Company action—such as a transfer to a different location, night shift work, etc.—course completion will be waived as a condition for reimbursement. If the course is not completed due to a Company action, the employee will receive payment for 100 percent of the cost of reimbursable items, provided the following conditions are met:

- The recipient is an employee of the Company at the time the courses would otherwise have been completed.
- Receipted bills for all reimbursable items are submitted.
- Application for a refund is made within a reasonable time after cessation of course work.

Reimbursable items include tuition, required books, printed course materials required in lieu of textbooks, registrations, laboratory, and other fees which the institution requires the student to pay, such as athletic, cap and gown, conference, enrollment, graduation (diploma), library or bookbinding, nonresident, matriculation, proficiency examination (if the employee passes examination and receives credit for courses not taken), student activity, and tests such as enrollment or late examinations. If any of these items is not required by the institution and the employee elects to pay it, it will not be reimbursable. Also, reimbursable are examination fees required for certification or licensing if the employee successfully completes the test.

Nonreimbursable items include equipment (such as radio parts, drafting equipment, and special laboratory equipment), application for entrance into college or university, class ring or pin, deferred payment or installment charges (including case discount forfeited by late payment), fraternity or sorority dues or initiations, interest charged on loans from banks or credit associations to pay tuition, late registration fees, parking permits or fees, program changes at employee's request, room and board, transfer of credits from one institution to another, and transcript of credits.

Application for Participation

An Application for Participation should be submitted for approval before the course is started. If submission is delayed due to extenuating circumstances, the application may still be approved.

When a course requires more than one semester or one quarter for completion, the Application for Participation will cover the first such period, and a separate application will be submitted for each subsequent period of course work.

When a correspondence course requires more than one year to complete, the Application for Participation will cover the first year or any lesser period in which a definite part of the course will be completed, and a separate application will be submitted for subsequent parts of the course. The estimated completion date for the part of the course covered by the application must be shown on that form.

The Application for Participation will require approval by the supervisor, the department head (which for the purposes of this program will be any high management level), and the program administrator. These approvals will be sufficient provided the total refunds to be paid, or previously paid, to the applicant in a calendar year will not exceed $2,000. In the event the total refunds will exceed $2,000, approval will also be required by the executive to whom authority to take such action has been delegated.

Tuition Advance

An employee may receive a cash advance for tuition expenses for a semester or quarter (or for a program requiring an annual upfront payment rather than a per course payment) which exceed 5 percent of the employee's annual salary. Request for a tuition cash advance should be submitted before the course is started, for approval by the appropriate member of the Management Committee of the Company or the executive to whom such authority is delegated. By receiving a tuition cash advance, the employee agrees to submit an Application for Refund immediately upon receipt of his or her grade at course completion. The employee also agrees to repay this advance to the Company if the employee fails to complete the course with a passing grade during his or her employment with the Company.

Application for Refund

An employee will pay the educational institution for expenses in connection with the courses taken, and when the course work is completed, submit an Application for Refund. Under ordinary circumstances, the application should be submitted within a month.

To qualify for a refund, all correspondence courses must be completed, except for unusual circumstances, within 60 days of the estimated completion date listed on the application.

Applications for refunds must be made when each semester or quarter is completed in courses which require more than one semester or quarter for completion.

In the case of correspondence courses which require more than one year for completion, an application for a refund must be made when the part of the course covered by each Application for Participation is completed. The refund will be calculated by proration of the total cost of the course. Verification of satisfactory progress for the part of the course completed must be obtained from the officers of the educational institution.

A refund will be approved for a review course the first time it is taken, even though the course is taken at a nonaccredited institution and no evidence of satisfactory completion is given at the conclusion of the course.

The refund will be mailed to the employees.

Program Administrators

Program administrators will review Applications for Participation with regard to course and institution to make sure that approvals are consistent with the terms of the program, will review such applications when they are considered unfavorably by either the supervisor or department head and express an opinion as to whether the application should receive further consideration, and will approve refunds up to a total of $2,000 per calendar year for an individual.

In the General Office, the Corporate Human Resources Department will act as program administrator. In field locations which have a Human Resources staff, a staff member will act as program administrator. In field locations without a Human Resources staff, the role of program administrator will be performed by the Corporate Human Resources Department. Questions pertaining to the interpretation and administration of the Program should be referred to the Corporate Human Resources Department.

A LARGE MIDWESTERN BANK

General

This plan is intended to provide for the educational development of qualified employees. Employees who receive tuition reimbursement are morally committed to remain in the service of the bank for reasonable lengths of time. It is also anticipated, but not assured, that better job performance will be realized, while enhancing an individual's advancement potential with the Corporation.

Eligibility

A. An individual must be a regular full-time employee or a part-time employee with a regularly scheduled work week of 20 hours or more.
B. The employee must be "satisfactorily" performing the duties and responsibilities of the present job.
C. The employee must have six months continuous service to be eligible for participation in this plan (i.e., before the course begins).

Courses

A. An educational course or program must be directly related to the employee's performance in his or her present position or enhance potential for advancement in the Corporation to a position which the individual has a reasonable expectation of achieving.

B. Courses or programs must be offered by an approved school, college, university, or correspondence school. The determination of approved institutions will be the responsibility of the Human Resources department.

C. Courses or programs must be scheduled outside of the employee's regular working hours. All work in the course must be accomplished on the employee's own time.

D. This policy is not intended to cover professional seminars or conferences which an employee attends at the discretion of the Employer.

E. No commitment will be made to provide for all courses leading to a degree. Each course must be applied for separately and should be evaluated on its individual merits in accordance with the requirements of this policy.

F. Full-time employees may take up to six credits per semester/ maximum 12 credits per calendar year.

G. Part-time employees may take up to three credits per semester/ maximum six credits per calendar year.

H. Part-time employees are not eligible for graduate degree reimbursement.

Forms

Tuition reimbursement forms are available in Human Resources. Signatures of the applicant, supervisor, manager, and Human Resources are required for approval. This form is to be submitted to Human Resources prior to the start of classes.

Reimbursement

A. Employees are reimbursed for the cost of tuition and professional review courses which meet the requirements of this policy, with the following limitations:

1. 100-percent reimbursement for qualified costs with a grade of "B" or better. 75-percent reimbursement for qualified costs with a grade of "C." Proof of payment and transcript is required.

2. Reimbursement for schools outside of Metro Milwaukee is limited to the local cost per credit.

3. If no grading system is used, the employee will submit evidence of satisfactorily having completed the course.

4. Books are considered to be personal property, and their cost is the employee's responsibility.

5. Lab fees, parking, mileage, etc., are not reimbursable.

B. Tuition reimbursements are processed through Benefits about the fifteenth of each month. A credit is issued to the applicant's checking account.

C. There will be no double payment under this policy. For instance, benefits under the G.I. Bill, an education grant, or a scholarship must be exhausted before reimbursement is made.

D. If an employee is terminated for reasons such as reduction in force or transfer to another assignment, reimbursement will be made for expenses authorized under this policy.

E. An employee who voluntarily leaves the bank or is terminated for cause prior to completing a course will be responsible for all expenses associated with that course and will not be reimbursed.

The Supervisor's Responsibility

A. The applicant's educational goals and the details of this Tuition Reimbursement Plan should be freely discussed with the employee. Additional information may be obtained from the Human Resources Department.

B. It is the responsibility of each supervisor to assure the eligibility of both the employee and the course before the application is approved.

A MAJOR INSURANCE COMPANY

A major U.S. insurance company supports continuing education and the Educational Assistance Program. However, the company does not guarantee career advancement based on course completion or graduation.

The Educational Assistance Program is administered by each department, subject to Company guidelines. Approval is not granted automatically. It is based on potential value of the course/degree to the applicant's career budgetary restrictions, and the criteria listed below. In addition, all employees working to receive reimbursement for courses covered by the Program should be encouraged to complete Courses I and II of the LOMA Insurance Education Program prior to applying.

Qualification Criteria

To qualify for tuition refund, an employee must meet the following qualifications:

1. Be employed by the company as a regular full-time or regular part-time employee for at least one full year. (Long-term and/or short-term temporary employees are not eligible.)
2. If a nonmanagement employee, have a performance rating of "Satisfactory," "Better," or "Best" for specific job-related courses; and "Better" or "Best" for degree programs. If a management employee, have a performance rating of "Capable," "Superior," or "Outstanding" for specific job-related courses; and "Superior" or "Outstanding" for a degree program.
3. Be employed by the company at the time the course is completed.
4. For graduate-level courses, be a management level employee or an NR on track to a management position.

Under special circumstances, exceptions to the above qualifications can be made only with department head approval after discussion with your department tuition refund coordinator.

Reimbursement Limits

If the above qualification criteria are met and the employee's application is approved, the employee is then eligible to receive reimbursement for tuition expenses, subject to the following limits:

1. A maximum of six credits per semester, if a full-time employee; and a maximum of three credits per semester, if a part-time employee.
2. For courses taken during the 1990-91 school year, a maximum of $195.00 per credit for undergraduate degree courses; and a maximum of $280.00 per credit for graduate degree courses.

Under special circumstances, exceptions can be made only with department head approval after discussion with your department tuition refund coordinator.

Application Procedures

To apply for the Educational Assistance Program an employee should:

1. Discuss the course/degree with immediate manager. Prior to beginning a degree program, complete a Planning Chart for Degree Candidates with immediate manager.
2. Select a school which is accredited. (If uncertain about the accreditation of a particular college or university, check with the Training and Organizational Development Division of the Human Resources Department.)
3. Select a course/degree that is work related; that is, related to the current position or potential career opportunities as identified by department management.
4. Complete an application for the company's Educational Assistance Program and obtain approval from and signatures of immediate manager, administrative officer, and departmental tuition refund coordinator. (Document receipt of other educational financial assistance on the application. The company will only reimburse the balance not covered by the other assistance.)
5. Submit the completed application for the company's Educational Assistance Program, with appropriate signatures, to the Training and Organizational Development Division of the Human Resources Department no later than one month after registering for a course. Late applications must be signed and approved by the department head.

The education and training coordinator of the Training and Organizational Development Division will notify the employee if the course/degree meets with Company policy.

Reimbursement Procedures

Upon successful completion of an approved course, complete the following for reimbursement:

1. Submit the final grade report to immediate manager for signature. The employee will be reimbursed only for courses for which he or she earned a final grade of C- (1.67 Grade Point Average) or above. (For courses in which a letter grade is not given, a "confirmation of attendance" must be submitted with manager's signature.)

2. Submit the following items to the Training and Organizational Development Division of the Human Resources Department:

- Copy of final grade report with manager's signature.
- Proof of tuition payment:
  - Copies of official school receipts *and*
  - Copies of cancelled checks (front and back to show they have been endorsed).

The reimbursement request will be processed by the Training and Organizational Development Division.

Table 6-1
Information for Applicants

What's Covered?	*What's Not Covered?*
• Obtainment of a general equivalency diploma/high school diploma • Required review courses • Independent study courses • Audit courses • A basic computer knowledge course • Associate degree courses* • Undergraduate degree courses* • Graduate degree courses* • Books for vocational technical school courses only	• Application fees • Assessment Center fees • Books (unless attending technical school) • Career counseling/placement services • Compulsory activity fees Enrollment fees (e.g., Marquette and UWM application fees) • Graduation fees • Laboratory fees • Professional licensing fees (e.g., state bar exam) • Late fees • Finance charges • Fines • Tools • Equipment and supplies (e.g., calculator, notebooks, pens) • Supplementary reading materials • Suggested or recommended references • Typing and clerical costs • Postal charges • Living and travel expenses • Parking fees • Data searches and research support

*These courses must be academic and part of a curriculum.

If you receive assistance from other financial sources such as veterans' benefits, scholarships, or fellowships, the company will make up only the portion not covered.

Noncredit courses from a nonaccredited institution such as Dale Carnegie or Evelyn Wood Reading Dynamics are not covered under the Tuition Refund Program. Short courses which offer continuing education units are also not accepted under this tuition refund policy.

Selected Reading

Selected articles and books can be provided to supervisors as another way to train and develop them. Some supervisors (probably a small minority) are anxious to read material on supervision, but most supervisors are not and will not read these materials if they can avoid it. If reading is to be an effective technique, three guidelines must be followed:

1. The reading material must be related to the supervisor's current job or a potential future one.
2. The material must be written so it can be easily understood by the supervisor.
3. The supervisor must be motivated to read it.

The first two guidelines are concerned with subject content. Someone must read available material and select articles, pamphlets, and booklets that relate to the supervisory job. Also, that person should seek material written in such a way as to be readily understood by the supervisor. Some material may be selected for one supervisor (with, say, an eighth-grade education) and a different kind of material selected for another supervisor (who may be a college graduate). The content may be substantially the same, but the reading level may be entirely different.

The third guideline—that the supervisor must want to read it—may be a real challenge, particularly for supervisors who don't like to read. There are several ways to create interest:

■ Show supervisors how they can benefit by reading the selected material.
■ Make it easy. Instead of suggesting that supervisors go to the library to get a book or magazine, give the material to them.
■ Follow up by asking for a report or by discussing the material with them, either individually or in a group meeting.

A personal example will indicate the challenge of getting people to read. When I was responsible for supervisory training at International Minerals and Chemical Corporation (IMC), I initiated a selected reading program for supervisors and managers. First, I carefully selected 100 management books that were pertinent to the management jobs at

IMC. Then I wrote a summary of each and indicated the reading level, as well as the content and approach of the author.

Next, I arranged for the books and summaries to be displayed in the IMC lounge. Each week, books on a different phase of management (e.g., communication, delegation) were featured. Finally, a notice was sent to all supervisors encouraging them to look at the display and borrow any books that seemed helpful. Several weeks later, I checked with the library to see the extent of borrowing by supervisors and managers. Practically none of the books had been checked out—a disappointing result.

Stimulating supervisors to read is a real challenge. The supervisor's boss is in the best position to motivate because he or she is the boss, and encouragement and suggestions will probably be more effective than those of a staff training person.

One organization that makes extensive use of selected reading is Web Converting of Cedar Hill, Texas. All employees, managers and nonmanagers alike, read selected books on company time. The supervisor and subordinates then discuss the book and its application in the department. According to Web president Robert Fulton, "Books play maybe the major role in the change-of-thinking process going on here." Whenever he found a book that excited him, he sent copies to the 12 corporate and plant managers, who then discussed it at a managers' meeting.

Computer-Based Training (CBT)

CBT involves the use of computers to deliver instructional materials to a central training facility or workplace. It can be effectively used to teach a variety of subject content, as well as to develop skills. It was originally planned as a means of presenting single-topic, stand-alone training programs. Today, it is usually combined with other training delivery systems.

One of the main advantages of CBT is that a student can select the time to learn from it and can do it at his or her own pace. This makes it a "tailor-made" approach and saves time and money. It can, however, be a lonely way of learning and lacks the interaction and stimulation that classroom training provides. Unless a student is highly motivated to learn, CBT is not effective.

Some CBT packages can be purchased that are related to supervisory needs. Programs can also be developed for in-house use. Both approaches are costly and require many people to use the program in order to be cost-effective.

According to Mitchell,[1] "In the training/learning universe, computers have both wonderful power and major limitations. They can bring much involvement and interaction into the learning experience. On the other hand, they can easily become demotivational and counterproductive experiences. This is particularly true when they are forced into the uncomfortable role of linear progressive tutorial instruction."

In supervisory training, the subjects that best lend themselves to CBT are problem solving and decision making. The format would be to create a situation and ask the learner to make a decision or solve a problem. All of the necessary information would be available in the computer, provided the learner asks for it. After the supervisor solves the problem or makes a decision, the computer provides feedback on the best solution. If the supervisor has not done well, the computer provides remedial action, and the learner can try again and again and again.

Summary

This chapter had identified six ways to train and develop supervisors. Most organizations use a combination of these. For example, most larger organizations have their own human resources trainers who plan, coordinate, and sometimes teach in-house programs for supervisors. They carefully select outside programs to meet the needs of certain individuals at all levels of management. Smaller companies that lack professional trainers often rely on outside programs for supervisory training and development.

Educational assistance programs exist in most organizations, regardless of size. Organizations that are located in cities usually take advantage of the many evening programs that local universities and colleges offer. Many organizations, particularly the larger ones, have libraries, although most of the books and periodicals in them are of a technical nature. Management books are usually located instead in the offices of human resources professionals.

---

[1]Garry Mitchell, *The Trainer's Handbook, Second Edition* (AMACOM, 1993). Reprinted by permission of the publisher from *The Trainer's Handbook: The AMA Guide to Effective Training, 2nd Edition* by Garry Mitchell, © 1993 AMACOM, a division of American Management Association, New York. All rights reserved.

Computer-based training is quite new and is not widely used to train supervisors. It is more typically used for technical training. Each organization should determine its needs for supervisory training and development, research the various ways it can be done, and use those approaches that are most cost-effective.

7

PLANNING AND IMPLEMENTING INTERNAL CLASSROOM TRAINING

Most organizations offer classroom courses to train and develop supervisors. They can be effective or ineffective, depending on a variety of factors. This chapter describes concepts, principles, and techniques to maximize the effectiveness of the courses.

Setting Objectives

Most classroom training programs are run for one purpose—to stimulate and teach proper supervisory behavior so that improved organization results will be achieved: the reduction of turnover, accidents, and costs; along with improved quality employee morale and satisfaction, and profitability.

To accomplish change in behavior and to improve results, the following specific objectives should be considered:

- ■ *Knowledge*—To improve supervisors' understanding of company policy rules, procedures, and the labor agreement if there is a union; theories, principles, and techniques of management; technical information related to the supervisor's job; and the backgrounds, attitudes, needs, and other characteristics of subordinates, typically referred to as "diversity of the work force."

- ■ *Skills*—To improve the supervisor's skill in such areas as inducting and training new employees; teaching effective communication, including listening, reading, speaking, and writing; team building; decision making; disciplining employees; delegating; motivating; planning; conducting performance appraisal interviews; and managing change.

- ■ *Attitudes*—To create proper attitudes of supervisors toward the company, their job, supervisors and staff people in other departments, and the employees who work for and with them.

The objectives of classroom training should be clearly set at the beginning. They should be oriented to the supervisors who will be in the class and related to the attitudes, knowledge, skills, and the behavior that those attending should have after the course. Robert Mager's book *Preparing Instructional Objectives* provides suggestions for determining needs and stating objectives.[1]

---

[1]Robert Mager, *Preparing Instructional Objectives*, 3rd ed. (San Francisco: The Center for Effective Performance, 1997).

Determining Subject Content

Once the objectives have been arrived at, it becomes relatively simple to determine the subject content of the course. Each objective indicates the kind of subject that needs to be taught if the objective is to be accomplished. For example, objectives that describe attitudes, knowledge, and skills of the trainees directly indicate the kind of topics, forms, and procedures that must be taught in the course. In the case of objectives dealing with behavior, however, there are some complicating factors that make it more difficult to determine subject content.

Let us assume, for example, we are teaching the supervisors the four-step method for effective on-the-job training. One of the objectives is to be sure that they know how to use this method when training employees. They will be taught how to do it in the classroom and demonstrate in the classroom that they know how to do it. If one of the objectives, however, is to be sure that supervisors *use* the four-step method when training new employees who come into their department, the job becomes more difficult. In addition to teaching supervisors the skill of the four-step method, we must also teach them an attitude that will make them want to use it on the job.

Even these two objectives are not sufficient to be sure they will use the four-step method on the job; we must also be concerned with what takes place from the time they leave the classroom until a new employee comes into the department. Perhaps the supervisor is tied up doing something vital when a new employee comes into the department. He or she feels that the task he/she is in the midst of is more important than applying the four-step method and may rationalize that the old way of training a new employee is good enough. To prevent such occurrences, the training program should not only (1) teach knowledge and (2) skills, but should also (3) stimulate the supervisor to apply the skills on the job and (4) be sure that the boss of the supervisor provides a positive climate for implementation.

An important consideration in transforming objectives into subject content has to do with the length of the program. A good approach for determining specific subject content is to list the possible subjects and topics, consider them in relation to the specific objective to be accomplished, and, finally, analyze and screen them in the light of the amount of time available for the training. This sorting-out process will help to determine the specific subject content for each session. Additionally, the advisory committee can be very helpful in making these decisions.

Some topics are appropriate in nearly any organization, particularly as a basic program—for example:

The Supervisor's Job. This topic emphasizes that the supervisor is part of management and it clarifies the objectives that he is expected to accomplish, including contributing to the profitability and effectiveness of the organization and maintaining high morale among subordinates. For the first objective, for instance, emphasis would be placed on quantity of work, quality, low cost, schedules, safety, housekeeping, and satisfied customers.

In addition to clarifying objectives, the session should describe the following functions that a supervisor performs in order to meet the objectives:

1.	Plan	6.	Delegate
2.	Organize	7.	Coach
3.	Communicate	8.	Innovate
4.	Train	9.	Manage paperwork
5.	Motivate	10.	Control

Styles of Leadership. This subject describes different styles and the pros and cons of each and stresses the need for tailoring the style to the culture of the organization and the specific situation.

Understanding and Motivating Employees. Here, the need for developing empathy—the ability to put oneself in the situation of subordinates—is stressed. Possible topics are the need for understanding employees, techniques for getting to know them better, recent research and theory in motivation, and application to the job of supervisor.

Effective Communication. Areas important include a definition of positive communication, along with barriers to effective communication, communication problems in the organization, and principles for effective communication—such as empathy and planning—and specific skills in listening, oral, and written communication.

Decision Making. The emphasis is on the amount of involvement and empowerment that is appropriate for the decision to be made, as well as the steps to follow in making a decision.

Orienting and Training New Employees. The subjects to cover include the need for proper orientation and training of new employees, the development of an orientation and induction checklist, principles of training new employees, and practice in how to induct and train new employees.

How to Manage Change. The need for empathy, communication, and participation in deciding on changes and seeing that they are accepted and implemented is the focus.

Total Quality Improvement. Because of increased competition and customer demands, this has become one of the most popular subjects for supervisory training and development. It teaches the attitudes, knowledge, and skills needed to obtain maximum quality.

A LARGE MIDWESTERN BANK

The following list of subjects chosen by a midwestern bank should be considered for an internal training program:

1. *Developing Effective Leadership Skills*—16 hours. Provides the new or soon-to-be supervisor with essential policy and procedure information as well as a foundation for positive supervisory skill development. A prerequisite for "FrontLine Leadership."
2. *Effective Interviewing and Selection Techniques*—14 hours. An understanding of current equal employment opportunity legislation, how to develop a strategy for choosing among applicants for interviews, a behavior-based strategy for the actual interview that allows the interviewer to go well beyond the typical "hypothetical interview," and how to choose the best probable candidate among those interviewed.
3. *FrontLine Leadership*—Series One—4 hours each session. A curriculum-based supervisory skill program where each session builds upon those sessions preceding it. The approach to each topic allows supervisors to establish action plans using their own actual supervisory situations. Each of the following represents one session. Additional units are added each year:

   - Basic Principles of Supervision
   - Recognizing Positive Results
   - Giving Constructive Feedback
   - Getting Good Information from Others/Getting Your Ideas Across
   - Dealing with Emotional Behavior

4. *Performance Evaluation and Goal Setting*—3 hours. Identifying critical job elements for evaluation, determining and communicating expected standards of performance, properly conducting

the performance appraisal meeting, and formulating an action plan for future development.

5. *Successful Business Writing*—2 hours. Fundamental guidelines covering the most common business writing situations.

6. *FrontLine Leadership—Series Two*—Prerequisite: "FrontLine Leadership—Series One."

   ■ Establishing Performance Expectations
   ■ Taking Corrective Action
   ■ Coaching for Optimal Performance
   ■ Clarifying Team Roles and Responsibilities

7. *Achieving Team Excellence—Part One*—8 hours. To open communication lines, establish performance expectations, and develop specific departmental goal plans, derived from the input of all members of the individual team.

8. *Running Effective Meetings*—4 hours. Explores strategies to maximize meeting effectiveness, understand meeting participant styles, develop effective meeting agendas, and use the appropriate leadership style based on the type of meeting being conducted.

9. *Valuing Diversity*—8 hours. Develops a heightened awareness of the impact and value of the multicultural, multiracial work force. Explodes stereotypes and provides a forum for developing a work environment where cultural, ethnic, and gender differences can be appreciated rather than being a source of potential conflict.

10. *FrontLine Leadership—Series Three*—Prerequisite: "FrontLine Leadership—Series Two."

    ■ Delegating Responsibility
    ■ Fostering Creativity
    ■ Managing Change in the Organization

11. *Achieving Team Excellence—Part Two*—8 hours. As an extension of the above, this program utilizes the Myers-Briggs Type Indicator to allow team members a better understanding of their personality preferences and its impact on how they handle their job responsibilities and how their preferences (and relative nonpreferences) impact the team's ability to accomplish departmental goals. Prerequisite: "Achieving Team Excellence – Part One."

12. *FrontLine Leadership—Series Four*—Prerequisite: "FrontLine Leadership—Series Three."

- Ethical Business Decisions
- Developing a Value-Driven Leadership Strategy for the Future

The list presented in this case study is only a suggestion. Each organization should select its own subject content based on needs.

Establishing the Schedule

The establishment of a proper schedule can be important to the effectiveness of the program. Schedules should be convenient for the participants so they feel that the time selected is a good one for them to attend. There are other considerations, of course, including the best time for them to be away from their jobs so that their bosses do not have negative attitudes toward the program.

Should programs be held on company time? The main consideration here is the attitude of participants toward attendance. If they feel that the company owes it to them or if they consider it an imposition to attend on their own time, then the program should probably be offered on company time. If the program is offered on employees' personal time and they are expected to attend, then they should be rewarded for attending. For instance, a Saturday program could be scheduled from 8:00 A.M. to 2:00 P.M. with breakfast, a morning coffee break, and lunch provided. This can lessen the feeling that the individuals are contributing too much and the company too little.

In general, if the participants can be spared, the program should be offered on company time. If it is important for them to be on the job all the time, however, or if their bosses feel that they should not be taken off their job, consideration should be given to having it on their own time. A combination of the two is possible. For example, a number of companies offer programs late in the afternoon so that part of the time is company time and part of it is the participants' own time.

How long should sessions be? It depends. They can vary from one-hour sessions held periodically (once a week, once a month) to a program that runs for a full week. One consideration is the amount of learning that occurs. Some educators believe that spaced learning is better and that sessions conducted periodically are better than one solid week of meetings. Others think that it is better to conduct a program in a continuous time period. Distance is another factor. If people gather from different locations, the sessions should be longer than if all people are located in the same place. A most common length of a session is from one and one-half to three hours—and a general rule is that the more participation from the learners, the longer the session should be.

How often should sessions be held? Supervisory training meetings are typically conducted once every two weeks or once every month to allow time between them for on-the-job application. In addition, sessions are not held so frequently as to interfere with production. Each organization must determine length and frequency to fit its own circumstances. An important factor is that supervisory training and development is a continuous process and not a one-shot approach.

Choosing Facilities

The facilities for classroom supervisory training must be large enough and comfortable enough so that the participants are in a proper climate for learning. If there are adequate facilities on the premises, this is probably the best location. Otherwise, meetings should be held at a nearby restaurant, hotel, or other location with satisfactory facilities. One advantage of holding meetings away from the workplace is to reduce interruptions and increase the level of concentration of the participants. A disadvantage is travel time. If the session is short (less than a half-day), it is probably better to use in-house facilities.

Deciding on a Room Setup

Every conference leader has a favorite room setup. Many prefer a U shape, with participants seated at the outside of the U (Figure 7-1). Others prefer a more traditional classroom setting (Figure 7-2). If supervisors are going to be involved in small group activities, a herringbone shape is probably the best (Figure 7-3). The setup depends on the size of the group and the size of the room, as well as the leader's preference.

Selecting the Participants

The size and the composition of the group must be determined before meetings start. Generally, there should not be more than 25 persons in a class in supervisory training, and some companies limit the size to 15. The optimum size depends on room size, as well as on the approach and conference skills of the leaders.

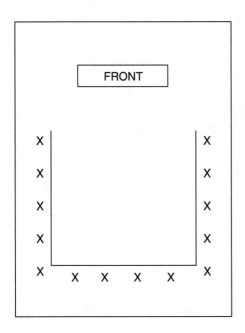

Figure 7-1. *U-shaped room setup for training*

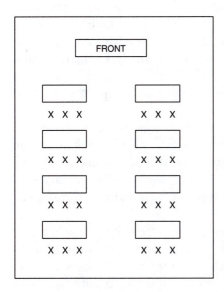

Figure 7-2. *Traditional classroom setup for training*

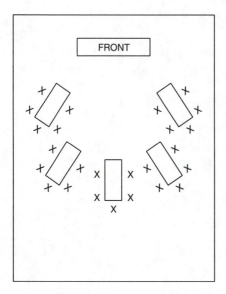

Figure 7-3. *Herringbone-shape setup for training*

In most organizations, the group consists of participants at the same level in the organization. For example, supervisory training meetings are limited to the first-level supervisors; higher management should not be in attendance. Some companies, however, have taken a different approach and have purposely included several levels of management. The American Telephone and Telegraph Company (AT&T), for example, frequently conducts sessions with "family groups:" groups in which several levels of management from the same department attend at the same time.

Generally, however, if the attendance of higher-level management people in supervisory training meetings inhibits the participation and learning that is taking place, it is better to restrict the attendance to the first-level supervisors. If the presence of higher-level management enhances the involvement and learning of supervisors, several levels should be included.

Another consideration regarding group composition is whether a meeting should be attended by all supervisors or only by those who can benefit from the subject matter. Most companies do not single out those persons who need the training most. They include all supervisors so that no stigma is attached to those who attend and so that those who are better supervisors can help in the teaching process. Some organizations make a number of courses available to supervisors on a voluntary basis.

Selecting Instructors

Careful attention should be given to the selection of the program teachers. Among the qualifications that should be considered are these:

- Subject knowledge
- A desire to teach
- A positive attitude toward the students
- Time for preparation
- Skills in presenting information and controlling discussion
- Tact, patience, and open-mindedness
- Respect from the participants

Whether to use persons within the organization or to hire consultants and teachers from outside depends on the qualifications of those inside. If persons inside have the qualifications just listed, there is no need to hire anyone from the outside. If this is not so, outside trainers should be hired. One caution is that outsiders should be carefully screened for effectiveness. For example, they may have most of the qualifications listed, but if they are weak in presenting information and leading discussion, the program is sure to be a failure. Therefore, when references about outside people as possible leaders for internal company programs are checked, specific information should be obtained regarding their previous experience and teaching effectiveness.

A number of years ago, I was asked by Allis-Chalmers Corp. to develop a lesson plan for a basic training program for supervisors, with emphasis on human relations, communication, and discipline. The plan was to select only line managers to do the teaching. I was surprised and concerned that my lesson plan might not be properly implemented by line managers and suggested that I conduct a short course with them to show them how to teach the course.

I think it was a mistake to insist that only line managers do the training. One or more of the seven qualifications might be absent, and the program would not be effective in terms of improving knowledge, developing skills, and creating positive attitudes on the part of those attending. In addition, if the line manager is not effective as a teacher, negative attitudes toward him or her might be created, which could adversely affect the job relationship. If line managers have all seven qualifications, use them. If not, select a leader who has them.

Determining Classroom Techniques and Aids

Supervisory training classes should be enjoyable, as well as beneficial. The first consideration for use of any technique is that it helps accomplish the objectives. Many different techniques and methods meet this criterion, and the participants will enjoy some of them more than others. Therefore, a variety of techniques should be used to accomplish the objectives and to make the sessions interesting and enjoyable. The participants' reaction can have an impact not only on what they learn at the meeting but also on how they apply it on the job. The teaching methods and techniques we will explore here are presentations, guided discussions, films and videotapes, case studies, role playings, the incident processes, tests and inventories, along with management games and exercises.

Presentations. The most basic technique used in a supervisory training course is presentation on the part of a leader to impart knowledge to the participants. This should be used whenever the leader has information that the group does not have. Barriers and practical tips are listed in detail in my book *No-Nonsense Communication*.[2] A number of ideas to make the presentation interesting and enjoyable, as well as beneficial, are as follows:

- Present the information in a way that is easily understood.
- Show the practical application of the information for the participants. Research and theory can be presented, but the connection between them and practical application should always be clear. In other words, the question "So what?" must be answered to the satisfaction of the participants.
- Be enthusiastic. Speakers are salespersons of ideas.
- Use visual aids to communicate effectively. Visual aids hold the participants' attention and help to convey ideas. They make use

---

[2]Donald L. Kirkpatrick, *No-Nonsense Communication*, 3rd ed. (Elm Grove, Wis.: Donald L. Kirkpatrick, 1991).

of the seeing sense in addition to hearing. Effective visual aids should be simple, pertinent to the subject content and objectives, as well as easy to read, and attractivly presented. The most common forms of visual aids are films and videotapes, overhead transparencies, slides, charts, illustrations on a chalkboard or easel, handouts, and specific objects. PowerPoint is one of the current most popular aids.

Questions and answers are usually a part of the presentation technique. When a question is raised, the leader should determine if the question is on the subject being discussed and if it is pertinent to others in the group. If the answer is no, the leader can indicate politely that the question can be answered after the class is over. If the question is of general interest, time should be spent answering it. Meetings should not end with a question-and-answer period. A summary of the major points, instead of an answer to a question, is a better ending.

The presentation technique is basic to effective supervisory training meetings. Presenters must maintain interest and attention, as well as communicate well if the session is going to accomplish the objectives set for it.

Guided Discussions. In a guided discussion, the supervisors participate under the guidance and control of the leader. It can be effective when participants have ideas to contribute. There are two approaches to the use of guided discussion in the classroom: (1) an open discussion in which the leader suggests a question or problem and volunteers, or selected people from the group, answer it and (2) small groups that allow for participation from everyone. The term *buzz groups* describes the situation in which subgroups of four to seven people are assigned a topic. To be sure that the buzz groups operate effectively, the meeting leader should see that:

1. Participants understand exactly what they are supposed to do and how much time they have to do it.
2. Each buzz group has a chairperson who is responsible for the performance and reporting of the group. The chairperson can be appointed by the meeting leader, selected by buzz group members, or selected by a criterion suggested by the leader.
3. Each chairperson understands that this role includes:

- Being sure that all members of the group understand the assignment.
- Getting everyone to participate.
- Keeping discussions moving toward the objective.
- Taking notes or delegating this role to another member of the group.
- Reporting or delegating this role to another member of the group.

For effective guided discussion, the meeting leader must prepare questions and assignments that will help to accomplish the objectives of the meeting. Getting people to participate is the first requirement. The second requirement is to control the meeting.

Scott Parry of Training House in Princeton, New Jersey, has described the following 16 techniques for getting responses from participants in a training program:

1. After asking a question, pause for 10 seconds before selecting a respondent. Look around the group. Restate the question. Give all trainees time to formulate responses in their heads. Then select a respondent.

2. Some questions are easy; everyone can answer out loud simultaneously. For example, "What color do we get when we mix red and yellow?" Orange. "When we mix yellow and blue?" Green. "When we mix red and blue?" Purple. "Which colors are called the primary colors?" Red, yellow, and blue. "Which are the secondary colors?" Orange, green, and purple.

3. With questions that require only a few words or numbers, have participants write the answers. You can circulate around the room to read some of the answers, thereby seeing if everyone got them right. That may also help you decide on whom to call.

4. From time to time, ask learners to take a guess on something you're about to give them.

5. Distribute a handout that contains a half-dozen questions and space for the answers. After each major stimulus (say every five minutes on the average), have learners respond to the next question. Then give them feedback before proceeding. This breaks a 45 minute lecture into eight or nine S-R-F links in an instructional chain.

6. Use a preprinted response sheet for trainees to complete throughout the lesson (perhaps a flowchart, checklist, schematic diagram, or list of pros and cons on which they must fill in words). Direct learners to the response sheet each time you cover a new item on it.

7. Distribute a self-assessment. This should be a self-scoring, quickly administered exercise that lets you and the learner know where she or he stands. It can tap knowledge, attitude, or skills, and serves to establish the "entering behavior" of your learners, on which you will build.

8. Ask for a show of hands. This is especially useful when you want to polarize the group on a dichotomous issue. For example, "How many of you think that preparing an inductive lesson is harder? How many think that a deductive lesson is harder to prepare?"

9. Have participants respond to each other, working in groups of two or three. For example, in a course on time management, you could say, "Turn to your neighbor and tell him or her what percentage of your time you think *is* and *is not* under your control."

10. When the group is large (say, more than 30 trainees), give each participant four colored, cardboard squares: red, yellow, blue, and green. Then pose a multiple-choice question from time to time; the four alternatives are color-coded. Trainees answer by holding up the corresponding cards, with the colors facing you. This gives you feedback, lets you know whom to call on, and shows you whether learners need more explanation.

11. When teaching interaction and communication skills (such as in sales, interviewing, counseling, training, and supervising), prepare a script of the interaction. Number each line and distribute copies to trainees. Elicit responses in a "notes" column by referring trainees to specific lines that illustrate concepts or techniques you've just dealt with. Ask whether they are good or poor examples, and why.

12. After every new topic, lesson, module, or sequence, have participants get out their action plan sheets. Ask them to write down what they plan to do back on the job to apply the things they've just learned. Have learners read the entries of the people sitting on each side of them. Have them give one another feedback.

13. If you're teaching a whole job, have each participant create a job description by making a new entry after you go over each duty, responsibility, and procedure. They should include criteria for performance. Have each trainee take this back to work to share with her or his supervisor.

14. Prepare mini role plays. You play the "foil" role and place trainees in the "critical" role. Have them make their responses to one another and evaluate each other after each interaction.

15. Allow time for silent decision making or for reflection on questions that don't require overt responses. For example, "When did you last write a note commending one of your workers for a job well done? When did you last ask your boss to send such a letter to one of your subordinates?"

16. At times, responses will be confidential. For example, they may cover topics such as how much trainees earned in commission last year, how they scored on the management style assessment, or how much time they spend with their bosses in a typical week.

In such cases, have learners respond on pieces of scrap paper, without giving their names. Collect the scraps in a box, shake them up, and draw them out for posting on a flip chart or chalkboard. Then you can discuss and process the data.[3]

Videotapes and Films. Videotapes are available from a number of producers. These aids come in several forms. Some are animated and tell a story that can be used for discussing supervisory principles and techniques. Some use live actors to provide a case study for discussion. Others feature an expert who makes a presentation, usually supplemented and illustrated by vignettes or case studies of situations that are pertinent to the subject.

The person who will be using the videotape should view it before showing it to the class. In most cases, a leader's guide is available to suggest ways in which it can be used effectively. So that it will be of maximum benefit, the leader should prepare an introduction that will relate the videotape to the subject being studied, conduct a discussion or use some other way to summarize the benefits from the videotape. The leader should also consider stopping the videotape partway

---

[3]Scott Parry, "An Equal Opportunity to Learn," *Training and Development Journal* (January 1991).

through to discuss a dramatized case study before proceeding with the rest of it. See the Bibliography for suggested sources.

Case Studies. Case studies assume a number of forms. Some are a five- to ten-page detailed description of an industrial or business situation. This type of case study requires a great deal of reading and study by participants, along with adequate time to discuss it and benefit from it. Case studies can also be short—not more than one page—and describe a particular situation for the group to discuss. Some case studies are presented on videotape or film instead of on paper. Usually dramatized case studies are more effective than written ones because the participants are better able to understand the situation.

Bradford Boyd set out the following six steps in writing a case study for use in supervisory training:

1. *Define the principles you are trying illustrate to a group.* This first step is essential as it provides the foundation upon which the case is to be built. A good instructor does not use a case simply to stir up activity; he or she uses the case to bring the group to the recognition of a principle he or she is trying to teach. In this first step, then, the trainer sets forth the direction for his plan:

   - Examples of a defined principle: Managers have a responsibility to keep others informed and cannot afford the attitude that communication is a one-way street leading to them.
   - Awareness of the need to communicate is the key factor in how well we communicate with one another.

2. *Establish a situation that illustrates the principle.* This step begins to give the plans for writing some substance. It creates the setting in which the case is to take place. Here is where [instructors] call upon our knowledge and experience of typical problems and problem individuals around us. An example would be an illustration about a manager who believes that people around him create an endless array of problems because they can't or won't communicate with him.

3. *Develop the symptoms.* Identify the symptoms that illustrate positively, negatively, or both, the principles to be taught. Consider what incidents and situations create or relate to the attitude

defined in Step 2 and illustrate the principle identified in Step 1, such as the following examples:

- The attitude expressed in the common complaint, "Nobody tells me anything."
- The attitude expressed in the feeling that people everywhere have to cooperate with me if I'm going to do my job.
- A subordinate goes over the supervisor's head to ask a favor of the department head.
- People misunderstand "simple" instructions and create disturbing foul-ups in the daily routine.
- We don't get cooperation when we ask for special effort.

4. *Develop the characters*. These might be "do-righters" or "do-wrongers." Either can be true to life and provide realism for the case. Developing the characters is somewhat like assembling the finishing materials for the construction job. Listen to trainees describe their bosses, employees, peers, and associates. We live in a world of case-study characters. Consider the following examples:

- Let's give the key person a name—Bill Newman is as good as any unless we are working with a group where names reflect a predominate nationality group. Then he might be a Stan Dombrowski or a Jose Martinez.
- Place him in the management hierarchy. For this situation, we might make Bill Newman a department head.
- What is his attitude or outlook? Make him a "do-wronger"— impatient, wrapped up in himself, always looking for others to blame when a problem arises, and typical of "the guy upstairs who needs this training."

5. *Write the case*. From here on it's simple: Build in the essentials. Describe the situation, the attitudes, the symptoms, and the characters but don't overburden the case with detail. If the preparation outlined in the first four steps has been carefully done, the writing is almost automatic.

6. *Conclude with questions*. They give direction to your group's thinking and provide your discussion with a pathway to the principle. Questions should state specifically what we want

considered and discussed so that trainees approach the problem
along the lines that the instructor intends to direct for the discussion.[4]

Following is a case study that I developed.

The Case of the Late Deliveries

You are Jim Marshall, general manager of a lumber yard
employing 25 people. Harry Brown, your yard foreman, supervises four truck drivers. He has worked for you for six years and
does an excellent job.

It has come to your attention that deliveries are not always
made as promised to customers. This morning, you received telephone calls from two angry customers: Tom Gibson, from Allied
Construction, and Bill Bailey, who is building a new home. Both
told you that yesterday's deliveries arrived more than two hours
late. Tom said that this has happened before and that he was
thinking of changing suppliers. What are your objectives in solving
this problem? What are you going to do?

This type of case study can be used in a training meeting on such
subjects as interpersonal relations and problem solving. It could be discussed in open discussion or assigned to buzz groups. Each group
could then report on its solution. This type of case also lends itself very
well to role playing.

The following three case studies can be used in a training program
on how to manage change.

The Case of the New Equipment

You are the supervisor in the accounting department. A new
computer is going to be installed to replace some of the manual
operations in your department in order to reduce costs. You have
looked at the new equipment and are still considering two different types. You have not yet decided which one to buy.

Your department now consists of 15 clerical and professional
workers. When the new computer is in operation, however, you

---

[4]Bradford B. Boyd, *Supervisory Training: Approaches and Methods* (a collection of
articles from the *Training and Development Journal*) (Alexandria, Va.: American
Society for Training and Development, 1976).

will need only seven people. You expect the new equipment to be installed in about six months.

You will find other jobs in your company for the eight people who will not be needed.

The Case of the New Policy

You are the foreman of a machine shop. Recently, your workers have been taking varying amounts of time to wash up and get ready to go home at the end of the shift. Some have taken as much as 30 minutes; others have taken as little as five. You have had no specific rules covering the amount of time they should take and have never told anyone that specific individuals were taking too long.

To increase productivity, top management and you have agreed to implement a new policy that workers will be allowed a maximum of 10 minutes to wash up before their shift ends.

The Case of the New Policy

You are a supervisor in an assembly department. When you received an order for a new product, you quoted a price that was based on assembling 130 units per day, a figure that had been determined in order to get the bid. Also, your engineers and top manufacturing management had agreed that it could be done. You, the supervisor, were not consulted on the number of units your people could assemble.

You have a long-term contract and you are losing money every day. You cannot change the price to the customer and you must increase productivity to stay in business.

If you have four subgroups in the meeting, one of these cases should be assigned to each. Or you could ask each person to volunteer to participate in the case in which she is most interested. Each group would then be given the following assignment:

1. Select a chairperson for your group who will be responsible for leading and controlling the discussion and reaching the assigned objectives.
2. Appoint a secretary who will be responsible for taking notes and summarizing the discussion that takes place.
3. Your specific objectives will be to discuss and decide how:

- Employees in your department would react to the specific change described in your case.
- You would communicate the change to the employees in your department.
- You would see that the change is effectively implemented in your department with emphasis on participation and teamwork.

This type of case study and approach can be readily adapted to any organization. Cases can be written to describe a typical situation that supervisors have faced or will face, with each group given from 30 to 45 minutes to analyze a case. The chairperson or another member of the group then reports to the entire group on the case. Next, the case study is opened to discussion by the entire group, after which the leader has the key role of supplementing and commenting on the principles, approaches, and techniques that have been explained, as well as tying the case study into the objectives of that particular session.

Role Playing. Role playing is a training technique in which one or more members of the supervisory training group assumes a role that is assigned. For example, in "The Case of the New Policy" described previously, one of the group members will be asked to play the part of a foreman. The conference leader can take the part of an employee who feels that 10 minutes is not enough time to wash up before the shift ends. In front of the group, the foreman then conducts a discussion with the employee. The rest of the supervisors observe the role playing and comment on it after it is finished.

In multiple role playing, all members of the supervisory training class participate at the same time. Half of them take the role of foreman and the other half the role of employee. After a period of multiple role playing, open discussions will analyze the situation from the standpoint of both the foreman and the employee. The multiple role playing can then be repeated, with each individual taking the opposite role. A modification of this approach is to divide the group into subgroups of three persons each, with the third person acting as an observer. After each role-playing situation, supervisors can see what happens and can discuss these events as a case study.

The Incident Process. A unique approach to the case study,[5] developed by Paul Pigors, formerly of the Massachusetts Institute of Technology,

---

[5]Paul Pigors, *The Incident Process* (Rockville, Md.: BNA Communication, 1961).

is the incident process—a method by which a group of supervisors can study problems and reach decisions by a systematic approach. When possible, the case selected is an actual one that has already been solved, so that the group decision can be compared with the real solution.

If a real case is used, Pigors suggests that it be unrelated to the jobs and problems of the participants. This facilitates the learning of principles, because the participants are not relating real people and problems to the case. Actual cases from their own organization can be effectively used after problem-solving principles and techniques have been learned.

In the incident process, participants receive a short written account of the problem (called the *incident*). Their assignment is to search for facts, weigh them in view of the circumstances, and decide what action should be taken. An example is given below.

The Incident

Joe Grimm, one of your employees, complains to you that Tom Jones is cheating the company. Joe claims that Tom often has someone else punch the time clock for him in the morning when he comes in late. Also, according to Joe, Tom abuses the company rules on break periods and wash-up time. You supervise both Joe and Tom. What would you do?

The method of analysis is divided into the following five phases:

1. *Studying the incident.* Individual members take time to discuss what approach they will take in progressing toward the decision.
2. *Fact finding.* Question are directed to the leader (the person with the facts) in an attempt to reconstruct the sequence of events. The leader answers all questions but does not provide any additional information. When the group feels that it has sufficient information to make a decision, a participant summarizes the key facts that have been brought out.
3. *Starting the issue.* The group decides what question it must answer in making a decision—for example, "Is discipline indicated under the circumstances, and, if so, to whom and to what degree?"
4. *Making a decision.* Each participant writes an answer to the issue with supporting reasons. The decisions are divided into pros and cons. Participants who think alike get together, appoint

a spokesman, and consolidate their thinking for a short debate. As soon as each side has debated the reasons for its position, the conference leader summarizes the actual decision.

5. *Learning from the case.* The conference leader moderates a discussion on what the case has taught and how effective the participants were in analyzing the problems.

The incident process can provide several benefits in supervisory training classes. Supervisors in the classes:

■ Have an opportunity to analyze actual problems by a practical method.

■ Share a group's accumulated experience in working with people.

■ Test their own decision-making and reasoning capabilities by comparing them with those made by other group members along with the historical (actual) decision if a real case is used.

■ Develop an appreciation of different viewpoints in approaching and solving problems.

■ Develop their abilities as leaders in the individual roles of team leader, observer, and discussion member.

Tests and Inventories. Tests and inventories can be used in determining needs, as well as specific subject content for supervisory training programs. They can also be used effectively as a teaching tool. I have used the following technique in teaching principles and methods for effective communication to supervisors in many organizations:

■ Administer the Supervisory Inventory on Communication (SIC) to the participants.[6] Eighty items are to be answered "A" (agree) or "DA" (disagree).

■ Select 10 to 20 pertinent items from the SIC. For example, the following items could be selected:

A. A good definition of communication is the sending of information from one person to another.

A   or   **DA**

---

[6]Donald L. Kirkpatrick, *Supervisory Inventory on Communication* (Elm Grove, Wis.: Donald L. Kirkpatrick, 1987).

B. A sender has failed to communicate unless the receiver understands the message the way the sender intended it.

A   or   **DA**

C. A sender has failed to communicate unless the receiver understands, accepts, and carries out the instruction.

A   or   **DA**

- Ask each buzz group of four to six people to reach a consensus on each item. (This is done before they have scored their test.)
- Have the reporter from each group give the results to the leader who records them on a flipchart.
- Tell them their score—the "correct" number according to the scoring key.
- Ask them to score their own tests.

This technique allows the participants to challenge and learn from each other. After they do this, they are very interested in the scoring-key answers and in voicing their opinions. The ensuing discussion becomes interesting and practical. This technique also can be used to precede presentations and guided discussions on any subject, and makes for a meeting that is interesting, enjoyable, and helpful. See the Bibliography for suggested resources.

When administering this test, remember to:

- Be sure that the test content is related to the subject content and the objectives of the session. Administer the test at the start of the program.
- Score the test and return it to participants, or allow participants to score their own and tell the leader how many items were wrong.
- Select items for discussion that will be of greatest interest and benefit to the group.
- During the discussion, encourage both sides of the question to be argued by participants.
- Provide the participants with the author's rationale for the correct answer.
- Summarize the discussion and the principle or technique that was illustrated by the test item.

Management Games and Exercises. When management games and exercises, commonly called *simulations* are used, the supervisors are divided into small groups and given a realistic situation to deal with. They compete with each other and are judged on their effectiveness (usually in terms of productivity, profits, sales, or similar criteria). Some management games are simple and require less than an hour of meeting time; others are complicated and use a computer. They can be created for a particular session or purchased. See the Bibliography for suggested resources.

Packaged Training Programs. There are two basic approaches to supervisory training and development. One is to develop a tailor-made program consisting of subject content, aids, and techniques developed by the human resources professionals in the organization. Previous sections of this chapter provide suggestions. The other approach is to purchase a program and implement it, with or without modifications by those planning and teaching the course. Again, see the Bibliography for suggested resources.

SUMMARY

Internal classroom training courses are developed and implemented by nearly every organization large enough to have 10 or more supervisors. They take all kinds of approaches. Some are continuous and others are one-shot programs; some are required, while others are voluntary; some use inside instructors, while others call on outside consultants to do the training; some develop their own content and aids, while others purchase programs. Some are effective, and others are ineffective. There is no one best way to develop and implement training courses. The training professionals and line managers in each organization must make their own decisions.

This chapter has described some principles and techniques that should be carefully considered so that internal courses have positive results in terms of reaction, learning, change in job behavior, and final results in improved productivity and morale.

Some of the case studies in Part II of this book describe successful in-house programs. An analysis of these can provide practical ideas for your program. In determining subject content, consider the topics described in the various case studies in Part II.

8

EVALUATING INTERNAL CLASSROOM TRAINING

Training programs should be evaluated to determine their effectiveness so that future programs can be improved, to decide if the program should be repeated, and to justify the value of the training department to top management.

This means that trainers must always evaluate their training and communicate its worth. Many different evaluation methods have been suggested and used to accomplish this goal. Some say that *real* evaluations measure the changes in behavior that take place on the job. Others claim that measuring changes in behavior is not sufficient; it's the results that count. Both of these groups usually view questionnaires and comment sheets as nothing more than "happiness" ratings. Other trainers and educators, however, feel that questionnaires and comment sheets can be helpful in evaluating training programs.

Evaluation can take many forms. Each can be helpful as long as the objectives and guidelines are understood. This chapter discusses areas to consider: reaction, learning, behavior, and results.[1]

REACTIONS

The first stage of the evaluation process is to measure the trainees' reactions to the training program—that is, how well they liked it. Evaluating reaction is the same as measuring the feelings of the conferee: it is a measure of customer satisfaction. It does not include a measurement of any learning that takes place. Because reaction is so easy to measure, it is the most common type of evaluation.

There are two important reasons for measuring reaction. In most instances, favorable reaction means that the learner is paying attention, enjoying the experience, and thus probably making an effort to learn.

The other reason for measuring reaction is to determine satisfaction. The participants are really customers. Favorable reaction means that the customer is happy and will probably "buy the product" again if it is offered. Additionally, a satisfied customer will tell other potential customers about the training program and will encourage those others to "buy the product." If the reaction is negative, the customer will probably tell others about the ineffective program and may not attend future meetings unless required to do so.

Favorable customer reaction is critical to organizations, such as universities, and to consultants that offer public institutes, seminars, and conferences. It is not quite as obvious that it is also important to training professionals who offer in-house programs. The situations are similar, however, unfavorable reaction in either case can mean that the people offering the program are out of business.

Guidelines for Measuring Reaction

1. Determine what you want to find out.
2. Design a form that will quantify reactions.
3. Encourage written comments.
4. Get 100-percent immediate response.
5. Get honest responses.

---

[1]Donald L. Kirkpatrick. *Evaluating Training Programs: The Four Levels*, 2nd ed. (San Francisco; Berrett-Koehler Publishers, 1998).

6. If desirable, get delayed reactions.
7. Develop an acceptable standard.
8. Measure reactions against the standard.
9. Take appropriate action.

A reaction sheet (Figure 8-1) was used to measure reaction at a national institute of the American Society for Training and Development. The planners of this program were interested in reactions to subjects, conference techniques, and the performance of each conference leader, and the form was designed accordingly. The conferees were asked to place a check in the appropriate spaces so that the reactions could be readily tabulated and quantified.

In Question 3, the designers of the form felt that a more meaningful rating could be given the leader if the conferees considered items A through G before checking the overall rating. This question was designed to prevent a conference leader's personality from dominating group reaction.

Question 4 encourages the conferees to suggest improvements. The optional signature was used so that follow-up discussions with conferees could be held. In this case, about half of the conferees signed their names. In all probability, the optional signature did not affect the honesty of the answers in this type of group. It is strongly suggested, however, that unsigned sheets be used in meetings held within a company to ensure truthful answers.

Figure 8-2 illustrates a simpler form that can be used for internal sessions. It should be completed by those attending at the end of each meeting unless the same leader is conducting a series of meetings on the same subject. In that case, the comment sheet should be given at the end of the second or third session, with the comments and suggestions taken into consideration to make the last sessions more effective. A final reaction sheet, such as that in Figure 8-3, should be used to obtain reactions to the total program.

Other types of reaction sheets can also be used to obtain valuable information. A form such as that in Figure 8-4 should be used where there are a variety of leaders who appear for a short time on a program. This form obtains the important separation of the participants' reactions to the subjects from their reactions to the leaders. It also provides space for comments and suggestions.

Text continued on page 137

Leader _____   Subject _____

Date _____

1. Was the subject pertinent to your needs and interests?
   ☐ No   ☐ To some extent   ☐ Very much so
2. How was the ratio of lecture to discussion?
   ☐ Too much lecture   ☐ OK   ☐ Too much discussion
3. How about the leader?

	Excellent	Very Good	Good	Fair	Poor
A. How well did he/she state objectives?					
B. How well did he/she keep the session alive and interesting?					
C. How well did he/she use the blackboard, charts, and other aids?					
D. How well did he/she summarize during the session?					
E. How well did he/she maintain a friendly and helpful manner?					
F. How well did he/she illustrate and clarify the points?					
G. How was his/her summary at the close of the session?					

4. What is your over all rating of the leader?
   ☐ Excellent   ☐ Very Good   ☐ Good   ☐ Fair   ☐ Poor
5. What would have made the session more effective?

_____
_____
_____
_____
_____

Signature (Optional) _____

Figure 8-1. *A conference reaction sheet*

Please give us your frank reactions and comments. They will help us evaluate this program for possible improvement in future programs.

Leader _____ Subject _____ Date _____

1. How do you rate the subject content?
   - ☐ Excellent   Comments:
   - ☐ Very Good
   - ☐ Good
   - ☐ Fair
   - ☐ Poor

2. How do you rate the conference leader?
   - ☐ Excellent   Comments:
   - ☐ Very Good
   - ☐ Good
   - ☐ Fair
   - ☐ Poor

3. What benefits do you feel you have received from this session?
   - ☐ New knowledge that is pertinent.
   - ☐ Specific approaches, skills, or techniques that I can apply on the job.
   - ☐ A change of attitude that will help me in my job.
   - ☐ Other:

4. How was the lunch?
   - ☐ Excellent   ☐ Very Good   ☐ Good   ☐ Fair   ☐ Poor

5. How were the meeting facilities?
   - ☐ Excellent   ☐ Very Good   ☐ Good   ☐ Fair   ☐ Poor

6. What would have made the session better?

Figure 8-2.
A simple reaction sheet for internal sessions

Name of program _____ Date _____

1. How do you rate the overal program as an educational experience?
   ☐ Excellent   Comments:
   ☐ Very Good
   ☐ Good
   ☐ Fair
   ☐ Poor

2. To what extent will it help you do a better job for your organization?
   ☐ Excellent   Comments:
   ☐ Very Good
   ☐ Good
   ☐ Fair
   ☐ Poor

3. What changes do you expect to make when you get back to your job?

   _____
   _____
   _____
   _____

4. Would you like to attend future programs of a similar nature?
   ☐ Yes   Comments:
   ☐ No
   ☐ Not sure

5. Would you recommend this program to other supervisors in your organization?
   ☐ Yes   Comments:
   ☐ No
   ☐ Not sure

6. Other comments and suggestions.

   _____
   _____
   _____
   _____

Signature (Optional) _____

Figure 8-3.
A final reaction sheet for the entire program

The purpose of this training program is to help you. Therefore, we need your reactions and comments to help us evaluate the program. It will help us decide the approach and content for future programs. Please use the following scale for your ratings.

5 = Excellent   4 = Very Good   3 = Good   2 = Fair   1 = Poor

I. Subjects and Leaders

Subject	Rating	Leader	Rating	Comments
A. Manpower Planning		Mason		
B. Technical Training Programs		Deady		
		Horwitz		
C. Pattern for Instruction		Fetteroll		
D. Audivisual Materials		Thomas		
E. Supervisory Training		Morgan		
F. Trainee Involvement		O'Brien		
G. Evaluation		Kirkpatrick		

Figure 8-4.
A sample reaction for multiple leaders

5 = Excellent   4 = Very Good   3 = Good   2 = Fair   1 = Poor

II. Other Aspects of the Program

	Rating	Comments
A. Schedule		
B. Location		
C. Meeting Facilites		
D. Food		
E. Room		
F.		

III. How do you rate the overall program?   Rating [ ]

a. What did you find most valuable?

Figure 8-4. *Cont'd*

b. Suggested improvements

_____

_____

_____

_____

IV. Your suggestions for future programs (subjects, location, schedule, etc).

_____

_____

_____

_____

Signature (Optional) _____

Figure 8-4. *Cont'd*

Figure 8-5 illustrates a practical approach used by chapters of the American Society for Training and Development. One part of the form is a simple reaction sheet. The other part is for participants to use for taking notes. At the close of the program, participants complete the reaction part and turn it in to the program coordinator, while keeping their notes.

Subject _____ Date _____

Speaker/Leader _____

Your reactions and comments will help us determine whether our programs meet your needs and interests. They will also provide a basis for program improvement.

1. Reaction to **Subject:**
   ☐ Excellent   Comments:
   ☐ Very Good
   ☐ Good
   ☐ Fair
   ☐ Poor

2. Reaction to **Speaker/Leader:** (if more than one, insert name next to rating)
   ☐ Excellent   Comments:
   ☐ Very Good
   ☐ Good
   ☐ Fair
   ☐ Poor

3. What did you find most valuable?

   _____
   _____
   _____
   _____
   _____

Figure 8-5.
A combined form for evaluating reaction and taking notes

4. Suggested improvements.

5. Suggestions for future programs: (subjects, speakers, locations, approaches, etc.)

Notes:

Figure 8-5. *Cont'd*

All of these forms provide data that can be tabulated and quantified so that program leaders and coordinators can measure the effectiveness of the program. At the Management Institute (MI), University of Wisconsin, acceptable standards of performance were established so that leaders and subjects could be measured against these standards. On a five-point scale:

      Excellent = 5
    Very good = 4
        Good = 3
         Fair = 2
        Poor = 1

The established MI standard is 4.7; a lower rating is considered unacceptable. The standard was established by gathering data from past performance of MI leaders and effective outside leaders. Each organization should gather such data and establish its own standards of performance. Leaders who do not meet these standards can be coached so that they can meet standards or otherwise be tactfully eliminated from conducting future meetings.

The planner and coordinator of a meeting may be able to give reactions that can be a helpful supplement to the reactions of conferees. Figure 8-6 illustrates the kind of form this person can complete after observing the meeting from the back of the room.

Rating _____ Date _____ Rater's Initial _____

Name of Leader _____ Subject _____

	Very much so	To some extent	No
A. Preparation 1. Did he/she prepare for the meeting?			
2. Was his/her preparation geared to the group?			
B. Conducting 1. Did he/she read the material?			
2. Did he/she hold the interest of the group?			
3. Was he/she enthusiastic/dynamic?			
4. Did he/she use visual aids?			
5. Did he/she help the group apply the material?			
6. Did he/she adequately cover the subject?			
7. Did he/she summarize during the conference and at the end?			
8. Did he/she involve the group?			

C. Constructive Comments

What would you suggest to improve future sessions?

_____

_____

D. Potential

With proper coaching, what would be the highest rating he/she could achieve?

_____

E. Additional Comments:

_____

_____

Figure 8-6.
A trained observer's reaction sheet

The combined reaction of the conferees and the coordinator should be communicated to the conference leader or speaker to help in understanding the feelings of the conferees and to improve conference leadership performance at future sessions. Care should be taken to communicate negative reactions in a constructive manner so that they will be accepted and considered in future sessions.

It is important to determine how people feel about the programs they attend. Decisions by top management are frequently made from one or two comments they receive from people who have attended. A supervisory training program may be cancelled if even one manager tells the vice-president that a program was "a waste of time." A quantitative tabulation of the comments from all supervisors can help to avoid decisions based on insufficient data.

Also, supervisors who like a training program are more apt to obtain maximum benefits from it. For maximum learning, you must have interest and enthusiasm. It is not enough to say, "Supervisors, here is the information, take it." We must make it interesting and motivate them to want to take it.

LEARNING

Enthusiastic reactions will probably lead to maximum learning but still do not guarantee that learning has taken place. The second stage of evaluation is to determine what knowledge, attitudes, and skills were learned in the training program.

Guidelines for Measuring Learning

1. Measure before-and-after attitudes, knowledge, and/or skills. Use a paper-and-pencil test for knowledge and attitudes and a performance test for skills.
2. Get a 100-percent response.
3. Statistically analyze the data.
4. Use a control group if practical.
5. Take appropriate action based on evaluation data.

These guidelines indicate that evaluation in terms of learning is more difficult than evaluation in terms of reaction. Because some knowledge of statistics is necessary, the evaluation should be designed by a person well acquainted with research design. Two methods of the many available to measure learning are *classroom performance* and *paper-and-pencil tests*.

CLASSROOM PERFORMANCE

It is relatively easy to measure the learning that takes place in training programs that teach skills—those, for example, in job instruction training, conducting performance appraisal interviews, work simplification, employment interviewing skills, reading improvement, effective speaking, and effective writing. Classroom activities—such as demonstrations, individual performances of the skill being taught, and discussions following role-playing—can be used as evaluation. The training coordinator can organize these so as to obtain a fairly objective evaluation of the learning that is taking place.

In a course that is teaching effective training methods to supervisors, for example, each supervisor will demonstrate the skills in front of the class. From the performance, the training coordinator can ascertain if the supervisor has learned the principles and can use them, at least in the classroom. In a work simplification program, each conferee can be required to fill out a flow-process chart, and the training coordinator can determine if the conferee knows how to go about this task.

In a reading improvement program, the reading speed and comprehension of each participant can be readily determined by classroom performance. And in an effective speaking course, each conferee can be required to give a number of talks, which can be recorded on videotape and then played back. A training coordinator and other participants can evaluate the amount of learning that is taking place by observing successive performances.

In these programs, an evaluation of the learning can be built into the course. If the evaluation is organized and implemented properly, the training coordinator can obtain a fairly objective measure of the amount of learning that has taken place and can set up before-and-after situations in which each conferee demonstrates the principles and techniques being taught.

PAPER-AND-PENCIL TESTS

When principles and facts, rather than skills, are taught, a paper-and-pencil test can be used. In some cases, standardized tests can be purchased to measure learning, but in others each organization must construct its own.

To measure the learning in human relations programs, for example, the Supervisory Inventory on Human Relations can be used.[2] (See Chapter 5 for sample items.) Standardized tests are also available to evaluate training programs that are designed to teach communication, safety, leadership, motivation, managing change, time management, decision making, performance appraisal, and coaching.

These inventories should be used as follows:

- They should be given to all conferees before the program as a pretest. If practical, they should also be given to a control group that is comparable to the experimental group.

- The pretests should be analyzed by the total score of each person, as well as the responses to each item of the test. A form can be used to get this information (Figure 8-7). There is no need to identify the person. The second tabulation (responses to each item) assists in evaluation of the program and provides some knowledge and understanding of the group before the program.

- After the program is over, the same test or its equivalent should be given to the conferees (as well as to the control group, if there is one). The total scores and individual responses of this posttest are then compared with those of the pretest to see what changes have taken place. Any changes in the responses of the control group must be deducted from those of the experimental group (those receiving the training). A statistical analysis will reveal the level of significance of the changes that have taken place because of the program.

Example 1 of Figure 8-8 shows that a positive gain of 9 was achieved by the experimental group, while the control group averaged a gain of only 2. The net gain was significant: 7. Example 2 shows a positive gain of 9 by the experimental group and a gain of 8 by the control group. The net gain, however, was not significant: 1.

---

[2]Donald L. Kirkpatrick, *Supervisory Inventory on Human Relations* (Elm Grove, Wis.: Donald L. Kirkpatrick, 1990).

Name of Inventory _____ Date _____

1. Please circle items that are "wrong" (different than the scoring key).

1	2	3	4	5	6	7	8	9
10	11	12	13	14	15	16	17	18
19	20	21	22	23	24	25	26	27
28	29	30	31	32	33	34	35	36
37	38	39	40	41	42	43	44	45
46	47	48	49	50	51	52	53	54
55	56	57	58	59	60	61	62	63
64	65	66	67	68	69	70	71	72
73	74	75	76	77	78	79	80	

2. Tabulate your *raw score* (number right), which is 80 minus the number wrong.

80 − _____ = [   ]

Figure 8-7
A form for analyzing inventories

Experimental Group: 25 Supervisors who completed the training program

Control Group: 25 Supervisors who did not attend the training program

		Experimental Group	*Control Group*
Example 1	Pretest	61	60
	Posttest	70	62
	Gain	9	2
	Net Gain	7	
Example 2	Pretest	61	60
	Posttest	70	68
	Gain	9	8
	Net gain	1	

Figure 8-8
A comparison of the scores of two groups on an inventory

Item 5	Correct	Incorrect	
	4	21	Pretest
	21	4	Posttest
	17		Gain

Item 10	Correct	Incorrect	
	6	19	Pretest
	8	17	Posttest
	2		Gain

Figure 8-9

A comparison of the change in responses on the pretest and posttest

Figure 8-9 shows two examples of the change in responses on individual items. Example 1 shows that on Item 5, four people answered it correctly on the pretest, while 21 answered it correctly on the posttest, for a significant gain of 17. Example 2 shows that on Item 10 of the test, the gain was only 2 from pretest to posttest. This would not be significant and would clearly indicate to the instructor a failure to teach the principle, fact, or technique covered by that item.

Unless the test or inventory covers the material presented, it will not be a valid measure of the effectiveness of the learning. Frequently, a standardized test covers only part of the material presented in the course, so only that part of the course covered is being evaluated. If certain items on the test are not being covered, no change in these items can be expected.

Some persons responsible for training programs have developed their own paper-and-pencil tests to measure learning in their programs. Training professionals at MGIC in Milwaukee developed a Product Knowledge Test consisting of 40 questions important to the job of supervisor. (See Chapter 5 for the test items.) The results of the pretest revealed the preprogram knowledge of participants. A comparison of pretest and posttest scores revealed what learning took place.

A pretest versus posttest design with a control group is very effective in training evaluation, although it does not completely eradicate the possible impact of factors other than training.[3] Taking a pretest may

---

[3]David A. Grove and Cheri Ostroff, "Program Evaluation," *in Developing Human Resources* (Alexandria, Va.: Society for Human Resource Management, 1991).

sensitize the supervisors to do better on a posttest measure. Additionally, many organizations are not static, so that events in an organization may have differential effects on the posttraining behavior of the experimental and control groups.

In summary, a paper-and-pencil test can be used effectively to measure the learning of attitudes and knowledge, while performance tests can measure skills. The evaluation should be systematic and statistically oriented. A comparison of before-and-after scores and performance should be made to measure how much learning has taken place.

BEHAVIOR

When I joined the Management Institute of the University of Wisconsin, my first assignment was to attend a one-week course on human relations for foremen and supervisors. During the week, I was particularly impressed by Herman, a foreman from a Milwaukee company. Whenever a conference leader asked a question requiring a good understanding of human relations principles and techniques, Herman was the first to raise his hand. He had all the answers in terms of good human relations. I was impressed and said to myself, "If I were in industry, I would like to work for a man like that."

A cousin of mine was working for that company, and, coincidentally, Herman was his boss. At the first opportunity, I asked my cousin about him and found that while Herman might have known all the principles and techniques of human relations, he didn't practice them on the job. He performed as the typical bull-of-the-woods who had little consideration for the feelings and ideas of his subordinates. I thus realized that there can be a big difference between knowing principles and techniques and using them on the job.

Even if supervisors learn, there is no assurance that they will change their behavior. Five basic requirements must exist to ensure a changed behavior:

1. The desire to improve
2. The required knowledge and skills
3. The right climate
4. Encouragement and help
5. Rewards for improvement

Items 1 and 2 can be accomplished in the classroom. The "right climate" in Item 3 refers to the situation that exists on the job—in other words, the climate for change that is created by the supervisor's immediate boss.

Five possible climates exist:

1. *Preventing.* The boss does not permit any change in behavior that has been taught and encouraged in the classroom.
2. *Discouraging.* The boss doesn't say, "You can't do it," but discourages any change unless he or she approves it.
3. *Neutral.* The boss doesn't seem to care. His or her attitude allows supervisors to do as they see fit, as long as it doesn't interfere with production.
4. *Encouraging.* The boss takes an interest in what was learned and offers to assist in the implementation.
5. *Requiring.* The boss is informed of the behavior changes that are taught and insists on their implementation.

It is obvious that little, if any change in behavior will occur if the climate is preventing or discouraging. Trainers should be aware of the existence of these climates and try to change them to "neutral" or better. One way to do this is to provide the bosses with similar training before the supervisors are trained. Another is to involve them in the planning and implementation of the program. Malcolm Knowles has stated, "Create a climate that is conducive for neutral planning. It is critical that a planning committee or task force be used which is representative of all the constituencies that the program is designed to serve."[4]

Items 4 and 5 are also important. Encouragement and help can come from the boss, human resources professionals, or both. And the most positive way to encourage change in behavior is a "requiring" climate established by the manager. One form of this is learning contracts recommended by Thomas Quick. He suggests contracts between:

1. The trainer and the manager whose subordinate supervisors attend the training
2. The trainer and the supervisors who attend
3. The manager and the supervisors[5]

---

[4]Malcolm Knowles, *Using Learning Contracts* (San Francisco: Jossey-Bass Publishers, 1986).

[5]Thomas Quick, *Training Managers So They Can Really Manage* (San Francisco: Jossey-Bass, 1991).

The first two contracts require a careful determination of needs by considering the suggestions of the trainees (supervisors) and those of the managers of the departments that the supervisors represent. The third contract should consist of agreement between supervisor and manager of what will happen as a result of the training. Discussions should focus on the department's needs and the supervisor's needs. These discussions and agreements should take place prior to the training program. Unfortunately, this kind of contract or even a brief pre-meeting discussion of the program is usually absent.

Knowles suggests that learners answer the following questions:

"What are you going to learn?" [*Objectives*]
"How are you going to learn it?" [*Resources and strategies*]
"What is your target date for completion?" [*Schedule*]
"How are you going to know that you learned it?" [*Evidence*]
"How are you going to prove that you learned it?" [*Verification*][6]

In a requiring climate, the boss of the learner would be involved in answering all five of the questions.

Guidelines for Measuring Behavior
1. Measure on a before-and-after basis if practical.
2. Allow time for behavior changes to take place.
3. Survey and/or interview one or more of the following:
   a. The trainees
   b. The bosses of the trainees
   c. The subordinates of the trainees (use caution)
   d. Others who know the behavior of the trainees
4. Get a 100-percent response of a sampling.
5. Use a control group (not receiving the training) if practical.
6. Statistically analyze data.
7. Repeat the evaluation at appropriate times (in three months, six months, twelve months).
8. Consider cost versus benefits.

The application of these guidelines requires knowledge of research design, as well as time and effort.

---

[6]Knowles, *Using Learning Contracts*.

Tom Newman, the international training manager for Johnson Wax, regularly evaluated the effectiveness of all the programs he conducted. In order to measure changes in behavior that resulted from a two-day seminar on leadership and influence (L&I), four areas were considered:

- Training skills used
- Changes in behavior
- Obstacles to use of the skills learned
- Benefits from the program

A follow-up questionnaire completed by 80 participants yielded these responses to the questions:

1. Which training skills have you used two or more times since the program?

Planned L&I tactics in advance	87%
Used the "Interaction Guide"	72%
Used the meeting checklist	57%
Completed the Interaction Planning Sheet	32%

2. What significant changes have occurred in your interaction with others?

Better organized, prepared	28%
Improved communication skills	20%
More receptive to others	17%
More self-confident	11%
Changes in behavior were positive	86%

3. To what extent has L&I training helped on the job?

A high degree	3%
Substantially	56%
Somewhat	31%
None	10%

Alexander Braun described an evaluation approach that asked each trainee, at the conclusion of each day, to write at least one realistic objective of how he or she would implement the day's learnings. The goal was to get participants committed to on-the-job changes in behavior and provide a basis for boss-subordinate discussion and implementation.[7]

T. K. Meier and Joseph P. Pulichene evaluated changes in behavior resulting from a course on assertiveness. The managers of those attending the course were given the questionnaire shown in Figure 8-10 before the course and again six weeks after the completion of the 15-hour course presented over a six-week period. The results were statistically significant in accomplishing three objectives: decreased passiveness, decreased aggressiveness, and increased assertiveness.[8]

Characterize your impression of the employee's behavior in various situations by using the following number scale:

Never or Rarely	Seldom	Sometimes	Usually	Almost Always or Always
-1-	-2-	-3-	-4-	-5-

_____ 1. Others may take advantage of him/her because he/she finds it difficult to refuse requests.

_____ 2. A reluctance to express his/her ideas hampers effectiveness on the job.

_____ 3. Downgrades his/her own work or attempts to offer excuses for his/her work even though it hasn't been criticized.

_____ 4. Seems to prefer giving other people the upper hand in a discussion rather than challenging their options or data.

_____ 5. During a performance review, he/she receives criticism without comment.

_____ 6. If he/she were genuinely overloaded with work in comparison to peers, he/she would try to complete the assignments alone regardless of the sacrifices required.

_____ 7. If you were treating him/her unfairly, he/she would do nothing, but wait for you to explain your intention.

_____ 8. He/She is able to discuss someone's criticism of him/her openly and constructively.

Figure 8-10
Manager's questionnaire for evaluating a course on assertiveness

---

[7]Alexander Braun, "Assessing Supervisory Training Needs and Evaluating Effectiveness," in American Society for Training and Development (ASTD), _More Evaluating Training Programs_ (Alexandria, Va.: ASTD, 1987).

[8]T.K. Meier and Joseph P. Pulichene, "Evaluating the Effectiveness of Assertiveness Training," in _More Evaluating Training Programs_.

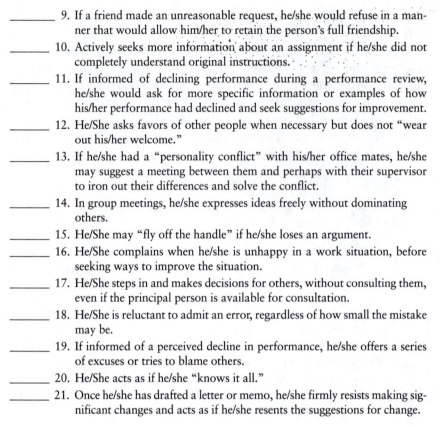

_____ 9. If a friend made an unreasonable request, he/she would refuse in a manner that would allow him/her to retain the person's full friendship.

_____ 10. Actively seeks more information about an assignment if he/she did not completely understand original instructions.

_____ 11. If informed of declining performance during a performance review, he/she would ask for more specific information or examples of how his/her performance had declined and seek suggestions for improvement.

_____ 12. He/She asks favors of other people when necessary but does not "wear out his/her welcome."

_____ 13. If he/she had a "personality conflict" with his/her office mates, he/she may suggest a meeting between them and perhaps with their supervisor to iron out their differences and solve the conflict.

_____ 14. In group meetings, he/she expresses ideas freely without dominating others.

_____ 15. He/She may "fly off the handle" if he/she loses an argument.

_____ 16. He/She complains when he/she is unhappy in a work situation, before seeking ways to improve the situation.

_____ 17. He/She steps in and makes decisions for others, without consulting them, even if the principal person is available for consultation.

_____ 18. He/She is reluctant to admit an error, regardless of how small the mistake may be.

_____ 19. If informed of a perceived decline in performance, he/she offers a series of excuses or tries to blame others.

_____ 20. He/She acts as if he/she "knows it all."

_____ 21. Once he/she has drafted a letter or memo, he/she firmly resists making significant changes and acts as if he/she resents the suggestions for change.

Figure 8-10. *Cont'd*

George Morrisey and William Wellstead evaluated a supervisory training program at McDonnell-Douglas. The supervisors who attended the program were required to commit themselves to specific objectives on how they would apply the learning on the job. In addition, they had to send in a progress report 60 days later in order to earn a certificate of completion. Getting the supervisors to make a written commitment to improvement action is a key element in the course. It resulted in "a tremendous return for a very modest investment," according to the authors.[9]

---

[9]George L. Morrisey and William R. Wellstead, "Supervisory Training Can Be Measured," in *More Evaluation Training Programs.*

Frederic Swierczek and Lynne Carmichael described their approach to evaluating learning and behavior changes. The program was the "Planning and Organization for Effective Supervision" workshops offered to public agencies in Florida by the University of South Florida Institute of Government. At the end of the workshop, participants were asked:

1. What skills did you learn in the workshop?
2. How will you apply these skills back at work?

In addition to Question 1, pretests and posttests based on a Likert scale were used to measure learning, and in addition to Question 2, a questionnaire was mailed to participants six months after the program. Some of the responses from 91 participants were:

Do my job better	43%
Delegate more	31%
Use skills with employees	26%
Communicate better	13%[10]

Terance Jackson suggests that changes in attitude are an important benefit that can result from a supervisory training program.[11] The following attitudes should be measured on a before-and-after basis, using the scale suggested:

Attitudes to Self (Self-Confidence, Drive, Ambition)

Has no self-confidence, drive, or ambition   0
Requires more self-confidence to do the job and more ambition
  to get on in the organization   .5
Has sufficient self-confidence to do a competent job; may progress
  through overambition   1.0
Has a certain self-confidence, drive, and ambition, which is shown
  much of the time   1.5
Has a great deal of self-confidence, drive, and ambition, which
  is shown all of the time   2.0

---

[10]Frederic William Swierczek and Lynne Carmichael, "The Quantity and Quality of Evaluation Training," in *More Evaluating Training Programs*.

[11]Terance Jackson, *Evaluation: Relating Training to Business Performance* (San Diego: University Associates, 1989).

Attitudes to Task/Job (Motivated by Current Job)

Is not motivated by current job   0

Is motivated a little by current job, which sometimes provides a small degree of satisfaction   .5

Derives a moderate amount of satisfaction from current job, which motivates from time to time   1.0

Mostly motivated by current job, which often provides satisfaction
      .5

Current job motivates very highly and provides a high degree of satisfaction most of the time   2.0

The attitude to self can be modified in classroom training, while changes in attitude toward the job probably require a positive job climate and possibly a change in job content, responsibility, and authority. Pretest and posttest measures of attitude should probably be done at a later date to also measure changes that could have occurred after the training program was completed.

Dana Robinson and James Robinson advise that the following scale be used on a questionnaire to measure changes in behavior.[12]

This is a behavior I never use.   **1**

This is a behavior I rarely use (less than 15% of the time).   **2**

This is a behavior I use very infrequently (less than 33% of the time).
      3

This is a behavior I use infrequently (less than 50% of the time).
      4

This is a behavior I use frequently (more than 50% of the time).
      5

This is a behavior I use very frequently (more than 67% of the time).
      6

This is a behavior I almost always use (about 90% of the time).
      7

This is a behavior I always use.   **8**

---

[12]Dana Gaines Robinson and James C. Robinson, *Training for Impact: How to Link Training to Business Needs and Measure the Results* (San Francisco: Josey-Bass, 1989).

Each behavior is described, and participants are asked to rate each one before the training program and again three months after the program is completed. A comparison of the response indicates the change in behavior as the trainee sees it.

RESULTS

The objectives of most training programs can be stated in terms of results to accomplish improved profits, reduced costs, improved quality, reduced accidents, improved customer relations, reduction in turnover, and improved morale.

Guidelines for Measuring Results

1. Measure on a before-and-after basis if possible.
2. Allow time for possible results to take place.
3. Use a control group (not receiving the training) if practical.
4. Statistically analyze data.
5. Repeat at appropriate time.
6. Consider cost versus benefits.
7. Look for "evidence" if "proof" is not possible.

The results of certain kinds of training programs are relatively easy to evaluate. For example, in teaching clerical personnel to be more effective in keyboarding, the measurement can be the number of words per minute before and after. Or, if the goal is to reduce grievances in a plant, the number of grievances before and after a training program on how to prevent grievances can be counted.

In most programs, however, it is difficult, if not impossible, to evaluate results because of the problem called the *separation of variables*. That is, many factors can affect results, and it may not be possible to isolate the effect caused by the training program. For example, a supervisory training course may be given to train foremen to induct and train new employees properly, with the objective being the reduction in the high rate of turnover among new employees. After the training program has been completed, a reduction in turnover may occur, but it must be proved that the training program caused the reduction in turnover. Other causes might be new employment practices, the tightness of the labor market, the season of the year, or recent wage increases.

Two graduate students at the University of Wisconsin used two techniques to measure the results of a Cost Reduction Institute conducted by the university's Management Institute. The first was to conduct in-depth interviews with some of the supervisors who had attended the course and with their immediate superiors. The other was to mail questionnaires to the remaining enrollees and to their supervisor.

Questions Used in Interviews With Trainees

1. Have you been able to reduce costs in the few weeks that you have been back on the job?

Yes	No	Noncommittal or Evasive	Did Not Answer
13	3	2	1

2. How?

The 13 trainers who answered "yes" said they made their cost reductions in different areas but with ideas that stemmed directly from the program.

Interviews With the Superiors of the Trainees. Eight of the cost-reduction actions described by the trainees were confirmed by the immediate superior, and these superiors estimated total savings to be from $15,000 to $21,000 per year. The specific ideas used were described by superiors and trainees.

Questionnaires Mailed to Trainees Not Interviewed. Questionnaires were mailed to those trainees who were not contacted personally. The results on the questionnaire were not as specific or useful as those obtained by personal interview, leading to the conclusion that a personal interview is better than a questionnaire to measure this kind of program.

One way to measure financial benefits versus costs is to use a formula:

$$TV = (T \times N \times I \times M) - (N \times C)$$

where:
    TV = training value
    T = duration of training effect
    N = number of supervisors trained
    I = impact of the training program
    M = monetary value of the impact
    C = cost of the training program

One large company used the formula to evaluate one of its programs. The results were:

$$TV = (1 \times 100 \times .67 \times \$30{,}000) - (100 \times \$7{,}200) = \$1{,}290{,}000$$

From this, they determined a payback period of three to four months and a return on investment of 179 percent.

Linn Coffman's article, "An Easy Way to Effectively Evaluate Program Results," details an approach that consists of a series of follow-up meetings with those who have been trained. They are asked for their input on what results have been accomplished because of attending the training program. In addition, their managers also provide input on what results they have seen.[13]

James Cullen and associates used an evaluation approach to assess the training investment in terms of cost-effectiveness by comparing training costs with benefits measured in monetary terms. They found the calculation of training costs and returns to be complex, with no single formula. Their model combined the economic reasoning of three cost-effectiveness models that have been used.[14]

Ann I. Kelley, Robert Orgel, and Donald Baer stated, "The bottom line is closer than you think!" They used before-and-after sales figures, as did C.E. Hahne.[15] They also used productivity improvement among production lines receiving various supervisory training.

---

[13]Linn Coffman, "An Easy Way to Effectively Evaluate Program Results," in *More Evaluating Training Programs.*

[14]James G. Cullen, Stephen A. Sawzin, Gary R. Sisson, and Richard A. Swanson, "Cost Effectiveness: A Model for Assessing the Training Investment," in *More Evaluating Training Programs.*

[15]Ann I. Kellley, Robert F. Orgel, and Donald M. Baer, "Evaluation: The Bottom Line Is Closer Than You Think," and C.E. Hahne, "How to Measure Results of Sales Training," both in *More Evaluating Training Programs.*

Robinson and Robinson suggest the following measures for evaluating results from a supervisory training program:

- Decreased rejection rate*
- Increased output*
- Reduced absenteeism*
- Reduced tardiness*
- Reduced number of grievances
- Reduced turnover
- Decreased waste*
- Increased number of employees' suggestions adopted
- Decrease in production costs*
- Reduced costs of new hires*
- Reduced overtime*
- Climate-survey data[16]

Those marked with an asterisk can easily be measured in dollars. The others require some effort to interpret in terms of dollars.

Figures 8-11 and 8-12 describe a case study of an organization that makes wood panels. Figure 8-11 shows how costs of training were determined (figures are from 1980), and Figure 8-12 represents the operational results twelve months after the training. The return on investment (ROI) of 6.8 was determined by dividing the operational results by the training costs.

It's obvious to most training professionals that results are relatively easy to measure for some kinds of programs and difficult in others. In sales, production, and safety, for example, specific figures can be readily compared on a before-and-after basis. When subjects like leadership, communication, motivation, decision making, and time management are offered, evaluation in terms of financial benefits is difficult, and maybe impossible, to measure. "Proof" is sometimes impossible to achieve. Evidence is much easier to obtain, and most top executives will be more than satisfied when this is presented.[17]

---

[16]Robinson and Robinson, *Training for Impact.*

[17]Donald L. Kirkpatrick, "Evaluating Training Programs: Evidence vs. Proof," in *More Evaluating Training Programs.*

Direct costs: The travel and per-diem cost is zero, because training took place adjacent to the plant. There is a cost for classroom space and audiovisual equipment, because these were rented from a local hotel. Refreshments were purchased at the same hotel. Because different supervisors attended the morning and afternoon sessions, lunch was not provided.

Indirect costs: The clerical and administrative costs reflect the amount of clerical time spent on making arrangements for the workshop facilities, sending out notices to all participants, and preparing class rosters and other miscellaneous materials.

Development costs: These costs represent the purchase of the training program from a vendor. Included are instructional aids, an instructor manual, videotapes, and a licensing fee. The instructor training costs pertain to the one-week workshop that the instructor attended to become prepared to facilitate the training. Front-end assessment costs were covered by the corporate training budget.

Direct Costs

Outside Instructor	$ 0.00
In-house instructor—12 days × $125	$ 1,500.00
Fringe benefits @ 25% of salary	$ 375.00
Travel and per-diem expenses	$ 0.00
Materials—56 × $60/participant	$ 3,360.00
Classroom space and audiovisual equiptment—12 days @ $50	$ 600.00
Food; refreshments—$4/day × 3 days × 56 participants	$ 672.00
Total direct costs	$ 6,507.00

Indirect Costs

Training Management	$ 0.00
Clerical/Administrative	$ 750.00
Fringe benefits—25% of clerical/administrative salary	$ 187.00
Postage, shipping, telephone	$ 0.00
Pre- and postlearning materials—$4 × 56 participants	$ 224.00
Total indirect costs (rounded to the nearest dollar)	$ 1,161.00

Development Costs

Fee to purchase program	$ 3,600.00
Instructor training	
Registration fee	$ 1,400.00
Travel and lodging	$ 975.00
Salary	$ 625.00
Benefits (25% of salary)	$ 156.00
Total development costs	$ 6,756.00

Figure 8-11.
Training cost analysis

Overhead costs: They represent the services that the general organization provides to the training unit. Because figures were not available, we used 10 percent of the direct, indirect, and program development costs.

Overhead Costs
General organization support
Top management's time

Total overhead costs	$ 1,443.00

Compensation for participants: This figure represents the salaries and benefits paid to all participants while they attended the workshop.

Compensation for Participants
Participants' salary and benefits (time away from the job)

Total compensation	$ 16,696.00
Total training costs	$ 32,564.00
Cost per participant	$ 581.00

Figure 8-11. *Cont'd*

Source: Dana Gaines Robinson and James C. Robinson, *Training for Impact: How to Link Training to Business Needs and Measure the Results* (San Francisco: Jossey-Bass Publishers, 1989).

Operational Results Area	How Measured	Results Before Training	Results After Training	Differences (+ or -)	Expressed in $
Quality of panels	% rejected	2% rejected 1,440 panels per day	1.5% rejected 1,080 panels per day	.5% 360 panels	$720 per day $172,800 per year
Housekeeping	Visual inspection using 20-item checklist	10 defects (average)	2 defects (average)	8 defects	Not measurable in $
Preventable Accidents	Number of accidents Direct cost of each accident	24 per year $144,000 per year	16 per year $96,000 per year	8 per year $48,000	$48,000 per year
				Total Savings:	$220,800.00

$$ROI = \frac{Return}{Investment} = \frac{Operational\ Results}{Training\ Costs} = \frac{\$220,800}{\$32,564} = 6.8$$

Figure 8-12
Operational results analysis

Source: Dana Gaines Robinson and James C. Robinson, *Training for Impact: How to Link Training to Business Needs and Measure the Results* (San Francisco: Jossey-Bass Publishers, 1989).

One word of caution: Be sure that the cost of evaluating is worth the possible benefits. If programs are expensive and will be offered many times, it is worthwhile to spend time and money to evaluate them. If they are offered only once or twice or they are economical to present, attempted evaluation of results may not be practical.

Summary

Evaluation of internal classroom programs may include all of the four stages: reaction, learning, behavior, and results. All programs should be evaluated in terms of reaction. This is easy to do and is important because it is a measure of customer satisfaction. If the supervisors (customers) are unhappy with the program (product), they will tell others (perhaps their boss and even higher-level managers), and the program will be eliminated. Also, the very process of asking for participant reaction tells the supervisors, "We want to help meet your needs, and we want you to tell us if we are doing it."

Evaluation of reaction has its limitations. It doesn't prove that learning has taken place and says nothing about changes in behavior and improved results. Therefore, as time, money, and skill permit, professional trainers should progress to evaluation in the other three stages.

Grove and Ostroff described the training evaluation strategy of one company as follows:

- Be determined by the overall strategic plan.
- Require specific training objectives.
- Obtain trainee reactions to every course.
- Evaluate behavior changes in "flagship" programs (high-volume, high-expense programs).
- Remember that some courses will not be evaluated beyond trainee reactions (it isn't worth it).[18]

This chapter offered guidelines and examples. Design, forms, and techniques can be borrowed and adapted to other organizations; results of the evaluation of other programs cannot.

---

[18]Grove and Ostroff, "Program Evaluation."

9

OUTSIDE SUPERVISORY DEVELOPMENT PROGRAMS

An effective way to train and develop supervisors is to send them to programs sponsored by outside organizations, such as universities, trade associations, professional groups, and consultants. Many benefits may result from participating in these programs. Those attending gain increased knowledge of the latest and best management philosophies and principles, improved management skills, and increased chances of promotion, salary increases, and other rewards. The organization also reaps benefits: improved attitudes, knowledge, and skills of individuals, resulting in better management; improved profitability because of

161

better management; and an improved image of the organization as being progressive, which can be important in attracting the best candidates for positions at all levels.

SELECTING PROGRAMS

The first step in selecting the best programs is to find out what programs are available. The bulletins sent to human resources managers and training directors are the best source of this information. The second step is to evaluate programs and pick the best. The careful reading of program bulletins will provide some indication of the program content, quality of leaders, and other pertinent information on cost and possible benefits. Remember, though, that subject content, qualifications of the leaders, and benefits may be exaggerated by some organizations in order to sell enrollments.

Probably the best way to judge the relative merits of different programs is to use a systematic method of evaluating participation. After each program, the participant should be required to fill out an evaluation form, such as that shown in Figure 9-1. Future participation can be based on an analysis of these forms.

One of the most extensive and best quality programs for training and developing supervisors is offered by the Management Institute, University of Wisconsin. The program was initiated in 1944 and has continued to grow in scope and quality. Currently it is being offered in both Madison and Milwaukee. Chapters 15 and 16 provide details.

SELECTING PARTICIPANTS

The human resources manager, training director, or other development person can determine which management development organizations offer high-quality programs at the least cost. The selection of the participants, however, should be a line decision, probably made with the assistance of a staff professional. In the selection process, the individual and/or the boss should study the program announcement and determine if the subject content is pertinent to the current or future job of the individual.

An organization should plan its participation for the entire year instead of waiting until the last minute to make a decision so that the participants can plan ahead, and so that fees and expenses can be budgeted.

Name _____ Title _____ Date _____

Program Attended:

Name of Program _____ Dates _____

Location _____ Fee _____

Organization Presenting Program _____

1. How accurately did the program announcement describe what was covered at the program?

☐ Very accurately   ☐ Fairly accurately   ☐ Inaccurately

2. To what extent did the subject content meet your needs and interests?

☐ Very well   ☐ To some extent   ☐ Very little

3. How effective were the speakers and conference leaders?

☐ Excellent   ☐ Very Good   ☐ Good   ☐ Fair   ☐ Poor

4. How were the facilities, meals, etc.?

☐ Excellent   ☐ Very Good   ☐ Good   ☐ Fair   ☐ Poor

5. What benefits do you feel you gained?

☐ Knowledge of what other companies were doing.
☐ New theory and principles that are pertinent.
☐ Ideas and techniques that can be applied on the job.
☐ Other (please explain).

6. How would you rate the entire program in relation to time and cost?

☐ Excellent   ☐ Very Good   ☐ Good   ☐ Fair   ☐ Poor

7. Would you like to attend a future program presented by the same organization?

☐ Definitely   ☐ Possibly   ☐ No

8. Would you recommend others from our company attend programs presented by the same organization?

☐ Yes   ☐ No   ☐ Not sure . . . If yes, who should attend?

9. Other comments.

Figure 9-1

Form for evaluating outside supervisory training programs

PREPROGRAM DISCUSSION

Those selected for an outside development program should be counseled before they attend. The participants' managers should be involved; someone from the human resources department may assist. The following checklist is a guide for this discussion:

1. Discuss the program with the supervisors. Show them that you are interested in their development, and see if they want to attend. If they are not enthusiastic, sell them on the benefits. (This discussion may be part of the process of selecting the programs to attend.)
2. Review the program details, including where and when.
3. Be sure that all necessary arrangements have been made in the department during the supervisors' absence.
4. Encourage supervisors to participate in the discussions during the sessions and in the off-hours.
5. If attending the program will necessitate being away from home one or more nights, show interest in the arrangements for their family.
6. If expenses are involved, discuss expense account arrangements.
7. Encourage supervisors to relax and enjoy the experience.
8. Explain what you expect on their return. This may include one or more of the following:

    a. A written report (evaluation plus content)
    b. An oral report (to the boss or to a group)
    c. A discussion with the boss
    d. On-the-job implementation of ideas learned
    e. Presentation to other interested supervisors

9. Answer any questions.

POSTPROGRAM DISCUSSION AND IMPLEMENTATION

To obtain maximum benefits from attendance, it is necessary to approach postprogram discussion and implementation systematically. The following checklist suggests items to be used; most of them should be handled by the supervisor's manager and some by the human resources department:

1. Obtain a written evaluation of the program. Use the same form for all participants (Figure 9-1).
2. Obtain a written and/or oral summary of what the supervisors learned, such as principles, approaches, and techniques.
3. Show an interest in the materials brought back.
4. Discuss any ideas that might be implemented on the job.
5. Give supervisors an opportunity to discuss the program at a meeting of interested persons.
6. Discuss possible follow-up (other programs or reading).

KEEPING RECORDS

It may seem obvious that records should be kept that show participation in supervisory development programs; however, it is common to find organizations in which no one knows what programs the supervisors have attended. These records are important to the supervisor, as well as to the organization, and should be kept in the human resources office or in some other place where they will be accurately maintained and readily available.

SUMMARY

All types of business, industry, and government organizations can benefit from participating in outside supervisory development programs. To maximize these benefits, a systematic approach is needed with the following steps:

1. Careful selection of quality programs
2. Careful selection of participants
3. Discussion with participants before they attend
4. Discussion with participants after they return
5. Encouraging and assisting participants in on-the-job application of what they have learned

This chapter has listed some specific factors to consider. If a systematic approach is to be used, someone in the organization should be selected as the coordinator. This person should:

- Screen bulletins and announcements to select high-quality programs.
- Work with line management to select participants.
- Handle necessary arrangements for enrollment, payment of fees, travel, and expense accounts.
- Coordinate preprogram discussion.
- Coordinate postprogram discussion and implementation.

Organizations that participate in outside supervisory development programs should realize that the time and money spent are an investment in the future of the individual and the organization and thus should try to get the best possible return. The systematic approach described here can maximize the return.

10

ON-THE-JOB PERFORMANCE APPRAISALS*

Middle- and upper-level managers are constantly training first-line supervisors by the examples they set. They are also coaching them by appraising their performance, formally or informally, and by telling them what they should do and what they should quit doing. Training professionals can provide guidance and assistance by planning and implementing a performance appraisal program. This chapter provides guidelines for doing it effectively. Chapter 11 provides principles and techniques for effective coaching.

In developing a supervisor, the manager should:

■ *Let the supervisor know what is expected*. Before subordinates can do an effective job, they must understand what they are expected to do. They should know their job duties, the standards

---

*This chapter appeared in slightly different form in Donald L. Kirkpatrick, *How to Improve Performance Through Appraisal and Coaching* (New York: AMACOM, 1982).

167

of performance they are expected to achieve, the objectives, goals, and targets, and what level of authority they have been given by the boss.

- ■ *Let the supervisor know how well he/she is doing.* Supervisors must know what they are doing well and not doing well. Appraisal and communication of performance should be related to duties, standards, objectives, and goals.
- ■ *Provide encouragement and help.* It isn't enough for managers to say to subordinates, "You're doing a poor job of quality control, and I expect you to do better." Bosses must provide assistance and help on how the supervisor can do better. They should explore with the supervisor specific ways to improve the quality of work.
- ■ *Reward the supervisor for performance.* Bosses should emphasize accomplishments and contributions rather than activities and energies expended. If subordinates are to be motivated to do their best, appropriate rewards, both monetary and nonmonetary, must be given.

Performance Appraisal and Review

To ensure that on-the-job development will be effective, a formal program of performance appraisal and review is probably needed. Four requirements must be met if this program is to be successful:

1. *The program must be well designed.* The program must fit the organization. It must consider the amount of paperwork and time required and the amount of staff help that is available for line managers to do the job. Well-designed programs are job oriented; they are concerned with the job to be done and how well it's being done—not with the personality traits of the person being appraised and developed.

2. *The program must be understood and accepted by managers.* This seems obvious, but in many cases it is not understood. Further, the managers should be enthusiastic about the program. If they believe that it is effective, they will act accordingly. If they understand it but do not accept it, they will probably do a poor job of implementation. Therefore, the program must be sold to managers as well as communicated to them.

3. *Managers must be properly trained to implement the program.* They must have the knowledge and the skills required to implement the program. For example, the program includes an appraisal interview, so

managers must be trained in conducting it effectively. A well-written manual will not accomplish the necessary training. Live training sessions, including role-playings and critiques, are needed.

4. *Proper administration and controls must be established.* If managers are required to complete the performance appraisal form on a regular basis, then administrative procedures must ensure that it will be done. In many organizations, managers who do not complete their performance appraisals discover that there are no serious consequences. They may not even receive a reminder, to say nothing about warnings or penalties. The program then becomes a "should do" instead of a "must do" part of their job. When this happens, many managers do not find the time to complete their appraisals and conduct the appraisal interviews.

One example of a control is the following policy: "Managers who do not complete their performance reviews as scheduled will not receive salary increases for themselves or their subordinates." This helps to give performance reviews a "must do" priority.

Another administrative control is constant reevaluation of the program—its approach, forms, and results. In addition, if information is provided for the personnel department, this information should be used in decisions such as salary increases, training, and promotion. Proper administration should also include the performance review training of new managers and the constant effort to keep the program sold. To accomplish all of these administrative controls, one person should be in charge. This person, usually in the human resources department, should report to a high executive in the organization who can take necessary action if the program is not operating in the way it was designed.

Program Design

Nearly every large company has designed and tried to implement some kind of performance appraisal and review program. Most of them have been quite unsuccessful in accomplishing their objectives. Human resources personnel, as well as line managers, are generally unhappy with the programs and do not consider them a success. The problem may be in the design. The following steps should provide the basis for the forms and procedures in order for the performance appraisal program to be effective:

1. The manager and the supervisor clarify the significant job segments that the supervisor performs. This is the "what" of the job.
2. The manager and the supervisor jointly develop standards of performance that the supervisor is expected to achieve in performing the job. This is the "how well" of the job.
3. The manager and the supervisor independently appraise the performance of the supervisor against the standards of performance that have been established. The following ratings can be used: "does not meet standards," "meets standards," "exceeds standards," and "outstanding."
4. An appraisal interview is conducted in which the manager and supervisor discuss the performance appraisals that each has completed. The interview has three goals:

   a. They reach agreement on a fair appraisal of performance for each standard established.
   b. The final appraisal is jointly analyzed to determine the strengths of the supervisor.
   c. The appraisal is jointly analyzed to determine the areas of weakness of the supervisor. These areas to be improved are ranked in order of priority, with top priority given to the one that most needs to be improved.

5. A written performance improvement plan (PIP) is jointly worked out by the manager and the supervisor in order to improve performance on the item with top priority. A personnel and/or training professional can assist in developing this plan. The plan includes on-the-job activities, as well as courses, books, and other approaches for improving knowledge, skills, attitudes, and behavior. The PIP should include what the manager can do, as well as what the supervisor can do, to improve the performance of the supervisor.

Human resources and training professionals usually spend considerable time deciding what forms to use in performance appraisal and review. Some forms are simple, and others are complicated, but all try to accomplish the same objective: to measure the performance of subordinates so that the boss can discuss performance with each one to help improve performance. The forms and procedures must fit the individual organization. If there is a shortage of clerical staff to help line management people, the forms and procedures should be simple. If clerical help is available, the forms can be more complicated, more extensive, and perhaps more useful to the organization.

Following are specific areas to consider when implementing the five steps:

Clarifying Significant Job Segments

In developing significant job segments, job descriptions can be helpful. Approximately six to eight segments should be selected. Figure 10-1 contains some examples from different types of organizations where the job description was used as the basis for selecting the significant job segments.

Developing Standards of Performance

There are eight characteristics of standards of performance:

1. *They are based on the job, and not on the person(s) in the job.* Standards of performance should be established for the job itself regardless of who occupies it. For example, the job of administrative secretary or production foreman may be one that a number of people perform. There should be one set of standards for the job—not one set for every person doing that particular job. Standards of performance are different from objectives. Objectives should be set for an individual rather than for a job, and a typical characteristic of an objective or goal is that it should be challenging. Therefore, a manager who has several subordinates doing the same job will have one set of standards for the job but may have different objectives for each person, based on that person's experience, skills, and past performance. For example, the objective for a mediocre performer may be the same as the standard, while the objective for an outstanding employee may be much higher than standard.

2. *They are achievable.* Practically all employees on the job should be able to reach the standard. (An exception is a new employee who is learning the job. The standard may not apply until the employee has passed the probationary period.) Most production standards are set so that practically everyone can meet the standard, and many employees can reach 125% of the standard.

(text continued on page 174)

POSITION TITLE: PAYROLL SUPERVISOR

Duties and Responsibilities

1. Supervises the following:
    a. Compiling of data.
    b. Tabulation of data.
    c. Computing of data.
    d. Preparation of summaries and control figures.
    e. Preparation of tax reports.
2. Assigns work to subordinates.
3. Interviews, selects, and trains employees.
4. Evaluates and counsels subordinates.
5. Recommends people for promotion.
6. Recommends salary increases.

Significant Job Segments

1. Data compilation, tabulation, and computing
2. Preparation of reports
3. Work Assignments
4. Personnel
5. Promotions and salary increases

POSITION TITLE: MACHINE SHOP SUPERVISOR

Duties and Responsibilities

1. Plans and coordinates precision machining of standardized components involving diversified operations and machine setups.
2. Interprets and directs compliance with the union contract and labor relations policies.
3. Enforces compliance with administrative practices and procedures.
4. Establishes budgets.
5. Maintains surveillance to ensure timely production that meets quality standards.
6. Keeps costs within established budget.
7. Interviews, selects, trains, counsels, promotes, evaluates, and assigns work to nonsalaried personnel.
8. Acts as liaison with other divisions.

Significant Job Segments

1. Planning
2. Union contract and policies
3. Practices and procedures
4. Budgets
5. Schedules
6. Quality
7. Personnel

Figure 10-1. *Examples of job descriptions*

POSITION TITLE: HEAD NURSE

Duties and Responsibilities

To Patients

1. Plan safe, economical, and efficient nursing care.
2. See that quality patient care is given to each patient in accordance with quality standards.
3. Formulate and utilize patient care plan to assist in resolving patient problems.
4. Act as liaison between patient, physician, and family.

To Medical Staff

5. Act as liaison between physician and patient care team.

To Own Nurse Manager

6. Share appropriate communications with unit personnel.
7. Ensure adequate staffing.
8. Make out patient care assignments.
9. Help with budget planning; operate unit within budget.

To Department Personnel

10. Hold regular unit personnel meetings.
11. Promote an environment in which the patient care team can work cooperatively toward objectives.
12. Provide an opportunity for personnel staff development.
13. Counsel personnel when necessary.

To Committees

14. Participate actively in selected committee activities.

To Other Organizations

15. Maintain membership in appropriate professional organizations.

To Self

16. Participate in continuing education programs.

Significant Job Segments

1. Patient Care
2. Medical Staff
3. Staffing
4. Budget
5. Meetings
6. Subordinate development
7. Self-development

Figure 10-1. *Cont'd*

3. *They are understood.* The standard should be clear to boss and subordinate alike. Unfortunately, there is often confusion between the two parties on the exact meaning of a standard.

4. *They are agreed on.* Both boss and subordinate should agree that the standard is fair. This is very important for two reasons: it motivates the employee, and it becomes the basis for evaluation.

5. *They are as specific and measurable as possible.* Some people believe that standards must be specific and measurable; they insist that they must be stated in numbers, percentages, dollars, or some other form that can be quantifiably measured. Every effort should be made to do this, but if it can't be done, the standard should be stated as specifically as possible even if subjective judgment must be used to evaluate performance against it. Early in a performance review program, it might seem impossible to state standards in measurable terms. With practice and experience, it may be possible to be specific on all or nearly all standards.

6. *They are time oriented.* It should be clear whether the standard is to be accomplished by a specific date or whether it is ongoing.

7. *They are written.* Both boss and subordinate should have a written copy of the standards that are agreed upon. In this way, they won't have to rely on memory, and the standard can be a constant reminder to both parties.

8. *They are subject to change.* Because standards should be achievable and agreed upon, they should be periodically evaluated and changed if necessary. Perhaps there are new methods, equipment, materials, or changes in other significant job factors. They should not be changed just because a performer is not meeting the standard.

Determining How Many Standards to Develop

There is no magic number to the number of standards, and there is no rule of thumb that says it all depends on the job. The main factor that determines the number of standards is the boss: How many standards does the boss feel are needed to clarify what is expected of a subordinate? If two standards will do it (say, quantity and quality), then that should be sufficient. If it takes 10 to 20 pages to do it, then that's how many there should be.

There is an advantage to having many rather than few: It gives a subordinate a clearer understanding of the total job and allows the boss to appraise many different facets of the job and pinpoint an employee's areas of strength, as well as those needing improvement. Therefore, an organization should not put a limit on the number of standards that should be developed for a job.

Figure 10-2 contains samples of standards of performance that have been developed for segments of different jobs in a variety of organizations.

(text continued on page 178)

POSITION: PRODUCTION FOREMAN

Significant Job Segments	*Standards of Performance*
1. Safety	1. Monthly safety meetings are conducted in accordance with company schedules.
	2. Safe operating procedures are followed by all employees.
	3. Regular monthly inspections are held in the department in accordance with the approved checklist.
	4. Action is taken within five days correct any unsafe condition.
	5. Monthly safety reports are submitted by the fifth of the following month.
2. Controlling costs	1. Waste and scrap are kept below 2% of total production.
	2. One cost-saving improvement per month is initiated and put into operation.
	3. Overtime costs are held to a maximum of 3% of direct labor costs.
	4. All purchases are made in the most economical manner according to a buying plan.
	5. Overhead costs are kept within budget limitations.
	6. Salary controls are exercised in accordance with the salary administration plan.
	7. The ratio of productivity to costs is improved by 1% every six months.

Figure 10-2. *Examples of standards of performance*

POSITION: PRODUCTION FOREMAN

Significant Job Segments	Standards of Performance
3. Developing subordinates	1. New subordinates are inducted and trained in accordance with a definite plan.
	2. Performance reviews are held with all subordinates on an annual basis.
	3. The appraisal and performance improvement plan aspects of the performance review program are reviewed with superior.
	4. Discussions are held with subordinates at least quarterly to see that performance improvement takes place according to plan.
	5. Responsibilities and authority are delegated to subordinates on a planned basis.

POSITION: OFFICE SUPERVISOR

Significant Job Segments	Standards of Performance
Written communication	1. All correspondence is answered, and a copy filed, within one week of receiving it.
	2. All written communication is handled so that there is minimal misunderstanding.
	3. All interdepartmental and intradepartmental memorandums are answered within two working days of receipt.
	4. All official memorandums are posted and/or circulated, initialed, dated, and returned to department head within one week of receiving them.
	5. Minutes of officially called meetings are distributed to participants within five days after the meeting.

POSITION: REGIONAL SALES MANAGER

Significant Job Segments	Standards of Performance
Developing subordinates	
A. Conducts performance reviews	1. Performance reviews are conducted with all subordinates according to the procedure approved by the sales manager.

Figure 10-2. *Cont'd*

POSITION: REGIONAL SALES MANAGER	
Significant Job Segments	*Standards of Performance*
Developing subordinates	
A. Conducts performance	2. For new employees, job duties and standards are clarified within the first three months of employment.
	3. A complete performance review is conducted within nine months of hiring each new employee.
B. Coaches	1. Subordinates are coached and worked with on a day-to-day basis to help them perform better on their current jobs.
	2. Follow-up is conducted to ensure implementation of performance improvement plan.
	3. Selected assignments are delegated to subordinates to help develop them for greater responsibilities.
C. Trains in products	1. Subordinates understand the products, procedures, programs, and policies that are pertinent to their work.
	2. District sales managers know how to use these items.
	3. District sales managers put pertinent items into operation.
D. Counsels	1. Subordinates feel that regional sales managers are readily available and glad to discuss problems with them.
	2. All personal conversations are kept confidential.
E. General	1. Subordinates clearly understand their jobs.
	2. Subordinates are qualified and skilled to perform their jobs.
	3. Subordinates know how well they are doing and what improvements need to be made.

Figure 10-2. *Cont'd*

Standards of performance are defined as conditions that will exist when the job has been done in an acceptable manner. They have two purposes. First, they guide the behavior of subordinates in accomplishing the standards that have been established. According to James L. Hayes, former president of the American Management Association and an internationally known expert on standards of performance, "If you go through the exercise of establishing standards of performance with your subordinates and clarify what your expectations are, it is a worthwhile exercise even if you never appraise their performance. This is because most people want to do an acceptable job."

The second purpose of standards of performance is to provide a basis against which the performance of an individual can be effectively and fairly appraised. Unless clear standards of performance are established, appraisals may be biased by feelings and subjective evaluation. Regardless of the approach and forms that are used in a program on performance appraisal and review, the process of clarifying what is expected is essential if the program is going to be effective. Standards of performance are the best way to do this.

Effective standards of performance are based on the job and are achievable, understood, agreed on, specific and measurable, time oriented, written, and subject to change. So that they can be properly set, with subordinates motivated to meet or exceed them, subordinates should be involved in setting their own standards. In cases of disagreement, the boss must make the final decision.

There is no minimum or maximum number of standards that should be set for a job, although having many standards helps the subordinate understand more clearly what is expected and helps the boss pinpoint specific strengths and areas needing improvement. The boss and subordinate should decide how many are appropriate and practical.

Appraising Performance

If an effective job is done in clarifying what is expected in terms of significant job segments and standards of performance, the appraisal by the boss becomes quite easy and objective. It is a matter of comparing actual performance with definite standards, and the more specific and measurable the standards are, the most objective the appraisal is.

In the book *MBO II*, George Odiorne warns that two kinds of flaws may exist in appraising performances if the standards are vague: the *halo effect* and the *horns effect*.[1]

The *halo effect* is the tendency of the boss to overrate a favored employee. This can happen for a variety of reasons:

- *Effect of past record.* Because the person has done good work in the distant past, performance is assumed to be adequate in the recent past, too. Good work tends to carry over into the current rating period.
- *Compatibility.* There is a tendency to highly rate people whom we find pleasing of manner and personality—perhaps more than they deserve. Those who agree with us, who nod their heads when we talk, or who—even better—make notes of our words: these people may get better ratings than their performance justifies.
- *Effect of recency.* The person who did an outstanding job last week or yesterday can offset a mediocre performance over the rest of the year by this single act.
- *The one-asset person.* The glib talker, the person with an impressive appearance or an advanced degree, or the graduate of the boss's own alma mater may get a more favorable rating than the person lacking these often irrelevant attributes.
- *The blind-spot effect.* The boss doesn't see certain types of defects because they are just like his or her own. For example, the boss who loves accounting may overrate another detail person.
- *The high-potential effect.* We sometimes judge the person's paper record rather than the accomplishment for the organization.
- *The no-complaints bias.* Here the appraiser treats no news as good news. The subordinate who has no complaints and says that everything is terrific is likely to go over well.

---

[1]George Odiorne, MBO II (Belmont, Calif.: Fearon Pitman Publishing Corp., 1979).

The *horns effect* is the reverse of the halo effect—the tendency to rate a person lower than the circumstances justify. Some specific causes of this are:

- *A perfectionist boss.* Because the boss's expectations are so high, he or she is more often disappointed and rates a subordinate lower than deserved.

- *A contrary subordinate.* Here the boss vents private irritation with the subordinate's tendency to disagree too often on too many issues.

- *The oddball effect.* Despite all the lip service to nonconformity, it seldom finds its way into practice when appraisal time comes around. The oddball, the maverick, and the nonconformist get low ratings because they are different.

- *Membership on a weak team.* A good player on a weak team ends up with lower ratings than he or she would have gotten if playing on a winning one.

- *The guilt-by-association effect.* The person who isn't known well by the boss is often judged by the company he or she keeps.

- *The dramatic-incident effect.* A recent goof can wipe out the effect of months of good work and give a person a lower rating than deserved.

- *The personality-trait effect.* The subordinate who is too cocky, brash, meek, passive, or otherwise lacks some trait the boss associates with a good employee suffers in the appraisal.

- *The self-comparison effect.* The person who does the job differently from the way the boss did it when he or she was back on that job suffers more than a person whose job the boss has never done.

If standards of performance have been effectively established, the halo and horns effects can be eliminated or at least drastically reduced. From one appraisal time to the next, a manager should be gathering information that will make the appraisal fair and accurate. Otherwise,

---

[2]J.C. Flanagan and R.K. Burns, "The Employee Performance Record: A New Approach and Development Tool," *Harvard Business Review* (September-October 1955).

the appraisal may be based on hazy memory or only on the most recent behavior and accomplishments of the subordinate.

J. C. Flanagan and R. K. Burns developed an objective approach for gathering data for the appraisal; they call it the *critical incident method*.[2] This technique relies on the collection of specific observable job incidents that are judged to be critical because they are related directly to either good or poor job performance. After the incidents are collected and tabulated, components are grouped under one of the headings in a specially designed performance record.

The performance record is accompanied by a manual that describes and illustrates each of the 16 critical requirements. The supervisor records each incident on the effective (blue) or ineffective (red) half of the page for the employee involved. The manual states that to be critical, an incident must be directly observed by the supervisor and must clearly show either outstanding, or less than satisfactory, performance.

In his experience with Delco-Remy Division of General Motors, Flanagan found that most of the recorded incidents were positive. There was speculation that the manager would be much more likely to record negative incidents, but this was not true.

The critical incident method has three basic steps: (1) completing the performance record as critical incidents occur, (2) summarizing them for the rating period, and (3) conducting a performance review interview with the employee. Flanagan and Burns recommend that this three-phase program be carried out at six-month intervals, and they suggest further that the performance review interview should take the average supervisor from half an hour to an hour. Summarizing the method, they said:

> A performance record is not a yardstick. It is not a rating method. It is a procedure for collecting significant facts about employee performance. These facts are gathered in such a way that they will be of maximum use to supervisors and management, both in improving the employee's understanding of the requirements of his present job and in developing his potential for more responsible positions. It is not simply a new form but a new approach.[3]

---

[3]Reprinted by permission of the *Harvard Business Review*. An excerpt from "The Employee Performance Record: A New Approach and Development Tool." September-October 1955. Copyright © 1955 by the President and Fellows of Harvard College. All rights reserved.

If the critical incident method is used, managers should be sure to look for both positive and negative incidents. Otherwise, the appraisal will become biased, and the subordinate will be unfairly appraised.

In gathering information, the manager should have one objective: to make an accurate appraisal of performance. This information comes from two major sources:

1. Performance records such as quantity of production, quality of work, meeting deadlines and schedules, safety, actual costs versus budget costs, absenteeism, and the number of complaints from customers or co-workers.

2. Other people who have had dealings with the subordinate. This could include the boss, staff personnel, people served by the subordinate, and even people in other departments with whom the subordinate works. If the organization uses project teams on which the subordinate has served, the project leader should be contacted. This should be as objective as possible. Instead of asking, "How do you feel about Harry?", it's better to ask, "What kind of service has Harry given you?", or, "How would you evaluate Harry's performance in regard to this issue?"

In other words, the more sources that are used, the better. Each source, however, should be carefully selected to provide objective data. All these data should then be analyzed and compared with the standards of performance to arrive at an accurate appraisal.

Preparing the Appraisal Form

There are almost as many types of appraisal forms as there are people designing the forms. One approach is shown in Figure 10-3, which uses the following key:

DNMS = Did not meet standard
MS = Met standard
ES = Exceeded standard
O = Outstanding

This form is based on the use of significant job segments and standards of performance, described earlier in the chapter.

Job Title _____

Name of Supervisor _____

Name of subordinate _____

Date _____

Significant Job Segments	Standards of Performance*	Appraisal				Comments on Performance
		DNMS	MS	ES	O	
	1.					
	2.					
	3.					
	1.					
	2.					
	1.					

*What conditions will exist when the job is performed in an acceptable manner?
DNMS = Did not meet standard   MS = Met standard   ES = Exceeded standard   O = Outstanding

Figure 10-3. *Performance appraisal form*

Performance Strengths

1.

2.

3.

Performance to be Improved

1.

2.

3.

Performance Improvement Plan

Performance to be Improved: _____

Action to be Taken	By Whom	When
1.		
2.		
3.		
4.		
5.		

Figure 10-3. *Cont'd*

Harnischfeger Corporation (a manufacturer of overhead cranes and hoists, mining shovels, draglines, hydraulic mining excavators, and related replacement parts) has modified this form to use a different key:

DNMR = Did not meet requirements
MR = Met requirements
ER = Exceeded requirements
O = Outstanding

The reason for the change was that the concept of standard of performance was too complicated to explain and implement. By using *requirements* instead of *standards*, the boss would have to explain the requirements in order to be sure that the subordinate understood what was expected.

Companies vary in their terminology. Some organizations use *unsatisfactory, satisfactory, outstanding,* and *superior.* Others prefer such terms as *unacceptable, acceptable, good, very good,* and *excellent.* Some military units use such words as *good, excellent, outstanding,* and *superior.* Here there are two words that mean something better than excellent. Some organizations prefer a five- or ten-point scale with 1 at the low end of the scale, meaning "poor" or "unsatisfactory," and 5 or 10 at the top level of the scale to mean "outstanding" or "superior." Still other organizations try to describe the gradations—for example:

Poor	Consistently unsatisfactory; doesn't come close to meeting standard
Fair	Occasionally meets standard; usually is slightly below standard
Good	Consistently meets standard; occasionally doesn't meet standard and occasionally is far above standard
Excellent	Consistently far above standard

Other categories and scales are used in the examples in Part II of this book.

If the purpose of performance appraisal is to improve performance, the word *average* should not be used because it invites comparison with other people rather than with the standard. In order to improve performance, it is important to identify, for each person, the level of performance for each standard. This will reveal strengths, as well as areas that need improvement. If the purpose of the appraisal is to determine salary increases instead of to improve performance, then the word *average* may be used. In this context, individuals' performances are compared with each other.

Using Self-Appraisal

The concept of self-appraisal is required in some organizations, left optional in some, and discouraged or prohibited in others. In a situation where the subordinate does not complete a self-appraisal, the boss makes out the appraisal form, meets with the subordinate for the appraisal interview, and tries to get from the subordinate both understanding and acceptance of the appraisal. The subordinate usually comes to the interview without any specific preparation (although he or she may have made an informal self-appraisal that may not be in writing) and may be fearful that it will be an unpleasant experience.

He or she is likely to be on the defensive because the boss may read off the appraisal and ask the subordinate to agree or to substantiate any disagreement. Many subordinates will not speak freely; they lack information to substantiate their self-judgments or are afraid to disagree with the boss. Therefore, they might very well express agreement—rather, refrain from expressing disagreement—even if they don't really agree—and the boss will naively conclude that both understanding and agreement have been reached.

If the subordinate completes a self-appraisal, preferably on the same form the boss uses, the two of them can sit side by side and compare their appraisals. This can create a relaxed climate in which the objective is to arrive at an accurate appraisal. If both have honestly tried to be as objective as possible and if the significant job segments and standards of performance have been clearly stated, the appraisals shouldn't be far apart.

The concept of self-appraisal says to the subordinate: "Your input is important. Maybe you know some things about your performance that I don't know. I want to be sure that you have a chance to communicate them to me. And I'll listen to you and consider your input before arriving at a final appraisal."

Several factors should be kept in mind if self-appraisals are going to be used:

■ Subordinates should be given enough advance notice—a minimum of three weeks—so that a fair self-appraisal can be made.

■ Subordinates should be told the reasons for the self-appraisal and how it will be used in the interview.

■ Specific instructions should be given to the subordinates on the form to use and what to do.

■ Subordinates should be urged to make an objective appraisal—not to be overly aggressive (rating themselves higher than justified) or shy (rating themselves lower than justified).

■ Managers should assure subordinates that the self-appraisal will be used to help them arrive at a fair appraisal.

The appraisal process must be done in a systematic and objective manner, first gathering data from various sources and then comparing performance with previously set standards. It is important for the subordinate to accept the appraisal as fair. The best way to accomplish this is to have the subordinate prepare a self-appraisal for comparison with the boss's appraisal. Free and open discussion will also help to arrive at a fair appraisal agreed on and accepted by both parties. In cases of disagreement, the boss must make the final appraisal. In most cases, however, agreement can be reached without the boss exercising this authority.

Conducting the Appraisal Interview

The manner in which this interview is conducted is critical to the success of the performance appraisal program. Following are suggestions of how to prepare, as well as how to conduct, an interview.

Preparing for the Interview. Both the boss and the subordinate should prepare for the interview. The boss has seven tasks:

1. *To decide on the best time.* The best time is when both parties are able to spend time together without interruption, so it is a good idea for the boss to suggest a time and get approval from the subordinate.

2. *To decide on the best place.* A private office is the best place—either the boss's office or a neutral place. It should be a private place where the door can be closed and people can't look in and

see what's going on. Finally, it should be a comfortable place where both parties can relax.

3. *To prepare the facilities*. Arrange the furniture so that the subordinates will feel at ease, perhaps with the chairs side by side instead of across the desk from each other. If possible, have coffee or water available.

4. *To gather information and materials*. Make a complete and objective appraisal. Have the forms and information on hand for the interview.

5. *To plan the opening*. Decide whether to talk about a current event—sports, politics, weather—or to begin by stating the purpose of the interview. Use whatever approach is most natural and will create the best climate for the interview.

6. *To plan the approach*. Here are some alternatives to consider:

   ■ Begin with strengths and then discuss job segments needing improvement.
   ■ Go straight through the form, give your appraisal, and discuss one item at a time to get agreement before going ahead to the next item.
   ■ Ask the subordinate for his or her appraisal before giving your own. You could do this for the entire form or for each item.
   ■ Alternate between yourself and the subordinate as to who gives the appraisal first.

   There is no right or wrong approach. Your approach might depend on whether the subordinate has made a self-appraisal. Remember that the objective is to get agreement, so use whatever approach is best for you.

7. *To give the subordinate appropriate advance notice*. The subordinate should have enough time to prepare for the interview and should clearly understand the time, place, objectives, and probable length of the interview.

The subordinate should begin to prepare as soon as the date is set. He or she should:

■ Gather information related to past performance. This includes specific data on activities and accomplishments, as well as reasons why certain things weren't done or were done incorrectly.

- Complete a self-appraisal if requested by the boss.
- Arrange for work coverage during the interview. This is important so that the subordinate can concentrate on the interview and not worry about whether the job is being done properly.

Conducting the Interview. The following general principles apply to all performance interviews regardless of the form that is used or whether a self-appraisal has been completed.

Establish and maintain rapport. Rapport can be defined as the climate in which the interview takes place. The location of the interview is important. It should be conducted in a place where both people can feel relaxed, with comfortable chairs, a minimum of noise, and privacy. If it would help to put the subordinate at ease, the boss and the subordinate should sit alongside each other rather than across the desk. The boss's verbal and nonverbal communications should make it clear that two-way communication will take place and that the subordinate should speak freely and frankly. A cup of coffee, for instance, might help to create this comfortable climate.

It is debatable whether to begin the interview by talking about hobbies or some current event or to begin by saying, "As you know the purpose of this interview is to . . . " If the two people have a common hobby that may be a good place to start, or if an unusual historical or sporting event just happened, that may also be a good opener.

Socializing for a few minutes is well worth the time if it creates rapport. The following list contrasts an interview climate of rapport to an interview climate without it:

Rapport	*Lack of Rapport*
At ease, relaxed	Nervous, fearful, anxious
Comfortable	Uncomfortable
Friendly, warm	Formal, cold
Not afraid to speak freely and frankly	Afraid to speak openly
Believing, trusting	Challenging, proving
Listening	Interrupting
Understanding	Misunderstanding
Open-minded	Close-minded
Accepting criticism without resentment	Resenting criticism
Disagreeing without offending	Arguing, downgrading

Clearly explain the purpose of the interview, and state it in positive terms, such as: "The purpose of the interview today is for us to discuss your performance and to agree on your strengths and areas that can be improved. Then we are going to talk about your future and how we can work together."

Encourage the subordinate to talk. The interview must include two-way communication. Some subordinates are ready to talk; others are reluctant because of shyness or fear. Establishing rapport will help to overcome this reluctance. In some situations, the boss must ask specific questions to get the subordinate to talk. In others, the subordinate will talk freely with little encouragement.

Listen and don't interrupt. By *listen,* I mean *really* listen. This means more than merely keeping quiet or not talking; it is an active process of finding out the thoughts and the feelings of the other person. If both parties start to talk at the same time, the boss should quit talking and encourage the subordinate to go ahead. Backing down is quite difficult for some bosses, but it pays off in maintaining two-way communication throughout the interview. It tells the subordinate, "What you have to say is more important to me than what I have to say to you!"

Avoid confrontation and argument. Even when differences of opinions are expressed, the boss should avoid confrontation and argument. Both parties know that the boss has more authority and power than the subordinate, so there is a chance of ending up in a win-lose situation (the boss wins and the subordinate loses). Winning by the boss might be very costly; it might destroy rapport and result in the subordinate's deciding not to communicate freely and frankly. If this happens, the interview will not achieve its objectives and might even do more harm than good. By keeping the discussion free and open, a win-win situation can be created so that the needs of both people are met.

Focus on performance, not personality. This is a performance appraisal interview, and emphasis should be on performance, not personality. This does not mean that such items as attitude, integrity, dependability, appearance, or initiative are not mentioned. It does mean, however, that these characteristics are mentioned only as they relate to performance.

Focus on the future, not the past. This does not mean that past performance will not be discussed, but the emphasis is on what can be learned from the past that will help in the future.

Emphasize strengths, as well as areas to improve. Every employee has strengths, as well as areas of performance that can be improved. Recognize and build on these strengths, and also discuss job segments that must be corrected if performance is to improve.

Terminate the interview when advisable. Don't hesitate to terminate an interview at any point if you think it's a good idea. Any number of reasons could justify the termination: loss of rapport, the boss or subordinate is anxious to go somewhere, quitting time has arrived, lack of progress being made, fatigue has set in, or an important interruption has occurred. If you end the interview before accomplishing all the objectives you set, agree on when the interview will continue.

Conclude on a positive note. Be sure that the subordinate leaves the interview in a positive frame of mind, instead of resentful toward the negative aspects of the discussion. After the interview is over, the subordinate should say (or at least feel), "Thanks. I'm glad we had a chance to get together and discuss my performance. Now I know where I stand and what I should do in the future. And I know that you are going to work with me."

A warm handshake at the conclusion of the interview is one way to end on a positive tone. Another is for the boss to say, "Thanks for coming in. I feel that this has been a very profitable discussion, and I know I can count on you in the future. I'll be glad to help you in any way I can."

Techniques for Successful Interviews. There really shouldn't be any great surprises in the interview if the significant job segments and standards of performance have been clarified and agreed upon as the basis for the appraisal. The subordinate's appraisal, whether mental or written, should be very close to the written appraisal by the manager. The problem the manager faces is to be sure that he or she receives honest agreement or disagreement from the subordinate on the appraisal. Obviously, the establishment of rapport is essential for this. Specific interviewing techniques are also important. Here are some specific suggestions:

1. *Be open.* Show the form to the subordinate. Don't hide it.
2. *Explain your appraisal.* Describe how you arrived at it. If you checked records or talked to other people, say so. If you did it by yourself, say so. Also, be sure to emphasize that you want frank comments from the subordinate because your appraisal may not be accurate. Admit, for example, that the subordinate may have done some things you've forgotten or don't even know about.
3. *Be sure that your appraisal is tentative.* Be willing to change your appraisal if the subordinate's input convinces you that you were wrong. Don't be afraid to admit a mistake.

4. *Summarize*. When the entire appraisal has been discussed, go over it with the subordinate. Have a copy made for the subordinate so that she has the same information you have.

All four of these techniques demonstrate to the subordinate that there is nothing secret about the process. A manager simply wants to come up with a fair and accurate appraisal that will make it possible to work with the subordinate and help improve performance. The manager may want to start with strengths or with the first item on the appraisal form and go straight down the form. Whatever way is most natural and comfortable is the best way. After completing the discussion, the entire appraisal should be summarized.

DEVELOPING THE PERFORMANCE IMPROVEMENT PLAN

In the first part of the interview, the boss and subordinate should accomplish the following:

1. Agree on a fair appraisal. If the subordinate feels that the appraisal is not fair, the process will fail.
2. Agree on the strengths that have been demonstrated by the performance. (Three is suggested.)
3. Agree on the weaknesses (areas to improve) that have been demonstrated by performance. (Three is suggested.)
4. Jointly select the one area that should be worked on first. The performance improvement plan will be based on this selection.

Most performance appraisal programs end without any plan of action. They sometimes offer suggestions to the subordinate on what and how to improve, but they don't develop a plan. If improvement is going to take place, a plan is necessary, and it should include what the manager will do, as well as what the subordinate should do. Often the lack of satisfactory performance by subordinates is caused by factors over which they have no control—and many of these factors are controlled by the manager. It is essential for the improvement of subordinates to be a joint venture between managers and subordinates.

An action plan should ask three questions:

1. What action will be taken?
2. By whom?
3. When?

In order to develop this plan, manager and subordinate should independently prepare a list of possible actions to be taken by each of them. In a meeting, the two of them will consider possible actions and integrate them into a plan.

Figure 10-4 shows a performance improvement plan that was jointly developed by Tom Severson, the manager, and John Green, his subordinate supervisor. It was based on the top-priority need of John: "Building an Effective Team."

Employee:	John Green, Supervisor
Boss:	Tom Severson, Department Head
Date:	October 1
Performance to be improved:	Building an Effective Team

Action to be Taken	By Whom	When
1. Evaluate each subordinate as a team player (5=high to 1=low)	John Green	October 20
2. If 3 or lower, determine why.	John Green	October 30
3. Read the following: Donald L. Kirkpatrick, *How to Improve Performance Through Appraisal and Coaching*, Chapter 5, "On-the-Job Coaching," (New York: AMACOM, 1982).	John Green	November 15
4. Attend a workship on "Team Building."	John Green	The next time offered by the Training Department
5. Talk with Supervisor Phil Taylor on his approach to building an effective team.	John Green	October 15
6. Talk with each subordinate rated 3 or below about ways to improve teamwork.	John Green	December 1
7. Set an example by being a good team player with peers in other departments.	Tom Severson	Starting NOW!

Figure 10-4. *Performance improvement plan*

SUMMARY

There are several objectives of performance appraisal programs. Most of them become the basis for salary administration. Nearly all of them provide information for personnel decisions on promotion, transfer, and termination, but few of them result in improved performance. Training professionals must realize that the typical performance appraisal program that concentrates on salary administration will not result in improved performance. The chart in Figure 10-5 compares programs aimed at salary administration and those with improved performance as the objective.

Training professionals should take an active part in the development of a program that will result in improved performance. This usually means that there are two different forms and procedures—one for salary administration and one for improved performance. The program described in this chapter is directly aimed at improved performance. The ingredients of such a program require that manager and subordinate agree on what's expected of the subordinate. This can best be accomplished by determining six to eight significant job segments and the standards of performance for each.

An appraisal against these standards should be made independently by manager and subordinate. In the appraisal interview, these appraisals are compared and discussed, and a final appraisal is agreed on. (If the subordinate feels that the appraisal is not "fair," the entire process

	Performance Reviews for Salary Administration	Performance Reviews for Improved Performance
Looking	Backward	Forward
Considering	Overall performance	Detailed performance
Comparing with	Other people	Job standards and objectives
Determined by	Boss, higher management, personnel department	Boss and subordinate together
Interview climate	Subjective, emotional	Objective, unemotional
Factors to consider	Salary range, total money available, inflation, seniority, performance, education	Performance

Figure 10-5. *A comparison of performance reviews*

fails.) The strengths, as well as the weaknesses, of the subordinate are agreed on, and priorities are established on performance to be improved. The top-priority need is analyzed, and a performance improvement plan is jointly developed that includes action to be taken by both manager and subordinate. No improvement has taken place yet, but a sound basis for coaching has been established.

If the program is going to be successful, the following steps must be followed:

1. Develop a program that is right for the organization.
2. Communicate it so that supervisors understand it.
3. Sell it so that supervisors are motivated to do it.
4. Train the supervisors so that they know what to do and how to do it.
5. Establish controls to be sure it is done.

One way (and probably the best way) to communicate and sell the program is to involve line managers in the development of the program. A good approach is to establish a performance appraisal task force consisting of line and staff personnel, with the training professional as the chairperson. If the training and personnel professionals don't involve line supervisors in the development of the program, line managers typically look at it as a "personnel program" that they must implement. When line managers are involved, they will see that it is a tool to help them do their job of working with subordinates to get maximum performance.

11

Coaching
for
Improved
Performance

Chapter 10 described the principles and techniques for planning and implementing an effective performance appraisal program designed to result in improved performance. The program ended with the development of a performance improvement plan, which involved communicating past performance and deciding what should be done in the future. The manager must now become a coach to be sure that improvement takes place. Part of the coaching effort must be aimed at implementing the performance improvement plan. The rest of it will be done on a daily basis.

Coaching on the Performance Improvement Plan

Figure 11-1 contains the coaching schedule for the performance improvement plan worked out between John Green, a supervisor, and Tom Severson, his boss. Tom does not wait to see whether John does what he agreed to do. Rather, Tom contacts him before the agreed-on date to remind him. The figure shows the contacts that Tom will make with John. Also, Tom does not expect John to buy the book he agreed to read. Rather, he gets the book for John. In other words, he encourages, helps, and follows up to see that the action plan is carried out. It is essential that Tom, the boss, does what he personally agreed to do.

Day-to-Day Coaching

In day-to-day coaching, the boss has to set the right example. In one of his essays, Ralph Waldo Emerson wrote, "What you are thunders so that I cannot hear what you say to the contrary!" This statement illustrates the importance of the example set by the boss. Supervisors are constantly looking at the attitude and behavior of their boss and wondering:

■ What does the boss do about self-development? Does he or she constantly try to keep up to date on technical and management subjects? Does he or she attend seminars and programs for personal growth?

■ To what extent does the boss support management development activities? For example, does the boss encourage and stimulate in-company programs that are designed to help the supervisor improve knowledge and skills? Does he or she encourage subordinates to attend outside management development programs?

Daily coaching is based on observing the performance of the subordinates. If the subordinate performs well, the manager provides positive reinforcement. If the subordinate fails to do something that should be done, the manager calls it to the attention of the subordinate to find out why it wasn't done and to see that it is done. And if the subordinate does something that should not be done, the manager must find out the reason for the mistake and take whatever action is appropriate.

Name: John Green, Supervisor   Boss: Tom Severson, Department Head

Date: October 1

Performance to be improved: Building an effective team

The Performance Improvement Plan   Coaching Contact by Tom Severson

Action to Be Taken	Performance Improvement Plan		Coaching	
	By Whom	When	When	Results
1. Evaluate each subordinate as a team player (5=high to 1=low)	John Green	October 20	October 18 October 21	Reminded John to do the evaluations. Went over the evaluations with John.
2. If 3 or lower, determine why.	John Green	October 30	October 25 October 31	Asked John for an update on the evaluations. Went over the evaluations with John.
3. Read the following; Donald L. Kirkpatrick, *How to Improve Performance Through Appraisal and Coaching,* Chapter 5, "On-the-Job Coaching," (New York: AMACOM, 1982).	John Green	November 15	October 5 November 1 November 12 November 16	Got a copy of the book and gave it to John. Asked John if he had read it yet. Reminded him of the November 15 date. Set a time on November 16 to discuss the book. Discussed the book with John and highlighted some specific things he should do.

Figure 11-1.

Coaching schedule for a performance improvement plan

Action to Be Taken	By Whom	When	When	Results
4. Attend a workshop on "Team Building."	John Green	The next time offered by the Training Department.	October 10	Found out from Phil Jackson, the Training Manager, that the next workshop will be held November 6. Discussed it with John and enrolled him.
			November 3	Reminded John about the course and told him I would discuss the program with him on November 8.
			November 8	Asked John what he had learned and discussed ways to implement the ideas with his subordinates.
5. Talk with Supervisor Phil Taylor on his approach to building an effective team.	John Green	October 15	October 16	Asked John what he had learned from Phil Taylor. Discovered that he had not talked to him. Set the date of October 20 to discuss his talk with Phil.
			October 20	Discussed with John what he had learned from Phil.

Figure 11-1. *Cont'd*

Action to Be Taken	By Whom	When	When	Results
6. Talk with each subordinate rated 3 or below about ways to improve teamwork.	John Green	December 1	November 24	Asked John what approach he was going to use in talking with those subordinates rated 3 or lower. He had not planned his approach yet. Set the date of November 28 to discuss the approach.
			November 28	Discussed John's approaches and offered suggestions.
			December 3	Asked John for a report on his discussions. Offered comments and suggestions.
7. Set an example by being a good team player with peers in other departments.	Tom Severson	Starting NOW!	October 3	Developed a plan to get together with other managers at my level to discuss cooperation and teamwork. Established a schedule of monthly meetings to discuss problems and suggestions on how we can better work together.

Figure 11-1. *Cont'd*

The key to effective coaching is to handle problem situations without causing resentment on the part of the subordinate. Resentment can easily be created by an eager coach who is overly anxious to correct an error. For example, a direct approach to pointing out the mistake and ordering the subordinate to do it right could well end up in resentment. To avoid resentment, a tactful approach is usually required.

If the manager sees an employee make a mistake, four possible courses of action can be taken:

1. Ignore the situation and hope that the subordinate will see the mistake and correct it.

2. Call immediate attention to the mistake and ask the subordinate to do the right thing.

3. Use an indirect approach such as, "How are things going?" If the subordinate knows about the mistake, he or she may frankly admit the mistake and tell the manager, "Don't worry. I'll take care of it." If the subordinate doesn't realize that a mistake has been made, however, the answer might be, "Fine. No problems." In this case, the manager will have to call attention to the mistake and ask, "What can we do to correct it?"

4. Use the sandwich approach: praise the subordinate for good work, call attention to the mistake, and end with a positive statement, such as, "I'm sure that this won't happen again." Some people ridicule this approach, saying that the subordinate will recognize the technique and, after the first words of praise, will immediately want to know what he or she has done wrong. Obviously, the success or failure of the sandwich technique depends on the frequency of its use. If the only time a manager praises a subordinate is to provide the first part of the sandwich, the approach will backfire. If praise is regularly used by the manager to recognize good work, however, the technique can be successful. In any case, it must be remembered that praise is recognizing good work that has actually been done—not just using complimentary words when they aren't true.

Among these four choices for correcting poor work, no guarantee exists that any will be successful or unsuccessful. For example, if the manager uses the first approach (doesn't say anything), the worker may or may not recognize the mistake and correct it. Similarly, the sandwich method may be successful with one employee but not with another. The important point is that the coaching must be done to correct the situation—now and in the future—and not cause resentment. Following are some specific suggestions that will help you achieve this.

If the employee has done a good job, the manager has a very pleasant situation. Positive reinforcement should be done immediately. If other people are within hearing distance, so much the better. They realize that the employee has done something well, and they are pleased to see a boss recognize it. Obviously, they hope to be treated in the same way when they do something worthy of praise. Even if the performance wasn't perfect, a compliment can be sincerely given—and complimenting improvement generally leads to continued effort by the employee and better results in the future.

Some managers compliment warmly when a job is well done. Others ignore it and act as if they think, "That's what we are paying you for. Why should I have to tell you that you're doing a good job?"

In sporting events, some coaches do not give praise when a player does an exceptionally good job. Other coaches openly show signs of enthusiasm and laud good work. Ara Parseghian is an example of the latter type of coach. When he was head football coach at Notre Dame, and a player made an exceptionally good play, Ara would jump up and down, give his player a hug or pat on the back, and pay him a nice compliment like: "Good play!" That spirit and outward expression brought out the best in his players.

If the employee has done a poor job, the boss should usually correct a situation as soon as it occurs. Sometimes, however, this isn't a good idea; it might not be the right time and place—there may be other people around—and the boss may be emotionally upset. In these situations, it is important to correct the employee in a timely manner, but in private. One good approach might be to say, "Can I see you in my office in five minutes?" This gives the manager time to cool down and to do a little preparation for the coaching interview: thinking of some good work the worker has recently done that can be mentioned, trying to determine the reason why the employee made the mistake, and thinking how the interview should conclude. The employee should say or think, "Thanks for calling this to my attention," rather than, "I'll get even with you."

"Coaching is not an option for managers," says Dennis Kinlaw. "It is a large part of their basic managerial functions. It is clear that superior managers and leaders engage in coaching and they do it well. The good news is that managers can learn the set of management practices that we call coaching."[1]

LEARNING TO BE AN EFFECTIVE COACH

Coaching is a word commonly used in the industry to signify what a manager should do to help subordinates achieve maximum performance. The term, of course, is borrowed from athletics. In order to identify principles and practices as athletic coaches see them, I wrote to a number of them and asked, "What are the characteristics of an effective coach?" Following are some of their direct statements:

J. Frank Broyles, Director of Athletics, University of Arkansas

In my opinion, an effective coach should be a living example of the virtues he teaches.

Paul F. Dietzel, Director of Athletics, Louisiana State University

The single most important ingredient is the loyalty the coach displays to his fellow coaches, to his team, and to the organization that he represents. In other words, does the coach have a genuine "like" for the people he or she coaches and an abiding interest in them after they are no longer able to participate for that coach? Maybe that could be spelled out in another way to be called, "Do you really want to be of service to young people?" Whatever it is, that ingredient…a genuine concern for the athlete . . . has to be of Number 1 importance.

John Erickson, Past President, Fellowship of Christian Athletes (former basketball coach, University of Wisconsin, and general manager, Milwaukee Bucks)

I have always felt that to be effective a coach must be an excellent teacher and a person of leadership qualities.

Elroy Hirsch, Former Director of Athletics, University of Wisconsin

He must not be afraid of having very sound, good people around him. He must not be afraid that someone underneath him is trying to take over his job. He must surround himself

---

[1]Dennis C. Kinlaw, *Coaching for Commitment* (San Diego: University Associates, 1989).

with strength, and of course, this requires him to be an effective manager of personnel.

Tom Landry, Former Football Coach, Dallas Cowboys

An effective athletic coach must be a teacher, a psychologist, and a motivator. He must possess leadership qualities and, at the same time, he needs the confidence and concentration to operate at maximum efficiency under great stress.

Ray Meyer, Former Basketball Coach, DePaul University

A coach must have patience. He can't expect too much too soon. He is a teacher. Probably the greatest quality a coach can have is understanding. He must understand that each player is an individual and must be treated as such. All players cannot be treated alike. Some you can improve by loud criticism, and others need encouragement. No coach can treat all players alike, for each one is an individual.

Tom Meyer, Former Baseball Coach, University of Wisconsin

A coach must create a climate where criticism can be expressed and viewed as healthy.

Tom Osborne, Former Football Coach, University of Nebraska

I believe that the qualities of an effective coach are: good organizational skills, a capacity to work long hours, an ability to communicate effectively with his athletes, an ability to maintain composure and to think clearly in pressure situations, and an ability to communicate a genuine sense of concern for the general well-being of his players.

Joe Paterno, Football Coach and Athletic Director, Pennsylvania State University

An effective athletic coach must possess sound moral values and the ability to relate to all types of people. He must be dedicated, loyal, and sincere about his beliefs and philosophies and must be willing to accept success and failure as part of the game. Above and beyond all things, he must have a true love for the sport and at all times realize the responsibility he has to his players.

Bart Starr, Former Head Coach, Green Bay Packers

To begin, I believe a coach is goal-oriented, has a plan by which to accomplish those goals, and a method by which to measure progress along the way. Additionally, he is extremely self-confident, very poised, has the ability to accept criticism and receive coaching himself, has a strong faith in God, and a good sense of humor.

John Wooden, Former Basketball Coach, UCLA

A coach must: communicate with those under his supervision; listen and not be disagreeable when there is disagreement; keep in mind that criticism is to improve, prevent, correct, or help and not to punish; make those under his supervision feel that they are working with him rather than for him; be more interested in finding the best way rather than having his own way; be well organized and not waste time; and be genuinely concerned about his players.[2]

When these statements are analyzed, the word *manager* can be substituted for *coach*, and the word *employee* substituted for *player* in nearly every case.

Lynne Tyson has described that an effective coach:

- Has faith in people and a belief that most can improve and grow in a suitable climate.
- Has a true interest in employees.
- Serves as a good role model for subordinates.
- Has a good understanding of leadership techniques.
- Uses these techniques.
- Has the ability to empathize with employees—caring enough to help them grow.
- Has knowledge of an effective use of rewards, including money, a pat on the back, a more challenging job, and a letter from the boss.

---

[2]Donald L. Kirkpatrick, *How to Improve Performance Through Appraisal and Coaching* (New York: AMACOM, 1982).

She then describes seven criteria for becoming a good coach:

1. Have a sincere unselfish interest in helping an employee grow on the job.
2. Develop a "game plan."
3. Earn and maintain team respect.
4. Remember that people learn best by doing.
5. Ask questions so that the worker can arrive at his or her own solution.
6. Establish sub-goals so that both supervisor and subordinate can see gradual progress.
7. Expect mistakes and use them as learning experiences and growth opportunities.[3]

Mike Phipps, a former quarterback, and T. W. Harvey provide the following suggestions for building good relationships with players:

- Treat all players fairly.
- After chewing a player out, be sure to stop by sometime that day and make him feel like coming back tomorrow.
- Support your players.
- Try to make every athlete feel important.
- If you criticize, do it to the player's face—not downtown. Always end your criticism with something positive about the individual.
- Stimulate a desire in the player to be the best.
- Always keep control of yourself and make sure your players keep control of themselves.
- Don't ever let an athlete loaf, no matter who he is.
- Coach before you criticize.
- What you teach is the most important, not what you know.
- Your practice plans are very important. Know what you are going to do in practice.
- Enthusiasm is contagious.
- Fundamentals are the most important factor for an athlete.

---

[3]Lynne R. Tyson, "Coaching," in William R. Tracey ed., *Human Resources Management and Development Handbook*, (New York: AMACOM, 1985).

- Coaches should never argue in front of players. Any disagreement should be dealt with after practice in the office. Never criticize another coach in front of an athlete, and never let an athlete be disloyal to a coach or teammate.
- Be concerned about injuries of any player.
- Don't ever threaten a player unless you plan to back it up.
- Work with every athlete in our program regardless of what problems may arise.[4]

Again, in nearly all these statements, the word *manager* can be substituted for *coach*, and the word *employee* substituted for *player*.

THE MANAGER AS COACH

The manager operates under a number of conditions that are related to coaching:

- The manager must get the best effort and performance from each subordinate.
- In many situations, the manager is concerned with a team of workers as well as with the performance of each individual worker (as in basketball, football, and hockey). In some situations, the manager is primarily concerned with individual workers because each person usually works alone (as in swimming, track, tennis, and golf).
- If individuals performing under a manager do not like the situation, they have options: letting up on performance, complaining, causing dissension among the other workers, and/or quitting.
- Managers have some employees who are better than others and therefore receive higher rewards. Sometimes the subordinates make more money than the manager.
- Managers are under constant pressure to produce with the people and resources that are available. Sometimes accidents, sickness, and other problems reduce the available human resources.
- Managers are concerned about competition. To stay in business, they must meet or beat the competition.

---

[4]Mike Phipps and T.W. Harvey, "A Coach's Guide to Good Player Relationships," *The Christian Athlete*, November-December 1987. Reprinted by permission from *The Christian Athlete*, official publication of the Fellowship of Christian Athletes.

- Managers are constantly trying to help subordinates improve for the benefit of the organization and also for the individual.
- Managers have the same opportunities and limitations for rewards that coaches have. Most of them are limited in how much money they can give, but they have ample opportunities to give nonfinancial rewards such as praise, more responsibility, more freedom, or to ask for ideas and give special job assignments.

Because the jobs of manager and coach are similar, the characteristics of an effective athletic coach apply to a manager. Just as athletic coaches have different types of players to work with, managers have employees with differences in attitudes, knowledge, and skills. In both situations, the challenge is to mold them into an effective team in order to accomplish the goals of the organization and to help them accomplish their own goals at the same time.

The coaching relationship between managers and supervisors is continuous. It begins with the setting of goals and follows through to see that the goals are achieved. An athletic coach has a broader objective than to win a game: It is to maintain high morale and teamwork among his or her players. The manager's role is similar in relationship to subordinates.

Managers need to evaluate their own performance as coaches. The coach's evaluation form in Figure 11-2 was prepared for this task.

No matter what is done to encourage, stimulate, and assist supervisors in their development, on-the-job coaching becomes a key factor. By example, the boss is constantly coaching subordinates and offering suggestions as to proper behavior. By words and attitudes, the boss is providing leadership, guidance, and direction for subordinates. For the most effective development of supervisors, it becomes essential that the manager does the following:

- Set an example by attitudes and personal behavior on the job.
- Set an example by self-development through professional organizations, reading, attending seminars and workshops, and other activities.
- Support management development activities inside and outside the company.

(text continued on page 211)

	Weak									Strong
	1	2	3	4	5	6	7	8	9	10
1. I praise my players whenever natural and possible.										
2. I maintain a good balance between being a friend and being the boss.										
3. I work at listening carefully to my players and not doing all the talking.										
4. I'm careful not to criticize in a manner that will alienate or demoralize.										
5. I find something positive to say after each practice and game.										
6. I discipline my players with their best interests at heart—not mine.										
7. I'm open to new ideas and techniques that will make the sport more fun.										
8. My players feel comfortable in sharing nonathletic concerns with me.										
9. The growth of my players as total persons is my highest priority.										
10. I let my injured players know I care about them, that they're still important to our program.										

Figure 11-2. *Coach's self-evaluation form*

	Weak									Strong
	1	2	3	4	5	6	7	8	9	10
11. I set a good example for my players by the life I lead off the field.										
12. I'm involved in outside activities that allow my players to get to know me and see my humanness.										
13. I act quickly to restore the relationship if I hurt a player through anger or pride.										
14. I make it a point to meet with each player at least once before and during the season.										
15. My former players keep in touch and encourage their children to compete.										
16. I don't push my faith on my players, but neither do I hide it.										
17. I'm willing to suspend or remove a star player who's disruptive to the team.										
18. Honesty is at the center of my player relationship.										
19. I encourage my players to think for themselves and not be afraid to fail.										
20. My relationship with God and my family come before my players.										

Figure 11-2. *Cont'd*

- Take a personal interest in the growth and development of subordinates by encouraging and recognizing any self-development efforts they make and by systematic coaching on the job.
- Provide a climate in which subordinates are able to use the new ideas and techniques they have learned. This climate features not only permission to change, but also encouragement and positive reinforcement.

SUMMARY

Coaching subordinates to help them improve their performances is one of the most important skills of a successful supervisor. This chapter has listed many of the qualities that characterize an effective coach. And it was made clear that the qualities of a successful supervisor are similar to those of an effective athletic coach.

The supervisor must coach on a regular basis. The purpose is to improve performance not only as an individual, but as a member of a team of workers. In addition, supervisors must coach as a follow-up to the performance appraisal process described in Chapter 10. In that chapter, a *performance improvement plan* (PIP) was developed as the last step in the performance appraisal program. Coaching must be done by the supervisor to be sure the plan is carried out.

12

SELECTING AND TRAINING NEW SUPERVISORS

Supervisors are the key to the productivity and future success of the organization. Selecting new supervisors to replace those lost through retirement, death, transfer, promotion, expansion, and other factors is a major challenge.

In selecting supervisors, special attention should be paid to the "Peter Principle": "In a hierarchy, every employee tends to rise to his level of incompetence."[1] According to Dr. Laurence Peter, when an

---

[1]Laurence Peter and Raymond Hull, *The Peter Principle* (New York: Morrow, 1969).

opening for supervisor occurs, the organization usually looks at the employees in that department to determine the most competent person on the job, and that person is usually picked as the supervisor. An analysis of hundreds of cases of occupational incompetence shows that competence in one position "qualifies" them for promotion. And given enough time and assuming enough ranks, each employee rises to and remains at a level of incompetence. A corollary is that people who are incompetent on a job are ineligible for promotion.

This condition of picking the best "doer" to be the supervisor is not as common as it used to be. More and more organizations realize that outstanding performance on a job should not be rewarded by a promotion. It should be a consideration, but not the prime requirement. Too many examples of the Peter Principle have occurred to believe that the best "doer" will make the best "manager."

A company can select a first-level supervisor in two ways. The first, and most common, way is to wait until the opening occurs and then select the best available person for the job. This person may be picked from inside, or the company may go outside to hire a qualified person from another organization.

Several problems usually exist with last-minute selection and placement. First, there is seldom enough time to use good selection techniques to pick the best person. There are pressures to find the person immediately and put him or her on the job. Also, emotions are usually high at the time an opening occurs. Many people are wondering, "Will Jane be promoted to the job?" And Jane has frequently been selected because she is the logical person with the most seniority and knowledge of the people and the jobs to be supervised. Many organizations believe that it is important to promote someone from within the department in order to maintain high morale.

There will be no time, however, to give Jane any prejob training. On Friday, she is a worker and, on Monday, she becomes a supervisor. Beginning Monday, her boss will try to provide extra help, coaching, and other on-the-job training to help her learn the job. The pressures to get work done are still there, though, and Jane is under a terrific handicap because of her lack of management training.

Often with last-minute selection and placement, the person selected is not eager to take the job. However, the manager talks he or she into it and promises all the help and encouragement needed. Often, he or she ends up a living example of the Peter Principle.

Many problems of last-minute selection can be solved by the second selection method: identifying and pretraining a group of potential supervisors, so that when an opening occurs, one of these people can be picked to fill the job. This method has three advantages: There is time to consider all candidates carefully; less emotion is involved, so the selection can be more objective; and some management training can be provided before the person takes over as a supervisor.

Selection Principles

The principles and approaches for an effective selection are just as important in picking candidates for a supervisor's job as they are for picking engineers or any other key persons. Seven items must be determined and implemented if a good job is to be done in selecting first-level supervisors.

1. *Determine the number of openings.* The first step in planning for this program is to estimate the number and type of openings that will occur in the near future (Six months? One year?). This figure should be based on the expected turnover among the current supervisors as well as on any growth—or contraction—that is expected. The best decision can probably be made by having several persons in key jobs, including the person in charge of a department, discuss the future. The human resources manager and others may also have helpful information concerning retirements, possible transfers, a supervisor's death, or job leaving.

2. *Prepare the job description.* When future openings have been determined, knowledgeable persons should spell out the duties and responsibilities related to those jobs—for instance: planning, communicating, maintaining the quantity and quality of production, maintaining the lowest possible cost, maintaining a good safety record, inducting and training new employees, coordinating work with other departments, handling complaints and grievances, assigning work properly, managing change, and the broad area of decision making. If up-to-date job descriptions are available in the company, these can be used with little modification. The importance of looking at the jobs is twofold: it serves as a basis for deciding what kinds of employees are needed and provides a basis for the training program that will be given.

3. *Ascertain the qualifications of candidates.* The candidates' qualifications should be determined from the job descriptions. For example,

if one duty is to plan and schedule the work, one qualification must be an ability to plan. If a job responsibility is to train new employees, a qualification must be the ability to teach and train employees. If a job responsibility is to communicate both orally and in writing, the person selected should have the ability to express himself or herself clearly. Other job responsibilities may mean a need for a certain level of intelligence, a certain emotional stability, health requirements, and an ability to get along with people. Other qualifications in line with company policy and future requirements may be related to experience and technical knowledge, a strong desire to be a supervisor, a positive attitude toward the company, and personal integrity.

4. *Specify how many candidates should be selected.* We have now determined the number and type of openings, job descriptions for these openings, and the desirable qualifications of candidates. How many candidates should be selected and trained? There are two different approaches. One is to train as many people as possible, even if most of them will never be promoted to a management job. This approach has the advantage of giving many people a management orientation and possibly developing better attitudes toward company management. It has the probable disadvantage of creating frustrations and negative attitudes by training many people who will not be promoted.

The other approach is to screen and train a limited number of candidates so that most of them will be promoted to supervision in a relatively short time. For example, if 10 openings are likely to be available in the next year, the company may decide to train 20 people for the job. This offers an opportunity to select from a fairly large group of candidates and to promote enough of them to maintain proper attitudes and morale among the rest of the trained candidates. This screening of candidates has the disadvantage of denying the training opportunities to those who are determined by management to be unqualified. Workers who are not selected for the training program may become dissatisfied.

The number of candidates to select is an important decision that must be made by any organization that implements a program for selecting and training potential foremen and supervisors. Generally, it is better to select a limited number of candidates (such as twice as many as will be needed during the next year) than to accept all who are interested and train them.

5. *Decide how to determine qualifications.* Certain selection criteria, such as education and previous work experience, are easy to

determine from available data. In other areas—such as intelligence, mechanical aptitude, knowledge of supervisory principles and practices, and personality—there may be little factual information, so other measures must be used. Qualified persons can give tests to measure some of these criteria effectively. Intelligence can be measured by a paper-and-pencil test, as can mechanical aptitude and a knowledge of principles and facts. Whether psychological tests are effective in determining personality is controversial. The personality of an individual can be determined by analyzing previous performance on jobs and behavior under various circumstances. Health can be measured by a medical examination. Leadership abilities and skills can be evaluated by analyzing leadership roles played by the individual, both inside and outside the company. Attitudes toward management, people, and various aspects of the company can be measured by interviewing that person.

In short, a number of different techniques should be used in determining the qualifications that have been established. Factual information should be supplemented with interviews, tests, medical examinations, performance appraisals, and other measures that will help predict one's future performance as a supervisor. If the organization does not have persons who can assess the qualifications of candidates, outside help should be acquired. Reputable psychological consultants can be called on to provide this service.

Some companies use assessment centers to determine an individual's potential for promotion. An assessment center is "a process in which potential supervisors participate in a series of situations similar to a job to which they might be promoted."[2] This individual's behavior is evaluated by several trained assessors, usually line managers, in a process that usually lasts two to four days. The simulation exercises used are related to the job of supervisor. They include individual problem analysis, including written reports to explain their actions; a one-on-one discussion between the assessor and the potential supervisor; an "in-basket" exercise followed by an interview conducted by an assessor; a leadership activity with two or more subordinates; preparation of a work schedule; and leaderless group discussion.

Participants are judged on such skills as planning and organizing, decision making, leadership, perception, adaptability, decisiveness, and

---

[2]Cabot Jaffee, Fredrick D. Frank, and James R. Preston, "Assessment Centers," in *Human Resources Management and Development Handbook* (New York: AMA-COM, 1985).

interpersonal and written communication. Typically, each assessor evaluates each of the participants, and the assessors pool their evaluation to arrive at a final assessment.

AT&T, a pioneer in developing the assessment center, identified 460 supervisors considered to be superior supervisors by their managers. From these supervisors, they identified the following areas as the most important:

- Planning the work
- Controlling the work
- Problem solving
- Providing performance feedback
- Creating and maintaining a motivational atmosphere
- Time management
- Informal oral communication
- Self-development
- Written communication
- Knowledge of the Bell System
- Career counselling
- Meeting communication

Care should be taken that the selection criteria and techniques adhere to equal opportunity and affirmative action government regulations.[3]

6. *Establish a procedure for the final selection of candidates.* If many qualifications are established and measures are set up to determine them, it is important to decide how the final selection will be made. If these criteria are objective, the selection becomes relatively automatic. If, however, subjective judgment will be important, then the authority and responsibility for selecting the qualified candidates should be clearly defined. Line management has the final responsibility and authority for selection, usually with the advice of human resources professionals.

---

[3]U.S. Department of Labor, Equal Employment Opportunity, 200 Constitution Ave., Room C-3325, Washington, D.C. 20210.

7. *Draw up procedures for communicating acceptance or nonacceptance of candidates.* If candidates are asked to volunteer or apply for supervisory jobs, it is important to decide how they will be notified concerning their acceptance for the program. If many people have applied, this is very important, especially for those who are not accepted. It is not sufficient, for example, to write a letter and say, "I'm sorry, but you have not been accepted." The letter should tell candidates why they were not accepted and what they might do to become qualified. The offer to discuss the reasons in a personal interview is always appreciated. Those who are not accepted may become discontented, so effective communication with them is important.

Bendix Products, Aerospace Division, South Bend, Indiana

I was instrumental in developing and implementing an effective approach for selecting first-level supervisors at the Bendix Products Aerospace Division. Although this approach was used in selecting foremen in a manufacturing organization, the principles and techniques can be easily adapted for selecting supervisors in a service or government organization. The only requirement is that the organization be large enough to select a pool of candidates for possible promotion to supervisor.

As the personnel manager, and in cooperation with the general manager and manager of manufacturing, I initiated, planned, and implemented a program for the selection and training of new first-level supervisors. The program contained five steps:

1. *Determination of need.* The following overall plan was developed to select and train new supervisors:

- Estimate the number of supervisory openings that would probably exist during the next year.
- Determine the number of candidates that should be selected and trained to provide a pool from which new supervisors would be selected.
- Determine the qualifications that new supervisors should have.
- Agree on the criteria for selecting the candidates for the pool.
- Develop a training program to be given to those selected.

- Announce the program to all concerned.
- Pick new supervisors from the pool of selected and trained candidates.

Based on the analysis of future growth and turnover among supervisors, it was decided that approximately 12 openings would occur within the next year, all of them at the foreman level, the first level of manufacturing management. It was generally agreed among management that approximately twice as many candidates should be selected for presupervisory training as would be placed within a year. Therefore, we decided to select between 20 and 25 candidates to be trained to become the pool from which new supervisors would be picked.

2. *Selection of candidates.* The job description of foremen at Bendix was used to determine the duties and responsibilities that a new foreman would have. The duties and responsibilities included planning and communicating; maintaining the quantity and quality of production; maintaining the lowest possible cost; maintaining a good safety record; inducting and training new employees; coordinating work with other departments, such as production control, industrial engineering, personnel, and accounting; handling grievances; and assigning work properly.

After discussion among the general manager, personnel manager, and manufacturing manager, it was decided that the following qualifications would be required:

- No person would be considered unless he or she completed an application blank showing a strong desire to be considered.
- Preference would be given to persons age 45 or younger. This was an arbitrary number that was selected because the present age of foremen was very high. The fact that some of these people would move into higher management was also considered. This figure was subject to change if there weren't enough candidates who met it.
- No candidate would be selected unless he or she was a high school graduate. (This was a well-established practice at Bendix.)
- No candidate would be selected unless he or she had above-average intelligence as measured by the Wonderlic Personnel Test.[4] (This, too, was a well-established practice at Bendix.)

---

[4]E.F. Wonderlic, *Wonderlic Personnel Test* (New York: The Psychological Corporation, 1983).

In addition, candidates were required to meet the following standards:

■ Be in good health.

■ Have good performances in past jobs.

■ Have a good attitude toward management and toward the company.

3. *Criteria for selection.* The desire to be a foreman would be measured initially by the fact that a candidate had completed an application blank. As part of this process, the applicant agreed to take a battery of tests and to attend training meetings on his or her own time. The age and education were determined from factual records in the personnel file.

Individual intelligence was measured by the Wonderlic Personnel Test, with a minimum score of 24 established as a cutoff point.[5] This was the same score that was used in selecting foreman prior to the pre-foreman selection and training program.

In addition, the Minnesota Paper Form Board Test was administered to the applicants to measure mechanical aptitude.[6] The scores were not used as criteria to select or reject a candidate. Rather, the test was given for possible use in future validation of the test.

The Supervisory Inventory on Human Relations was administered to the candidates to provide information concerning the candidates' knowledge and understanding of human relations facts, principles, and approaches.[7] Responses to each of the 80 items were tabulated to determine which facts and principles should be emphasized in the training program. The test was administered again at the completion of the program to evaluate the effectiveness of the training.

Appraisal forms completed by supervision provided criteria concerning past performance, the ability to communicate, one's attitude toward the company, any ability to get along with other people, and other pertinent factors. The health of the individual was measured by the medical records filed in the Industrial Relations Department.

---

[5]Ibid.

[6]*Minnesota Paper Form Board Test* (New York: The Psychological Corporation, 1970).

[7]Donald L. Kirkpatrick, *Supervisory Inventory on Human Relations* (Elm Grove, Wis.: Donald L. Kirkpatrick, 1990).

Three criteria (age, education, and score on the Personnel Test) were used as the first screening device, with preference given to those meeting these three criteria. Those who did meet the major criteria were further evaluated by appraisals obtained from immediate supervisors, present and past (see Figure 12-1), and by medical records. These additional data were discussed among the general manager, the manufacturing manager, and me. Twenty-three candidates met all of the criteria and were selected for the presupervisory training program. The following chart shows the selection statistics:

Number of potential candidates for foremen (hourly employees)	2,000
Number of employees who completed application blank	130
Number of employees who completed the test	93
Number of employees who met the criteria of age, education, and intelligence	29
Number of employees selected for the training program	23

(text continued on page 223)

Name of candidate _____

Length of time under my supervision: Years _____

Months _____

1. Job performance?
   ☐ Very Good   ☐ Satisfactory   ☐ Unsatisfactory

2. Supervision required?
   ☐ A Great Deal   ☐ Average   ☐ Very Little

3. Attitude toward management?
   ☐ Very Good   ☐ Average   ☐ Negative

4. How well get along with others?
   ☐ Very Well   ☐ Average   ☐ Poorly

5. Does he/she create problems for supervision?   ☐ Yes   ☐ No

   If yes, explain _____

   _____

   _____

Figure 12-1.
Performance appraisal form, Bendix Products, Aerospace Division

6. Absence: ☐ Never   ☐ Occasional   ☐ Frequent

   Tardiness: ☐ Never   ☐ Occasional   ☐ Frequent

   Health: ☐ Excellent   ☐ Good   ☐ Poor   ☐ Don't Know

Comments: _____

_____

_____

7. Do you have any evidence that this person has leadership ability? (on the job or outside evidence)   ☐ Yes   ☐ No

If yes, give details _____

_____

_____

8. How would he/she be in regard to the following items:

Yes/No		*Yes/No*	
_____	Would be a good communicator.	_____	Would accept responsibility.
_____	Would be too bossy.	_____	Would be a good organizer.
_____	Would be easily influenced by employees.	_____	Would stand up for subordinates.
_____	Would be a "Yes" person.	_____	Would give credit.
_____	Would be overly concerned with details.	_____	Would be loyal to company.
_____	Would be a good trainer.	_____	Would be helpful to any employee having a problem.
_____	Would give instructions clearly.	_____	Would be capable in handling grievances.
_____	Would be a "buck passer."	_____	Would let employees know where they stand.
_____	Would be cost-conscious.	_____	Would be likely to show favoritism.
_____	Would be able to influence his/her boss.	_____	Would have respect for subordinates.
_____	Would be well liked by subordinates.		

Figure 12-1. *Cont'd*

9. To what extent would you recommend this person as a foreman?

☐ Strongly Recommend ☐ Mildly Recommended

☐ Do Not Recommend ☐ Uncertain

Additional factors (favorable or not) that should be considered: _____

_____

_____

_____	_____
Date	Signature of Foreman

_____	_____
Date	Signature of General Foreman

NOTE: The signature of the General Foreman doesn't necessarily mean agreement with the appraisal by the foreman. It simply means that he has seen it.

Figure 12-1. *Cont'd*

After the final selection of 23 candidates, the general manager sent a letter to each person who had applied for the program. Those who were accepted were told that they had been accepted and were given the schedule for the training program. For those who were not accepted, a letter from the general manager told them that they had not been accepted for this first program. It also told them that if they had any questions and wanted to know why they had not been accepted, they should contact the training supervisor, who would discuss it with them. One-third of those who were rejected did contact the training supervisor to discuss the reason for not being selected.

Figure 12-2 is a copy of the letter that was sent to all 2,000 hourly employees. Figure 12-3 is a copy of the application form.

(text continued on page 226)

TO: Aerospace Hourly Employees
SUBJECT: Preforeman Training Program

As mentioned in my recent letter, we are now ready to offer preforeman training to our employees. This is a program whereby we want to select and train employees who have the potential to become foremen. Then, when new jobs open up, we will fill them from this group. We believe in promotion from within and are going to try this program as a way of putting into practice what we believe. Here is our program:

1. All candidates will be carefully screened to determine those we feel have the best potential for the job.

   a. The candidate will be given three paper-and-pencil tests to give us an indication of mental ability, mechanical aptitude, and knowledge of supervisory principles.
   b. We will get a performance appraisal from foremen who have supervised the candidate.
   c. The candidate may be given a medical exam.

2. Candidates will be selected by the general manager, manufacturing manager, and the personnel manager.

3. A training program will be given on the candidate's own time. It will include such subjects as:

   a. The Foreman's Job
   b. Planning and Organizing Work
   c. Understanding and Motivating People
   d. Training Subordinates
   e. Labor Relations
   f. Communications
   g. Aerospace Division Policies and Procedures

4. Graduates of the program will be considered for such positions as openings occur.

Please understand that candidates for this program will be selected on the basis of their potential to become foremen. If you are selected for the training program, we cannot guarantee you a foreman's job after successful completion of the course; however, your chances of being chosen for the position will be greatly enhanced.

We feel that there are many people interested in improving themselves. They will want to complete the enclosed application and return it to Don Kirkpatrick, our Personnel Manager. Your application will be kept in strict confidence. Your applications must be received by December 3 to be considered.

Figure 12-2.
*Letter informing employees of preforeman training program,
Bendix Products, Aerospace Division*

If you have further questions, please contact Don directly.

Sincerely,

R.E. Whiffen
General Manager

P.S. Even though the program is designed to select and train future foremen, some of the candidates may be offered other salary jobs in manufacturing, quality control, and production control.

Figure 12-2. *Cont'd*

1. Name _____ Department _____

2. Street address _____ City _____ Phone _____

3. Date of birth _____ Date employed by Bendix _____

4. Jobs held at Bendix: _____
   _____
   _____
   _____

5. Jobs held at other companies: _____
   _____
   _____

6. Education
   a. Please circle last grade completed:

   1 2 3 4 5 6 7 8 9 10 11 12   1   2   3   4
           Grade and high school   College

   b. List any special courses you have taken (night school, correspondance, vocational school, etc.)

   Name of course _____ School _____ Year ____
   Name of course _____ School _____ Year ____
   Name of course _____ School _____ Year ____

Figure 12-3.
Application form for preforeman training program,
Bendix Products, Aerospace Division

c. Other comments on education: _____

_____

_____

7. Leadership activities (list any offices held and other leadership activities):

_____

_____

_____

_____

_____

8. Other information that might be important when considering for you a foreman's job:

_____

_____

_____

I understand that this application will be held in strict confidence. I also understand that there is no guarantee that I will become a foreman even if I complete the training.

_____   _____
　　　　Date　　　　　　　　　　　　　　　　　　　　　　　　Signature

Figure 12-3. *Cont'd*

4. *Preplacement Training*. After supervisory candidates are selected, a training program should be planned to prepare them to take the big step from doer to manager; they must be able to see that work is done through others. There are two approaches. One is to provide on-the-job training by a current supervisor. This can be successful if the teacher is an effective supervisor and coach, but it is not practical in most organizations. The other method is to provide classroom training, either internally or at outside supervisory development programs. This was the approach we took at Bendix. The factors we considered in developing the 18-hour preplacement training program are common to all such programs.

What are the objectives? The objective of the training program is to prepare the candidates for management jobs. The participants have to learn about management attitudes as well as approaches and techniques that supervisors use. At Bendix, we identified three objectives: (1) to orient participants toward the management job of a foreman, (2) to improve their understanding of the duties, responsibilities, and desired qualifications of a foreman, and (3) to develop some skills foremen need.

What subjects will be taught? The goal of the subjects taught is to aid in reaching training objectives. The general subject content for Bendix was determined jointly by the general manager, the training supervisor, and me, with suggestions from current foremen, general foremen, and superintendents. The specific topics were selected by the training supervisor and me, with pretest responses to the Supervisory Inventory on Human Relations analyzed to determine specific items to discuss.[8] Suggestions for other topics came from various other people who were interested in the training program.

What schedule will be followed? The program was scheduled from 4:00 to 5:30 p.m. on 12 consecutive Tuesdays. The first shift ended at 3:30, and employees attended on their own time and were not paid. Special arrangements were made for the few people who worked the second and third shifts.

A number of considerations went into this decision. First were state and federal laws regarding the training of hourly people for management jobs. In most states, hourly people can be trained without pay if meetings are held outside working hours, attendance by employees is voluntary, the course is not directly related to the employees' current jobs, and the employees do not perform any production work during the meetings. The schedule also had to be convenient for all the candidates.

The length of each meeting, the length of the program, and the frequency of meetings were arrived at by considering the objectives of the program and the convenience of candidates.

Where will the meetings be held? The meetings were held in the plant conference room, which was convenient for all participants and was comfortable.

---

[8]Ibid.

Who will conduct the meetings? Leaders should be selected for their subject knowledge plus, most importantly, their ability to communicate effectively. They can come from both management and the personnel and training department and/or from outside. In this program, all of the leaders were Bendix employees. The following training program schedule gives details on leaders as well as subjects:

Subject	Leaders
The Foreman's Job	Don Kirkpatrick, Personnel Manager
Management Philosophy and Organization	Richard Whiffen, General Manager, plus major department heads in engineering, manufacturing, marketing, and finance
Effective Communication, I	Don Kirkpatrick
Effective Communication, II	Irv Margol, Training Manager
Planning and Organizing Work	Irv Margol
Understanding People	Don Kirkpatrick
Motivating People	Don Kirkpatrick
Assigning Work	Irv Margol
Delegation	Irv Margol
Training Employees	Irv Margol
Labor Relations	Lou Tiege, Director of Industrial Relations
Discipline and Control	Don Kirkpatrick
Awarding Certificates and Comments	Richard Whiffen

What techniques will be used? This training program used a variety of methods. Presentations by the leaders were accompanied by aids and techniques, including the following:

- *Blackboards and flipcharts.* These tools helped the trainer to emphasize the important points made by the group as well as by the leader.
- *Films.* During the program, three movies were shown.
- *Group discussion and involvement.* The trainees participated extensively in buzz groups with six persons in each group, contributed freely in asking questions and giving opinions, participated in projects to get them to "learn by doing," and discussed various items of my Supervisory Inventory on Human Relations and Supervisory Inventory on Communication.[9]

---

[9] Ibid.

- *Case studies.* Several case studies were given to the group in order to get them to think in terms of practical application of the principles discussed.

How will the program be evaluated? Participants completed a reaction sheet at the conclusion of the training program. Figure 12-4 shows their positive reaction.

1. How did the course match your expectations?

   __0__ Just what I expected.
   __22__ Generally what I expected.
   __1__ Not at all what I expected.

Comments: _____

_____

2. Was the course held at the proper time?   __20__ Yes __3__ No

If not, when should it have been held: _____

_____

3. How was the approach?

   __1__ Too much theory
   __20__ Right combination of theory and practical application
   __2__ Not enough theory

4. Were the subjects properly covered?

	Should have spent more time	Should have spent less time	OK
1. The supervisor's job	1	0	22
2. Aerospace Organization	8	0	15
3. Communications (two parts)	0	0	23
4. Planning and organization work	3	0	20
5. Understanding employees	1	1	21
6. Motivation	0	0	23
7. Assigning work-delegation	4	1	18
8. Training	8	0	15
9. Discipline and control	5	1	17
10. Labor relations	3	0	20
11. Meeting the department heads	11	0	12

Figure 12-4.
Sample reactions to the preforeman training program, Bendix Products, Aerospace Division

5. What have been the results of the program as far as you are concerned? (Check as many as apply to you.)

<u> 23 </u> Better understanding of Aerospace management, problems, etc.

<u> 20 </u> Better understanding of the foreman's job

<u> 13 </u> More desire to be a foreman

<u> 0 </u> Less desire to be a foreman

<u> 15 </u> Better attitude towards my job as an hourly employee

_____ Other (please describe): _____

6. Would you be interested in a follow-up program?

<u> 19 </u> Yes   <u> 0 </u> No   <u> 4 </u> Uncertain

7. Other comments and suggestions:

_____

_____

_____

_____
Signature

Figure 12-4. *Cont'd*

There are other ways to evaluate, too. If the Supervisory Inventory on Communication is given at the start of the program, it can also be administered at the end of the program, and a comparison can be made of pretest and posttest responses. Another worthwhile, but more difficult, way is to compare the performance of supervisors selected from this program with that of supervisors picked in other ways.

5. *Placement in supervision.* The selection process was developed and implemented by the manufacturing manager, the general manager, and me. We agreed that future foremen would be taken from the pool of candidates with any exceptions approved by the general manager.

The selection of a specific person to fill a specific opening became the decision of the manufacturing manager. He would consult with his superintendents and general foremen. In order to help him in the decision, a looseleaf notebook was prepared that contained the following information on the candidates in the pool, including each individual's:

- Original application showing education, experience, and other information prior to Bendix employment.
- Work history at Bendix showing all departments in which the person worked and jobs performed.
- Completed application to apply for the preforeman program.
- Appraisal forms completed by the current and past immediate supervisors.

This information could be studied and the candidate interviewed by the manufacturing manager and anyone else he chose. Usually, the interviewing was jointly done by the manufacturing manager and the general foreman, to whom the new foreman would report.

When the person had been picked, the manufacturing manager and I agreed on the offered salary, with the figure depending on the salary range for the job, the current salary of the candidate, and the salaries of other foremen doing comparable jobs. I then contacted the candidate and explained salary, benefits, and opportunities.

During the first year of the program, 12 of the 23 candidates were promoted—10 as foremen and two as salaried personnel in production control. All except one accepted the position and salary that was offered. This person had been working in an experimental production department, where the wages of workers and the salary of the foremen were higher than in the production department. He was offered a job as a regular production foreman when he would have preferred the job of foreman in an experimental department. He was assured that if he turned down this job, he would still remain in the pool of candidates. He did turn down the offer. As it happened, an opening occurred as foreman in the experimental department about two months later. He was offered the job and accepted it.

During the first year, only one exception was made to the policy of selecting all new foremen from the pool. In one department, extensive metallurgical knowledge was required on the part of the foreman, and none of the 23 candidates had this knowledge. Also, the position was only temporary; the foreman would be returned to the labor force after about six months. Because of these circumstances, the general manager approved the recommendation of the manufacturing manager that a person from that specific department be promoted, but only on a temporary basis.

6. *Evaluation of the program.* The program at Bendix was one of the most effective and satisfying programs that I have been involved in.

No one seemed to be unhappy with it. The union had no objections or negative comments about the program. We kept them informed but did not ask for their input or reactions.

We were very careful to involve the current foremen, the general foreman, and the superintendents in the program. We explained our approach and asked for their suggestions. We asked them to encourage their good workers to apply for the program. We kept them informed of all aspects of the program and welcomed their comments.

Although the manufacturing manager was reluctant at first to have me, as personnel manager, interfere in his right to select his own foremen, he accepted the program well and became enthusiastic, particularly when he realized that he still had the authority to make the final selection.

Although I do not have tangible data on the success of the program, the overall impression was that the newly selected foremen were well qualified and performed well. During the two years I was at Bendix, none of them left his or her new job.

The Bendix program was intended as a pilot. If the general manager and I had remained at Bendix longer, we would undoubtedly have repeated the program, with a few changes perhaps. We would have opened it up to salaried, as well as hourly, employees and probably would have changed the criteria for selecting the pool. We would also have continued the three essential elements of the program:

- Look first for those who have a desire to be a foreman.
- Develop a pool of selected people.
- Provide management training before they are placed on a management job.

Two more case studies give examples of similar approaches to training future supervisors. The selection of candidates for the pool was basically the same as the Bendix approach. Following are brief descriptions of the training.

Note: This case study took place in 1962. Since that time there have been many changes in the characteristics that can be considered in deciding promotions. For example, age can no longer be considered a factor. However, the case has been described as it took place and will provide concepts, principles, and techniques that can be adapted to any organization.

INLAND STEEL PRODUCTS COMPANY, MILWAUKEE, WISCONSIN

The preplacement training program consisted of 12 sessions of one and a half hours each, according to Inland Steel Products personnel manager R.O. Tjensvold. All the meetings were scheduled after working hours on the applicant's own time and without pay for that time. The subject matter had been selected by the plant manager and personnel director in consultation with other interested managers.

During the program, emphasis was placed on informality rather than a schoolroom atmosphere and on group participation instead of lecture. All meetings were conducted by management personnel from the plant with the exception of the session on "Understand People," which was led by an outside psychologist. Details are described in Figure 12-5.

Class attendance, like all other aspects of this program, was entirely voluntary; however, every participant had to attend Sessions 1 and 12, plus at least eight others, or else he could be jeopardizing chances for further consideration. Class participation was encouraged, and lack of interest and involvement became a negative factor when considering

(text continued on page 235)

Inland Steel Products Company

Session and Date	Subject to Be Covered	Leader
One	**Why we are here . . . and what's ahead**	R.C. McLean
Nov. 8	There are many aspects to the job of the foreman. Most people have to learn this job by trial and error. Here is an opportunity to learn through the accumulated experiences of others.	
Two	**Survey of Company Organization**	R.O. Tjensvold
Nov. 15	The organization charts show the company structure in its ideal form; the actual relationships are more complex. Job descriptions, especially those of the supervisor, will be reviewed.	

Figure 12-5.
Preplacement training program schedule. Inland Steel Products Company

Inland Steel Products Company

Session and Date	Subject to Be Covered	Leader
Three Nov. 22	**Internal Relationships and Interdependence** The manufacturing department does not operate by itself. It is part of that larger organization—the company. The various departments are considerably dependent on each other to get the total job done.	J.W. Hendricks
Four Nov. 29	**Understanding People** Everything we do is done through people and by people. Therefore, what is basic to doing every job is our need to understand people.	Dr. E. Russell
Five Dec. 6	**Principles of Communications** People are motivated to act mainly by what they hear or read. How can we improve our skills in communicating in order to get things done?	R.O. Tjensvold
Six Dec. 13	**Employee Attitudes and Discipline** Some situations call for disciplinary action; many do not. How do we identify what our problems are and how best to deal with them?	L.J. Dunlap
Seven Dec. 20	**Paperwork of the Supervisor** Among the necessary though time-consuming tasks of the supervisor are those of handling mounds of paperwork. Insight is given on why paperwork is necessary and what is involved.	J.W. Jendricks
Eight Jan. 3	**Planning and Organizing Work** Without an organized approach, important tasks may be left unfinished because of time devoted to nonessentials. Let's consider how to identify the important and get it done first.	R.O. Tjensvold
Nine Jan. 10	**Job Instruction** One of the most important duties of a supervisor is training his people. Job instruction training presents a helpful guide to supervisors for this task.	R.O. Tjensvold

Figure 12-5. *Cont'd*

Session and Date	Subject to Be Covered	Leader
Ten Jan. 17	**Analyzing Problems** Before a problem can be solved, it must be identified. Then it can be analyzed for possible solutions.	R.O. Tjensvold
Eleven Jan. 24	**Basic Economics** Part of our understanding of how our company may be a profitable concern depends on our knowledge of basic economics applied to the organization.	D.R. Axtell
Twelve Jan. 31	**Final Review and Questions** A summary session briefly reviews the many subjects already touched on, relating them to each other and to the job of the supervisor. Questions from the participants will be answered.	R. C. McLean

Figure 12-5. *Cont'd*

the person for promotion. A certificate was given to the 14 who completed the course.

There were a number of indicators of the success of the selection and training program at Inland Steel Products:

■ The record of attendance at the 12 training sessions exceeded 95 percent, a clear indication of the continued interest among the participants.

■ After the twelfth session, the participants were asked to comment on the effectiveness of the program as they saw it. Their comments were highly favorable, with some practical recommendations for improvement among the instructors.

■ The objective of the program was to provide a cadre of potentially promotable candidates for supervision. With the exception of the two who left the company before they might have been promoted, all the graduates of the program moved up within 18 months from the end of the preplacement training program. Nine went to tasks as production foremen, one moved to an office supervisory job, and the remaining four were upgraded to salaried jobs outside the manufacturing department.

■ Top management agreed that the program would be repeated whenever future supervisory needs developed.

■ Other supervisory training was developed at the request of older supervisors who felt that if the program was good enough for trainees, it was good enough for them.

When the results of the evaluations were analyzed, changes in future programs were planned. The most significant changes were in the content of the sessions in order to make them more directly applicable to the specific job of the first-line supervisor. Also, teaching techniques were improved to use more group participation and more audiovisual aids and to do less lecturing. The approach to the selection process, by self-nomination and screening, remained unchanged, however, because management and candidates felt it was effective.

Kearney and Trecker Corporation, Milwaukee, Wisconsin

According to company vice president, Dave Coverdale, the training of presupervisory candidates at Kearney and Trecker involved three major thrusts: internal understudy training, external management training, and internal and/or external technical training.

Employees were scheduled into various functions of the organization on a rotational basis for assigned time periods. These schedules were tailored to the background and experience of each trainee so that no one was assigned to a session in an area in which he or she already possessed expertise or experience. The purpose of this internal understudy-type training was twofold: To teach trainees the inner workings of the department, its functions, and its major procedures; and to help trainees identify the people in the organization who make things happen and get to know them as human beings they can communicate with in person—rather than as voices at the end of the telephone.

Following an orientation program of a series of half-days rotating through the major manufacturing functions, the employees were assigned to areas such as payroll, industrial engineering, employee relations, and labor relations. These jobs were interspersed with assignments to provide temporary relief help to supervisors in various departments to gain first-hand supervisory experience.

This periodic return to the manufacturing environment kept the trainees aware of what was happening in the manufacturing areas and gave them opportunity to practice the skills and experiences they had picked up during the training program. Moreover, it served to strengthen their identity as future supervisors.

From time to time, requests were made by various operating departments to have a trainee assigned for a special project. The criteria for such an assignment were the project's length and that it was a learning experience. In other words, the purpose was to provide training, not just to get the job done. This evaluation was made jointly by the training manager and the manager of manufacturing. Such assignments included a special plant layout project, the revamping of a payroll reporting system, and preparation for an arbitration.

The first 20 weeks were spent in areas relating directly to manufacturing supervision. The following 18 weeks were spent primarily in areas giving a broader viewpoint of the company's overall operations, such as marketing and engineering.

The second part of the program involved outside management training. Kearney and Trecker is close to the facilities of the Management Institute, the University of Wisconsin, Marquette University's adult education program, and other fine academic educational institutions. Two courses offered by the Management Institute were required: "Supervisory Skills" and "Leadership Methods." These three-day seminars proved to be invaluable in the development of new supervisors. Also, depending on the need, time, and availability, supervisors were scheduled to attend sessions at the University of Wisconsin and Marquette University on such subjects as problem solving and decision making, time management, training new employees, interviewing skills, grievance handling, and discipline.

Candidates were encouraged to continue their education through utilization of the corporation's tuition reimbursement program. Several candidates worked on a degree or two-year certificate program from various institutions.

The third part of the program was to develop technical skills in areas where it appeared that the employee might be eventually assigned. To this end, Kearney and Trecker's Technical Training Department provided training in various machining functions or other areas of shop expertise such as the customer training school programs on numerical/control programming, maintenance, and the like. Various outside technical institutes provided training that was not available at Kearney and Trecker.

Summary

Many supervisors are ineffective because they do not have the necessary qualities. In most organizations in past years, the primary qualities for being promoted to supervisor were a strong performance in one's present job, seniority, and cooperation with bosses. A promotion to supervisor was considered a reward for outstanding performance. Typically, the search for a supervisor was restricted to workers in the department that the supervisor would manage.

More and more organizations are realizing that outstanding performance as a "doer" is not a good predictor of performance as a "supervisor." This chapter has suggested concepts, principles, and techniques for selecting first-level supervisors. It has encouraged organizations to avoid "last-minute" selections and to develop a plan for selecting. It has also suggested that new supervisors receive some management training *before* they assume the role of supervisor. Emphasis has been placed on the desire to be a supervisor as well as other qualifications.

Case studies from Bendix, Inland Steel, and Kearney and Trecker have illustrated successful ways to select and train supervisors, especially in large organizations.

PART II

CASE STUDIES OF SPECIFIC PROGRAMS

Note: Some of these case studies were written a number of years ago and changes have been made. They are important because they provide concepts, principles and techniques that have proved successful. Readers should look for ideas that can be adapted to their own organization. They will find many!

239

13

A
COMPREHENSIVE
IN-HOUSE
PROGRAM

Many companies do supervisory training on a hit-or-miss basis, conducting programs that they feel are needed. These are usually crisis programs developed to meet an immediate need or to solve a critical problem.

Other organizations have well-planned programs. One of the best-planned and implemented programs is at Deere & Company, a maker of agricultural, construction, and consumer products and financial services. The following case study sets out the company's mission statement, philosophy, programs, and the action steps it took to stimulate changes in job behavior.

DEERE & COMPANY, MOLINE, ILLINOIS

Statement of Mission and Basic Philosophy

Harry E. Litchfield, Manager of Worldwide Learning, has said that the fundamental purpose of the Employee Training & Development (ET&D) Department is to enable individuals, groups, and organizations within the John Deere network to improve their overall efficiency and effectiveness. To accomplish this, we help them anticipate needs, adapt to changes, and improve their skills to meet present and future job requirements. To this end, we provide a broad range of quality education and training programs as well as consulting and facilitating services.

In support of this mission, we believe that:

- Training and organization development must be viewed as a process rather than a singular event.

- A systematic approach must be used to determine individual, group, and organization needs before considering appropriate training or other interventions.

- All programs and services must reflect state-of-the-art concepts, skills, and methodologies.

- The use of internal and external resources is determined by individual customer needs, in-house capabilities, and cost-effectiveness.

- Managers and supervisors must prepare employees and teams before the training or intervention, and actively support their efforts to apply what has been learned.

- The evaluation of training and consulting should involve measuring the learning, behavior changes on the job, and genuine value added to the organization.

- Continuing self-development of ET&D staff is critical to maintaining leadership in the development and delivery of quality programs and services.

External Education and Training

All training needs cannot be fulfilled through internal programming and services. Therefore, we provide assistance in determining appropriate external resources, enrollment, and seminar evaluation.

We subscribe to the Seminar Clearinghouse International (SCI). This is a national service and centralized file of seminar feedback evaluations and training resources. We use this service and *Bricker's International Directory*, as well as our own files, to search education and training resources at employees' requests.

Available Programs

Many programs are offered for all employees. With the assistance of their bosses, they select the ones that best meet their needs. The following programs, however, are specifically for supervisors.

Developing Communication for Increased Collaboration

Scope

This two-day seminar will provide supervisors with the communication skills required to communicate one on one more effectively, to facilitate team meetings, and to collaborate within the work group and among other work areas.

Content

The content of the seminar includes the following subjects:

- Four Basic Communications Skills
- Behaviors That Encourage Open Communication
- Communication Attitudes
- The Communication Inventory
- Team Focus
- Participation
- The Bargaining Game
- Principled Negotiation/Collaboration
- Negotiation Case Study

Participants

Maximum 24, minimum 18. Designed for first-level supervisors who have a minimum of three months' experience on the job.

Goals

To provide participants with opportunities to:

1. Increase their meeting effectiveness.
2. Keep teams focused on tasks.
3. Increase collaboration by using a five-step collaboration/negotiation process.
4. Enhance ongoing relationships among departments.
5. Practice effective communication skills.

Objectives

Upon completion of this seminar, participants will be able to:

- Identify a framework for understanding how to interface with other departments regarding ways to accomplish work.
- Apply a simple strategy for collaboration that enables them to pursue their departmental goals without giving in or getting into futile confrontations.
- Follow a preparation procedure that covers a crucial step in negotiating with other departments and work groups.
- Apply a process for solving interdepartmental issues.
- Develop a meeting plan and facilitate a group in carrying out the plan.

Developing Employees

Scope

This two-day seminar focuses on the skills required to motivate employees and manage their performance (setting goals, coaching, and evaluating performance). Discussions on training and employee development will also be included.

Content

The following subjects are covered in this seminar:

- Understanding the Leadership and Motivation Model
- Measuring Your Leadership with the Leadership Survey
- Writing Mission Statements
- Constructing Goals
- Conducting Objective-Setting Sessions
- Providing Performance Feedback
- Observing, Documenting, and Coaching Employees
- Recognizing and Rewarding Accomplishments
- Supporting Employees
- Creating Performance T-Charts
- Action Planning

Participants

Maximum 24, minimum 12. Designed for first-level supervisors who have a minimum of three months' experience on the job.

Goals

To provide participants with opportunities to:

1. Learn that motivation is internal.
2. Foster the conditions that increase motivation and empower their direct reports to work beyond their job descriptions.
3. Increase their own motivation as a supervisor.

Objectives

Upon completion of this seminar, participants will be able to:

- Assess their motivational leadership as a process of influencing others' behavior.
- Develop their skills as first-level supervisors in promoting continuous improvement.

- Write performance goals and objectives and practice objective-setting skills.

- Identify the importance of coaching in the context of performance management.

- Practice conducting a coaching session.

- Plan for ongoing employee development, recognition, and support for their direct reports.

- Identify their personal strengths and opportunities for improvement using their results from the prework Leadership Survey.

- Assess the social styles of their direct reports and use that to develop action plans to improve their performance.

Developing High-Performance Teams

Scope

This two-day seminar will provide participants with the skills required to be effective team leaders. They will learn the stages of team development and what their role is throughout those stages.

Content

This seminar will cover:

- Achieving Excellence Through Shared-Responsibility Teams
- Analyzing the Changing Work Environment
- Empowering Employees
- Changing Team Leadership Styles
- Understanding the Manager As Developer
- Building a Shared-Responsibility Team
- Developing Vision Alignment
- Providing Individual Development
- Understanding the Stages of Group Development and the Manager's Role in Each
- Learning the Principles of Innovation
- Analyzing the Innovation Styles Model

■ Understanding the "Creative Journey": A Step-by-Step Process for Generating and Implementing Innovative Solutions

Participants

Maximum 24, minimum 18. Designed for first-level supervisors who have a minimum of three months' experience on the job.

Goals

To provide participants with opportunities to:

1. Re-examine their roles as supervisors to better fit today and tomorrow's world.
2. Learn how to empower employees.
3. Develop plans to build a shared-responsibility team.
4. Understand their team leadership style.

Objectives

Upon completion of this seminar, participants will be able to:

■ Identify the techniques to implement effective and efficient team development.

■ Increase responsibility and accountability for department objectives.

■ Identify ways to improve quality.

■ Describe the importance of a tangible vision.

■ Practice leading teams in a way that is more appropriate for today's business.

Developing Self-Leadership

Scope

This two-day seminar focuses on providing participants with the skills required to manage themselves and others through change. Participants will learn techniques to minimize the "people breakage" (anxiety, frustration, or anger) that sometimes accompanies change. And, they will also learn how to develop a vision to enhance the acceptance of change.

Content

This seminar will cover:

- The Three Phases of Change
- Handling "People Breakage"
- Your Role in Supervising Change
- The "Never End" Exercise
- The "Change Response Scale"
- The Four Reactions to Change
- Observing Change Response
- The Perceptions/Self-Talk/Behavior Model (PSB)
- The Stop/Challenge/Focus Technique
- The Clarify/Share/Engage Support System
- Vision Versus Planning and Organizing

Participants

Maximum 24, minimum 18. Designed for first-level supervisors who have a minimum of three months' experience on the job.

Goals

To provide participants with opportunities to:

1. More effectively direct themselves and their reports through change.
2. Practice self-management techniques to contend with change.
3. Manage their emotions and the emotions of their direct reports through change.

Objectives

Upon completion of this seminar, participants will be able to:

- Define the role of a leader in a changing environment.
- Identify the three phases of change.
- Identify the different kinds of reactions to change.
- Assess reports reactions to change using the Change Response Scale.

- Practice techniques for managing change.
- Develop a plan to overcome resistance to change.
- Explain the effect of vision on the motivation to accept and support change.

Training and Development Philosophy

Instructional Methods

Lectures, question-and-answer discussions, case studies, small-team activities, role playing, and other structured participative activities are used in all programs to ensure participant interaction and involvement. Programmed instruction techniques are also used. Many learning aids and handout materials are made available. Most programs are conducted by Employee Training and Development instructors or by unit trainers who have been certified by our department.

The "Certified Trainer Process" is the hallmark of our department. Its purpose is to provide timely access for an increased number of employees to obtain quality delivery and content of selected programs. In addition to completing an extensive "training-the-trainer" curriculum, candidates for certified trainer status enroll in certified trainer workshops. In these workshops, they are assisted in achieving student-oriented learning results through colleague observation, co-training experiences, classroom feedback, and information sharing.

The developmental needs of supervisors should be driven by the appraisal/performance management process. Gaps, comparing present skills vis-à-vis competencies for the position, are identified and individual development plans are determined. When training is appropriate, the programs outlined above are offered. Other development experiences such as job assignments, on-the-job training (OJT), and "e-learning" are also utilized.

Application on the Job

Using what has been learned and applying it to the job is of great importance to us as training people. Too often, we blame circumstances within the work environment for the participants' inability to use their new knowledge or skills "back at the ranch." In order to do this, the instructors are told to build at least two methods into a training program that will help initiate or reinforce in-class learning back on the job.

Here are suggested approaches:

Before the Program

- Have participants evaluate program goals and objectives.
- Have participants clarify seminar expectations with their supervisor.
- Tie program objectives to on-the-job management objectives.
- Focus on back-home problems and individual motivation.
- Have participants spend some time doing necessary background reading and other prework.
- Have top management kick off the program or attend key sessions.
- Have a preseminar meeting of participants' bosses to help explain program content and their role in the training process.
- Make programs consistent for vertical cross-sections of management.

During the Program

- Have participants frequently answer the questions, "What have I learned?" and "How will I use it?"
- Have participants identify and deal with problems or obstacles of on-the-job applications.
- Design modules such that the instructors must move consistently and hold participants accountable for their activities.
- Get participants to grade their involvement and contribution each day.
- Provide retention aids as back-home reminders.

After the Program

- Have each participant make an individual contract or action plan, and send each a copy of it later.
- Ask participants' supervisors to review their subordinates' action plans.
- Have participants send the seminar evaluations through their supervisor.

■ Conduct follow-up interviews for review and evaluation, and include each participant's supervisor.

■ Send out "reminder" mailings of reinforcing information on various program skills at short intervals after the program.

■ Conduct a postseminar meeting of participants to discuss or test program skills application.

14

COACHING TO WIN: A MANAGEMENT TRAINING PROGRAM

Training professionals at the National Service Center (NSC) of Hartford Life Insurance Company developed and implemented a training program to improve the coaching skills of their supervisors and managers.[1] The program was requested by the Vice President of

---

[1]Internally developed and implemented by Gordon Dozier, Heather McAllister, Sue Muehlbach, and Kirk Friedman.

Operations, who made it mandatory for all his people. An overview of the proposed program was presented to him and his direct reports for approval before finalizing the course. The course lasted for one day and was divided into three modules.

Case studies were based on real situations and class participants played the parts of "manager" and "employee" in role-playing situations. A "Training Evaluation" form was used to measure reaction (Level 1), and each participant was assigned a "peer coach" during and after the class for accountability. In order to evaluate changes in behavior (Level 3), brown bag luncheons ("coaching forums") would be held so that program participants could share how they had applied the principles and technique that were taught.

The training staff planned two follow-up programs to increase the effectiveness of this course and coaching in general: A "Leading to Win" course for Senior Managers and Directors, and a "Playing to Win" course for nonmanagement employees.

The content of the Coaching to Win program is described as follows:

NATIONAL SERVICE CENTER, HARTFORD LIFE INSURANCE COMPANY, MINNEAPOLIS, MINNESOTA

The Opportunity

The pressure to perform at high-performance levels in business today has become increasingly greater. Coaching employees is essential to developing a high-performance team, organization, and culture. The NSC wants to continue to develop successful teams and employees and the Coaching to Win program helps to ensure this success.

What is coaching? Coaching is a planned and purposeful interactive process between managers and employees to enhance behavior, skill, and overall performance. Just like legendary sports coaches leave behind a legacy of inspiration, we want our managers to provide employees with the skills, knowledge, and motivation to perform at the highest level to help beat the competition in customer service, products and processes, distribution, and quality of service.

The Project

The course goals are to:

- Identify the role, qualities, and attitudes of a successful coach.
- Use the "Winning Coach" model to instruct, inspire, and guide employees to "win" as a high-performance team.
- Identify and implement effective ways to communicate to employees in both good and poor performance situations.
- Improve coaching skills through practice and application using real-life case studies.

The course is divided into three modules:

1. Coaching Basics
2. The Practiced Coach
3. Practical Coaching

Achievement and Goals

The goal is to roll the Coaching to Win course out to all levels of management along with a future peer coaching program for employees. The first coaching course was offered in October 1999. To date, the program has been delivered to 20 of the 40 associate managers at the NSC.

Why Coaching Now?

- Coaching employees is essential to developing a high-performance team, organization and culture.
- Coaching is a healthy, positive, and enabling process that develops the capacity of people to solve problems.
- Ongoing changes with people, teams, technology, and leadership require ongoing training and professional development at all levels of the organization.
- Progressive leaders and companies are choosing coaching as a fundamental part of creating high-performance teams.

Course Goals

After completing this course, participants will be able to:

- Identify the role of a coach on a team.
- Use the Winning Coach Model as a tool to both assess and meet the needs of team members.
- Identify and implement "The Practical Coach."
- Improve coaching skills.

COACHING TO WIN

Coaching Basics—Module 1

Coaching Basics

- Define "coaching"
- Explore the characteristics of a "Winning Coach"
- Introduce the "Winning Coach Model"

What Is a Coach?

The three roles of a coach:
1. Instruct a team to win
2. Inspire a team to win
3. Guide a team to win

Sports and Business Coaching Parallels[2]

- Both sports and business coaches strive to motivate, inspire, and get the "extra mile" from their players.
- Both demand *commitment*, *action*, and *results* for the team and the stakeholders that support the team.
- Both build trusting relationships with their players.
- Both need focus and vision.
- Both play to win.

---

[2]James S. Doyle, *The Business Coach* (New York: John Wiley & Sons, 1999).

Bosses vs. Coaches[3]

Boss	Coach
• Pushes and Drives	• Supports and Inspires
• Tells/Directs/Lectures	• Inquires/Guides/Listens
• Focuses Only on Errors	• Encourages Excellence
• Talks *at* People	• Initiates "Two-Way Street"/ Dialogue
• Knows the Answers	• Seeks the Answers
• Strives for Results-Only Focus	• Stresses Processes & Results
• Instills Fear As Dominant Motivator	• Inspires Commitment
• Delegates Responsibility	• Models Accountability
• Creates Structures & Procedures	• Creates Vision & Flexibility
• Does Things Right	• Does the Right Things
• "Gets the Most"	• "Gets the Best"

A Coach's Job Description

- Get to know people as people.
- Understand enough about people's roles, goals, and challenges.
- Make sure performance expectations and goals are clear.
- Delegate to develop skills and competencies.
- Observe people's work closely enough to give relevant feedback.
- Provide timely and specific feedback.
- Reinforce progress toward goals, rather than wait for perfection.
- Offer constructive suggestions for performance enhancement.

Winning Coach Model

Three roles of a winning coach:	Three needs of a winning team:
1. Instruct	1. Knowledge
2. Inspire	2. Motivation
3. Guide	3. Skills

[3]Thomas Crane, *The Heart of Coaching* (San Diego: FTA Press, 1998).

What types of knowledge, motivation, and skills are needed by a winning business team?

Instructing Your Team
1. Communicating the "goals."
2. Communicating expectations.
3. Striving for continuous learning.

Communicating the Goals
1. What will "winning" look like to your team?
2. How do you communicate your goals to your team?

Goal Setting
Most people would divide the relative importance of goal setting[4] and managing consequences into 75 percent and 25 percent, respectively. The reality is just the opposite: 25 percent of what impacts performance comes from setting goals, and 75 percent comes from what happens after goals are set. Performance is influenced most by consequences—that is, the response from a coach who is on the scene.

Communicating the Expectations

Human Level	Business Level
• Professional attitude/ demeanor	• Products or "outputs"
	• Process/workflow
• Communication	• Standards of quality—
• Professional appearance	timeliness and accuracy

Brainstorm! What are your own expectations?

Striving for Continuous Learning
■ Cross-training

■ Formalized on-the-job training (OJT)

■ Internal classes

■ External classes

---

[4]Don Shula and Ken Blanchard, *Everyone's a Coach* (Grand Rapids, MI: Zondervan Publishing House, 1995).

- Professional associations
- Media/intranet/Internet
- Self-study
- Peer coaching
- Periodicals
- LOMA
- Attending seminars

> "Leadership and learning are indispensable to each other."
>
> — *John F. Kennedy*

Inspiring Your Team

1. Choosing a "winning attitude."
2. Modeling a "winning performance."
3. Providing the "winning motivation."

Winning Attitudes[5]

- Keep winning and losing in perspective.
- Lead by example.
- Go for respect over popularity.
- Value character as well as ability.
- Work hard but enjoy what you do.

Inspiration to Motivation

Inspiration	Motivation
• Thoughts, Feelings	• Will to Act

Guiding Your Team

1. Creating the context for success.
2. *Being present* to encourage high performance and challenge low performance.

[5]Ibid.

Formula for Reaching the Goal

Process +	*Business Tools +*	*Knowledge & Motivation +*	*Environment =*	*GOAL*
• Workflow • Defined functions/tasks	• Systems • Job aids	• Training & coaching • Incentives	• External issues • Ergonomics	
• The service provided • How it's performed	• Procedures	• Consequences	• Organizational/team	
	• Information		• Team culture • Staffing • Physical layout	

"Management by Walking Around" MBWA[6]

It is being in touch with customers, suppliers, and your people. It facilitates innovation and makes possible the teaching of values to every member of an organization. Listening, facilitating, and teaching and reinforcing values, what is this except leadership? Thus, MBWA is the technology of leadership. Leading is primarily paying attention.

When Am I Needed as a Coach?[7]

- When things are going well and I can recognize, reinforce, and reward positive behavior.
- When I would like to suggest small, subtle mid-course adjustments.
- When things are not going well and clear corrections need to be made.
- When breakdowns, significant behavior and attitude problems, skill gaps, or performance issues exist and must be addressed.

Coaching Challenges

- What are some of the challenges you have faced as a coach?
- How were they handled?
- What was the outcome?
- What might you do differently?

Offense vs. Defense

Offense	*Defense*
• "The Team" • "Players" and "Coach" united by a common goal . . . to win!	• "The Obstacles" • Prevent or delay team from reaching its goal • Lack of communication, consequences, and conditions

---

[6]Tom Peters and Nancy Austin, *Passion for Excellence* (New York: Random House, 1985).

[7]James S. Doyle, *The Business Coach* (New York: John Wiley & Sons, 1999).

Defensive Lineup
- Lack of communication
- Lack of consequences
- Lack of conditions

The Practical Coach—Module 2

Coaching Good Behavior
1. When you see it, say it!
2. Be specific.

Coaching Poor Behavior
1. Make it private, make it positive.
2. Ask questions.
3. Show your concern for them personally and professionally.

Coaching Feedback Tips
- Know and respect your audience.
- Be aware of the "Power of Perspective."
- Be constructive. Focus on the problem and solution—not on the person.
- Make the feedback specific (who, what, where, when, how).
- Discuss cause and effect.
- Make the feedback timely.
- Make honest statements.
- Watch for verbal and nonverbal clues to gauge the internal response.
- Actively listen to your audience.
- Plan what you will say.

"The Two-Minute Challenge"[8]
1. **State** what you've observed.
2. **Wait** for a response.

---

[8]Media Partners, 911 Western Avenue, Seattle, WA 98104

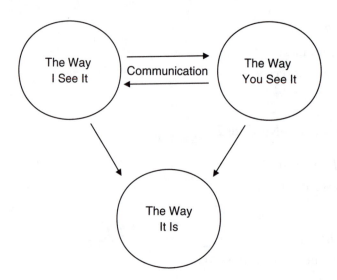

Figure 14-1. *"The Way It Is" Model*

3. **Remind** them of the goal.
4. **Ask** for a specific solution.
5. **Agree** together.

Sidetracks!

Four Natural "Defense" Techniques

1. The Stall
2. The Self-Inflicted Wound
3. The Guilt Trip
4. The Attack

The Two-Minute Challenge

Words to Say

Step 1—State: You state: "This is what I saw..."
Step 2—Wait: You wait for a response from the employee.
Step 3—Remind: You state: "This is what I need to see . . . "
Step 4—Solve: You ask: "What can we do to make sure this happens?"
Step 5—Agree: You re-state: "So we agree . . . "
Step 6—Follow-up and encouragement.

The Stall

This usually appears after you have stated (and demonstrated to your team member) the new action you want to see. Get their involvement on how to solve the problem and agree with a mutual solution.

- ■ "OK."
- ■ "Sure."
- ■ "That's a good idea."
- ■ "I'll work on that."

The Self-Inflicted Wound

Sometimes a team member will begin to criticize himself before your message is even completed. Try to refocus the discussion and work through how to solve the problem. Use phrases such as:

- ■ "I know, I know, I do that."
- ■ "You know what's even worse is I do this."
- ■ "I just can't seem to get it right."
- ■ "I'll work on that."

The Guilt Trip

The Guilt Trip is just how it sounds. It is intended to try and make you feel guilty. The key is to recognize the sidetrack and simply stick to the facts.

- ■ "You always seem to be picking on me."
- ■ "I'm doing my best."
- ■ "What more can I do?"
- ■ "I'm sorry it is never enough for you."

The Attack

A team member attacks your authority, and sometimes the attack is personal. The key here is to stay calm even though you may feel like striking back. Stick to the facts. It may be necessary to continue the conversation at a later time.

- "Who are you to tell me?"
- "You don't do that yourself. Why should I?"
- "Yeah, it's easy for you to say. You're not the one out here doing the work."

Coaching Drills

1. What was the scenario?
2. What were your expectations and goals? (How were you going to solve the problem?)
3. What happened? What was the need? How did they respond?
4. How did you demonstrate your concern for the employee?
5. Was anything said that changed your perspective?
6. What was the agreement? Did it address the need?
7. Did the employee use a sidetrack? If so, which one? How did you respond?

Proactive Coaching—Module 3

Coaching Employees

- Proactive Employee Coaching (Development)
- Reactive Employee Coaching (Feedback on Performance)
- Coaching Various Personality Types
- Coaching Drills

Teamwork

A team's performance is the collection of individual performances.

Proactive Coaching

1. Review competencies and objectives.

   - Position description
   - List of employee competencies

2. Measure current performance.

   a. Observation

      - Observe employee performance (MBWA—Management by Walking Around)
      - Team/peer feedback

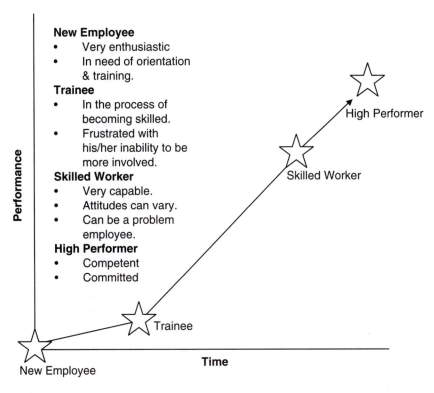

New Employee
- Very enthusiastic
- In need of orientation & training.

Trainee
- In the process of becoming skilled.
- Frustrated with his/her inability to be more involved.

Skilled Worker
- Very capable.
- Attitudes can vary.
- Can be a problem employee.

High Performer
- Competent
- Committed

Figure 14-2.

- Customer feedback (internal & external)
- Employee's perception

b. Documentation
  - Performance metrics
  - Coaching sessions/discussions
  - Coaching documentation

3. Develop plan to "bridge the gap" (see Figure 14-2).[9]

---

[9]Donna Berry, Charles Cadwell, and Joe Fehman. *Coaching for Results* (Amherst, PA: HRD Press, 1996).

Coaching Documentation Tips

- When coaching an employee on any topic, including positive feedback, development planning, performance improvement, progressive discipline, or behavioral concerns, always document the discussion.

- This documentation is for your supervisory/employee file. It does not belong in the personnel files in Human Resources.

- The documentation will most often be brief and concise—even in bullet-point format.

- Complete the documentation immediately after the meeting while everything is fresh and current.

- The documentation should "stick to the facts" of the meeting/dialogue. If you are unclear what is appropriate, please contact your manager or HR personnel.

- The purpose of documentation is to assist you as a coach/manager to be in a better position to provide a consistent/pro-active follow-up with each employee situation.

- Documenting "positive" coaching sessions is equally important as documenting those sessions that might be considered "negative."

- Lack of documentation is the number-one error made by coaches and managers in the areas of development planning, performance management, and progressive discipline.

- You need to determine with each individual coaching meeting whether or not to provide a summary/overview of the meeting to the employee. Again, if you are not sure, ask your manager or HR personnel.

Coaching Personality Types[10]

1. Front & Center

   - They love to be out mixing with people.
   - They like to try new methods. Their lives are often about extremes—emotional and otherwise.
   - They push their ideas, and they push the rules.

---

[10] Media Partners, 911 Western Avenue, Seattle, WA 98104.

- They live for recognition.
- They are usually self-starters who thrive on applause.
- At times, they are oblivious to their weaknesses.
- When they "slump," they can get very down.

2. In the Wings

- They live for approval and prefer an informal interaction.
- They want to be appreciated with greater access to you.
- They love to feel included. They are rarely in a hurry, and they dislike pressure.
- They tend to be cautious and want to work with others in accomplishing goals.

3. Behind the Scenes

- They don't want the limelight.
- They don't crave applause; they crave appreciation.
- They are low key. They need to know that they can trust people in leadership.
- They are hard on themselves when they "mess up."

Rewards & Recognition[11]

1. Applause & Awards

- Public praise for good performance.
- Receiving tangible awards.

2. Appreciation

- Personal or written "thank you's."
- Posted list of individual & team accomplishments.

3. Access

- More one-on-one time with their coach.
- A commitment from their coach to work on their concerns.

The coaching relationship grows from the inside out. It is not a role you can pick up and put on like a uniform. It comes from a commitment to be a coach, not just a desire to act like one. Being a coach

---

[11] Ibid

means having to demonstrate competencies and attitudes that inspire team members to grant you authority as their coach.[12]

Transitioning from Boss to Coach[13]

Rhonda was a self-made executive. She was one of the few senior executives working for a particular food manufacturer who had risen through the plant organization. She had held production, supervisory, and plant manager positions prior to moving to the corporate headquarters. Now, as vice president of procurement, she found herself in the paradoxical position of looking back over her 33 years in the industry with the firm, and looking forward to the twilight of her career. Rhonda wanted her legacy to include passing on her knowledge, experience, savvy, and passion for the business to her younger protégés. She found herself in a new role—advisor, mentor, and coach.

It hadn't always been like that, however. Rhonda was from the old school and had done more than her share of "kicking butt and taking names" as part of her management heritage. Something motivated her to be different, though. Tina had both admired and feared Rhonda's reputation prior to their working together. As time passed, however, Tina sought out Rhonda's advice and counsel regularly. Rhonda then found herself in a unique position of being able to extend her own efforts through the success of Tina's. It was truly a win-win situation for both.

Rhonda made adjustments to her driving, directive style and listened more, asked more questions, made allowances for Tina's mistakes, and encouraged her to take risks. Tina, sensing trust and mutual respect, responded even more favorably to the environment of openness, clarity of expectations, and support.

"I don't know any other way to lead but by example."

— *Don Shula, former professional football coach*

---

[12]James S. Doyle, *The Business Coach* (New York: John Wiley & Sons, 1999).
[13]Ibid.

Training Evaluation

Class title: _____ Date: _____

Student name (optional): _____ Instructor: _____

Circle one number for Questions 1 through 7. Please submit the completed form at the end of class to the instructor.

	Strongly Disagree	Disagree	Neither Agree Nor Disagree	Agree	Strongly Agree
1. The course content and materials were organized and well prepared.	1	2	3	4	5
2. The course content met my expectations.	1	2	3	4	5
3. The information presented will help me do my job better.	1	2	3	4	5
4. Participants' questions and concerns were addressed appropriately.	1	2	3	4	5
5. The trainer(s) kept the class moving and on track.	1	2	3	4	5
6. The trainer(s) demonstrated a thorough knowledge of the subject.	1	2	3	4	5
7. The trainer's instructions were clear and concise.	1	2	3	4	5

8. What information was most useful?

9. What areas need improvement?

10. What comments would you like to make about the course and/or instructors?

15

A 10-DAY CERTIFICATE PROGRAM FOR SUPERVISORS

Few organizations use a well-thought-out approach to supervisory training and development. Typically, training professionals decide to put on a program because of a specific need or pressure from a chief executive who has heard about a program that another organization has offered—such as "Leadership," "Diversity in the Work Force," "Empowerment," or "Total Quality Improvement."

The Management Institute (MI) of the University of Wisconsin uses a different approach. In 1944, MI offered a program called "Human Relations for Foremen and Supervisors." Because of requests and research on the needs of supervisors, MI continually revised and added programs to cover all of the topics that supervisors need to be effective. This resulted in a 10-day program that benefits supervisors in all types and sizes of organizations. It is beneficial to new supervisors as well as those who have been in supervision for many years but have never been taught how to be "managers" instead of "doers." Following is a description of this program.

Management Institute, University of Wisconsin, Milwaukee, Wisconsin

Organizations have discovered that first-line supervisors are the key people in accomplishing maximum results, according to program director Ronald J. Bula. They influence not only how the job gets done, but also the morale and culture of the organization. In addition to having a management perspective and the "right" attitude, they need up-to-date knowledge and skills in performing their jobs. They need to know how to work with people to get the job done.

In most cases, however, they have been promoted from "doers" to supervisors with little or no training on how the new job differs from the previous job. Because of the lack of understanding about their new roles and responsibilities, they frequently become frustrated and do not perform well.

Organizations that invest in their supervisors, though, receive a real payoff. Not only will these supervisors learn the knowledge and skills needed to do their jobs, but they will also have a feeling of confidence, importance, and loyalty to upper-level management who have demonstrated their concern to help them be successful.

The supervisors are told that "management" is "a science and an art." The "science" of management is concepts, theory, principles, and techniques. This they will learn in the programs. The "art" of management is application back on the job. They must keep this constantly in mind so that the organization's investment pays off in improved performances.

Program Content

Ten days of training are required to complete the certificate. The recommended parts of the program can be met in two ways. Supervisors can attend two three-day programs or a one-week workshop. The remaining days can be selected from a list of elective courses. This allows supervisors to focus on programs that meet their particular needs. Following are the details.

Recommended Courses

Six days of recommended courses comprise Unit 1 (three days) and Unit 2 (three days). Units 1 and 2 can also be combined in a week-long seminar called "The Total Supervisor."

Unit 1, Leading and Working with People

The following subjects are covered in this three-day program:

1. **Making It in Management**—Supervisors look at the whole picture of what it means to be a successful supervisor and how it's different from being a worker. Learning what is required and why it's important gives the participants a wide-angle view of their expectations and performance. This covers such issues as:

- Dealing with the responsibilities, roles, and pressures of managing
- Developing the management perspective
- Understanding, developing, and adopting your leadership style

2. **Growing Personally as an Ongoing Process**—It's not enough to attend a management seminar if development stops there. There has to be a challenge to keep growing. This session provides an incentive for supervisors to see how and where to keep improving. Participants complete a plan for personal development, including a step-by-step guide for future improvement in their performance. This area covers such topics as:

- Introducing the elements of life/work planning
- Identifying personal and professional goals
- Developing a strategy for greater life and work satisfaction

3. **Understanding and Getting Along with People on the Job**—
Employees are people with feelings, hopes, and fears. Supervisors
who understand this are powerful assets to their organization. They
manage employees as individuals, helping them overcome their weaknesses and develop their strengths. This also covers:

- Identifying what supervisors should know about their people
- Getting to know them
- Learning the essentials of human relations
- Assessing yourself and your interpersonal style

4. **Creating the Climate for High Motivation and Achievement**—
This session shows supervisors practical ways to provide leadership
that creates a climate for high performance. It also covers:

- Understanding the elements of an effective job performance, rewards, and job satisfaction for employees
- Identifying what the supervisor can do to create a climate of high motivation
- Handling today's motivational problems and opportunities

5. **Improving Your Communication Effectiveness**—Knowing with
whom to communicate, why, when, and how are as important as
what's being communicated. In this session, supervisors have an
opportunity to learn and practice effective communication—written,
oral, and nonverbal. This also includes:

- Clarifying the meaning of communication
- Identifying communication barriers
- Learning the requirements for effective communication
- Planning for effective communication
- Learning methods and techniques
- Getting feedback to verify understanding

6. **Managing Change Without Anxiety**—Change is an everyday
fact of life, and so is the anxiety that goes with it. Planning and
preparing to manage change is a critical management function. This
session teaches managers how to obtain their employees' acceptance
of change and contribute to its successful implementation. This also
involves:

- Understanding the supervisor's role in managing change
- Understanding why employees resist/resent change

- Understanding why employees accept/welcome change
- Understanding the three keys for managing change

Unit 2, Mastering Supervisory Skills

The following subjects are covered in this three-day program:

1. **Solving Problems and Making Decisions**—This key part of the supervisor's job is covered in depth with case histories, group assignments, and practice sessions to build understanding and confidence. Supervisors learn specific techniques that improve their abilities as problem solvers and decision makers.

- Understanding systematic approaches to problem solving
- Defining problems and analyzing causes
- Generating, selecting, and weighing alternatives
- Implementing decisions
- Deciding when to use participative problem solving

2. **Preventing and Handling Complaints and Grievances**—Every organization, whether union or nonunion, faces problems that lead to complaints by employees and that can turn into serious problems or grievances. Supervisors learn the important differences between complaints and grievances and how to recognize common sources and causes. They acquire practical concepts and skills for handling complaints so that these situations don't get out of control. Issues include:

- Defining gripes, complaints, and grievances
- Determining relationships and causes
- Understanding prevention versus cure
- Investigating complaints and grievances to arrive at an acceptable resolution

3. **Maintaining Order and Discipline**—Discipline is not a reaction to something bad that's already happened. It's a continuing process of recognizing, preparing for, and dealing with small situations that can develop into major problems. Once supervisors start thinking of discipline as problem prevention rather than punishment, they're more comfortable and adept at handling it in a consistent and fair manner.

- Developing an enlightened approach to discipline
- Establishing order through modeling: clarifying expectations and building rapport

- Communicating corrective actions and praise to produce the right results
- Handling major disciplinary problems

4. Orienting and Training Employees—The first few weeks on a new job can make or break an employee. Through good orientation (introducing employees to policies, procedures, and the organization—as well as effective training based on objectives, follow-through, and evaluation), supervisors hold the key to the new employee's success. Learning the systematic approaches that are presented in this session enables supervisors to perform their role effectively. This area includes:

- Understanding why it is necessary to orient and train employees properly
- Understanding how employees learn
- Learning the principles of instruction
- Learning the four-step method for training
- Practicing the four-step method

Elective Courses

The second part of the certificate program is designed so that participants can structure their own learning experiences around the topics that most closely meet their needs. They can select programs that enhance or expand their supervisory skills. Most of the supervisors who complete the 10-day requirements attend a week-long course called "The Effective Manager." Subjects in the course include:

Developing Administrative Skills

The following themes are covered:

- Planning and Organizing
- Time Management
- Direction and Delegation
- Improving Performance through Appraisal and Coaching

Improving Communication Skills

The following subjects are covered:

- Interviewing Skills That Produce Results
- Managing Conflict
- Organizing Productive Teams
- Communication Barriers, Principles, and Approaches
- How to Conduct Productive Meetings
- How to Write Effectively

The following additional elective programs allow the participants to select topics that more closely meet their personal needs:

The Supervisor and the Union (two days)
Dealing with Difficult People (two days)
Developing an Effective Leadership Style (two days)
Managing Technical People (two days)

Instructors

The full-time faculty and ad hoc instructional staff not only have the educational background and teaching experiences needed to make programs top quality, but they also have a broad range of ongoing "real world" business experiences. They are, or have been, practitioners in their areas of expertise. It is a combination of theory, practical experience, and teaching skills that make the courses effective.

Methods and Techniques

The latest concepts, theories, principles, and techniques are presented and discussed in the programs. The instructors make the meetings interesting, enjoyable, and practical by using much group involvement. The most frequently used aids and techniques are videotapes, case studies, supervisory inventories, exercises, and buzz group assignments. The participants learn from each other as well as from the instructors. Practice is included in many of the sessions.

Certificate

A paper certificate is awarded for each program. A supervisor who completes the 10-day requirement receives a wooden plaque for the office wall.

Evaluations

In every program, the participants complete reaction sheets that ask for their evaluation as well as comments and suggestions. The ratings are consistently in the "very good" to "excellent" range. These reaction sheets are carefully analyzed by the instructors to be sure that they are meeting the needs of the participants. Probably the best measure of the effectiveness of the programs is that most participants return to complete the 10-day certificate. In addition, their recommendations back at the office or plant result in additional people attending. Many organizations have sent all of their supervisors (and even their bosses) to the programs.

SUMMARY

The Management Institute has gained a reputation for presenting high-quality programs that meet the needs of the supervisors who attend. During 1999, for example, 191 supervisors attended. Forty-eight percent of them came from states other than Wisconsin.

For detailed information on these programs, contact:

Ron Bula, Program Director
Management Institute, University of Wisconsin—Milwaukee
161 W. Wisconsin Avenue Suite 6000
Milwaukee, Wisconsin 53203
(414) 227-3218

16

AN EVALUATION OF A TRAINING PROGRAM

To review, Chapter 8 described four stages for evaluating the effectiveness of training programs:

- *Reaction*—How well did the participants like the program (a measure of customer satisfaction)?
- *Learning*—What attitudes were changed, and what knowledge and skills were learned?
- *Behavior*—What changes in behavior took place as a result of attending the program?

278

■ *Results*—What final results (increased production, reduced costs, improved quality, reduced turnover, increased return on investment, increased sales, reduced accidents) occurred because of attending the program?

Following is a case study of an evaluation of a program that was conducted numerous times by the Management Institute, University of Wisconsin. The purpose of the evaluation was to determine the amount of behavior change that took place when the participants returned to their jobs. In addition, an attempt was made to measure results.

In reading the following case, note especially the research design that can be adapted to any evaluation of this type.

MANAGEMENT INSTITUTE, UNIVERSITY OF WISCONSIN, MILWAUKEE, WISCONSIN

Since 1944, the Management Institute of the University of Wisconsin has presented three- to five-day institutes for foremen and supervisors. These programs have been attended by representatives of companies throughout the midwestern United States. Each program has been evaluated from the standpoint of the reaction of the participants. Consistently, the participants have been enthusiastic about the subjects, the leaders, and the benefits.

Evaluations have also been made of the learning of the participants. Pretests and posttests have been given to measure the amount of learning of the principles, facts, and approaches that has been taught. These evaluations revealed significant changes in knowledge and attitudes.

Following is a description of an evaluation project designed to measure changes in behavior that took place on the job as a result of participating in a supervisory training program. The evaluation was planned and implemented by Dr. Donald Kirkpatrick, Professor of Management.

The Program

The institute's program called "Developing Supervisory Skills" was presented in Milwaukee, Wisconsin, on three consecutive Tuesdays and then repeated for a different group on three consecutive Wednesdays. In attendance were 57 lower-level management people from various organizations in southeastern Wisconsin.

The program featured six three-hour sessions covering the following topics:

1. Order Giving
2. Training Employees
3. Appraising Employee Performance
4. Preventing and Handling Grievances
5. Decision Making
6. Initiating Change

The leaders were staff members of the Management Institute, the University of Wisconsin. Teaching methods included lecture, guided discussion, buzz groups, role playing, films, case studies, and other visual aids.

Research Design. A questionnaire was completed by each participant to obtain information on the participant, his company, and his relationship with his immediate supervisor. Specific information was obtained on:

- *The participant*—His job, experience, education, age, why he is attending the program, and what he hopes to learn.
- *The company*—Size, type, and climate for change.
- *The participant's boss*—Years spent as boss, the climate he sets for change, and his involvement in sending the participant to the institute.

Interviews were conducted with each participant within two to three months following the institute. The interviews were conducted in the participant's company to obtain information regarding changes in behavior that had taken place on the job. In addition, interviews were conducted with the participant's immediate supervisor as another measure of possible changes in the participant's behavior.

The Group Being Evaluated. Complete information was obtained from 43 of the 57 participants in the institute. Only these 43 are included in the research results. The following data describe the 43 participants and their organizations. The information was obtained from the questionnaire they completed at the start of the program.

Organizations of Participants

1. Size

      4   0-100 employees

      3   500-1,000 employees

      10   100-500 employees

      26   More than 1,000 employees

2. Products

      15   Consumer use

      11   Industrial use

      12   Both

      5   Other

3. How would you classify top management?

      31   Liberal (encourages change; invites and responds to suggestions)

      3   Conservative (discourages change)

      9   Middle-of-the-road

4. How would you classify your boss?

      35   Liberal

      0   Conservative

      8   Middle-of-the-road

5. How often does your boss ask you for ideas to solve departmental problems?

      19   Frequently

      19   Sometimes

      5   Hardly ever

6. To what extent will your boss encourage you to apply the ideas and techniques you learn in this program?

      14   To a large extent

      14   To some extent

      1   Very little

      14   Not sure

Participants

1. Title

    33   Foreman or supervisor

    8   General foreman or superintendent

    2   Other

2. Education

    12   Less than high school

    21   High school

    10   More than high school

3. Previous attendance at University of Wisconsin institutes

    38   None

    2   One

    1   Two

    1   Three

    0   Four

    1   Five

4. Before attending this institute, how much were you told about it?

    3   Complete information

    8   Quite a lot

    20   A little

    12   None

5. Attendance at in-plant training programs?

    28   Yes

    15   No

6. How many people supervise?

    1   0-5

    9   6-10

    6   11-15

    8   16-20

    19   More than 20

7. Whom do you supervise?

   26   All men

   11   Mostly men

    6   Mostly women

    0   All women

8. What kind of workers do you supervise?

   14   Production (nonskilled)

   13   Production (semiskilled)

   11   Production (skilled)

    2   Maintenance

    9   Office

    4   Other

9. To what extent do you feel that you will be able to improve your supervisory performance by attending this program?

   21   To a large extent

   22   To some extent

    0   Very little

Research Results

The purpose of the research was to evaluate changes in on-the-job behavior that resulted from attendance at the institute. It was felt that information from both the participant and his immediate supervisor would contribute to the research. A comparison of responses from participants with those of their supervisors was also considered part of the research—in other words, how much agreement on changes in behavior was observed by the immediate supervisor in comparison with the changes in behavior expressed by the participant himself.

The results were described below in two categories: "A" related to those relating to overall behavior, and "B" related to those relating to each of the six subjects covered in the institute.

The following figures given are percentages. Wherever two figures are given, the first figure is the percent of the response from participants, and the second figure is the percent of response from the participants' immediate supervisors.

Overall Changes in Behavior and Results

1. To what extent has the program improved the participant's working relationship with his boss?

   To a large extent 23 – 12

   To some extent 51 – 32

   No change 26 – 56

   Made it worse 0 – 0

2. Since the program, how much two-way communication has taken place between the participant and his subordinates?

   Much more 12 – 5

   Somewhat more 63 – 46

   No change 25 – 44

   Somewhat less 0 – 0

   Much less 0 – 0

   Don't know 0 – 5

3. Since the program, is the participant taking a more active interest in employees?

   Much more 26 – 5

   Somewhat more 67 – 49

   No change 7 – 44

   Somewhat less 0 –0

   Much less 0 – 0

   Don't know 0 – 2

4. On an overall basis, to what extent has the participant's job behavior changed *since* the program (Figure 16-1)?

5. In regard to the following results, what changes have been noticed *since* the participant's attendance in the program (Figure 16-2)?

(text continued on page 287)

Supervisory Areas	Much Better	Somewhat Better	No Change	Somewhat Worse	Much Worse	Don't Know
a. Order giving	25–12	70–65	5–14	0–0	0–0	0–9
b. Training	22–17	56–39	22–39	0–0	0–0	0–5
c. Decision making	35–14	58–58	7–23	0–0	0–0	0–5
d. Initiating change	21–9	53–53	26–30	0–0	0–0	0–7
e. Appraising employee performance	21–7	50–42	28–36	0–0	0–0	0–12
f. Preventing and handling grievances	12–7	42–40	46–46	0–0	0–0	0–7
g. Attitude toward job	37–23	37–53	26–23	0–0	0–0	0–0
h. Attitude toward subordinates	40–7	42–60	19–30	0–0	0–0	0–2
i. Attitude toward management	42–26	26–35	32–37	0–0	0–0	0–2

Figure 16-1. *Changes in participants' job behavior*

Supervisory Areas	Much Better	Somewhat Better	No Change	Somewhat Worse	Much Worse	Don't Know
a. Quantity of production	5–5	43–38	50–50	0–2	0–0	0–5
b. Quality of production	10–7	60–38	28–52	0–0	0–0	0–2
c. Safety	21–7	28–37	49–56	0–0	0–0	0–0
d. Housekeeping	23–14	32–35	42–46	0–5	0–0	0–0
e. Employee attitudes and morale	12–7	56–53	28–32	2–5	0–0	0–2
f. Employee attendance	7–2	23–19	67–77	0–0	0–0	0–0
g. Employee promptness	7–2	32–16	58–81	0–0	0–0	0–0
h. Employee turnover	5–0	14–16	79–79	0–5	0–0	0–0

Figure 16-2. Other changes noted in participants' behavior

The responses to these five questions indicate that the program improved relationships between the participant and his boss, as well as those between participants and subordinates. In nearly all instances, the participant indicated more of a positive change than his supervisor did. In Questions 1 and 2, for example, approximately 75% of the participants indicated a positive change, while 51 percent of their supervisors indicated a positive change.

In Question 3, there is a large difference of opinion (93% of the participants expressed a positive change while 54% of their supervisors indicated a positive change). In Question 4, all nine of the items revealed a positive change on the part of more than 50% of the participants—as expressed by participants, as well as their supervisors. The most significant changes were expressed in "order giving," "decision making," and the attitude of the participant toward his job.

Question 5 shows less positive change than was revealed in Questions 1–4. Employee attitudes and morale showed the highest positive change, while employee attendance, promptness, and turnover showed the least positive changes.

Changes in Behavior Relating to Each Subject. The responses to the questions on "order giving" (Figure 16-3) reveal a high degree of positive change, particularly as expressed by participants. These changes cover all aspects of the order-giving process.

As many as 28 percent of the participants' supervisors answered "don't know" to items dealing with the participant and his dealings with subordinates. It is interesting to note that approximately 90 percent of the supervisors are personally involved in training their new and transferred employees (Questions *b* and *c* in Figure 16-4). Sixty percent train the workers "usually" or "always." The situation did not change as a result of the program.

Questions *d* through *i* indicate that the participant is expending more effort and time to see that the training is done more effectively. Question *a* shows that these efforts are paying off in terms of better-trained employees. According to Question *a* in Figure 16-5, approximately two-thirds of the participants conduct formal appraisals with subordinates. As a result of the institute, the greatest positive change

(text continued on page 293)

Order Giving	Much Better	Somewhat Better	No Change	Somewhat Worse	Much Worse	Don't Know
a. *Since* the program, is the participant taking more time to plan his orders?	17–23	58–60	16–12	7–0	0–0	X–5
b. *Since* the program, is the participant taking more time to prepare the order receiver?	24–17	71–57	5–19	0–0	0–0	X–7
c. *Since* the program, is the participant getting more voluntary cooperation from his employees?	26–0	37–56	37–23	0–0	0–0	X–21
d. *Since* the program, is the participant doing more in the way of making sure that the order receiver understands the order?	51–21	44–44	5–7	0–0	0–0	X–28
e. *Since* the program, is the participant taking more time to make sure that the order receiver is following instructions?	21–16	60–58	19–12	0–0	0–0	X–14
f. *Since* the program, is the participant making more of an effort to praise his employees for a job well done?	24–X	50–X	26–X	0–X	0–X	X–X
g. *Since* the program, is the participant doing more follow-ups to see that his orders were properly carried out?	37–21	39–42	23–26	0–0	0–0	X–12

Figure 16-3. *Changes in participants' order giving*

Training Employees	Yes	No	Not Sure
a. *Since* the participant attended the program, are his or her new or transferred employees better trained?	63–46	9–0	23–43
No new or transferred employees: 6–11			

Training Method	Participant Always	Participant Usually	Participant Sometimes	Participant Never
b. *Before* the program, who trained the workers?	16–13	42–45	34–31	8–11
c. *Since* the program, who trained the workers?	15–18	45–42	3–229	8–11

Progress in Training Effective	Does Not Apply	Much More	Somewhat More	No Change	Somewhat Less	Much Less	Don't Know
d. *Since* the program, if someone else trains the employees, has the participant become more observant and taken a more active interest in the training process?	14–11	22–16	40–27	24–30	0–0	0–0	X–16

Figure 16-4.

Changes in participants' involvement in training new employees

Progress in Training Effectiveness	Does Not Apply	Much More	Somewhat More	No Change	Somewhat Less	Much Less	Don't Know
e. *Since* the program, if the participant trains the employees, is he or she making more of an effort to see that the employees are well trained?	8–5	42–24	42–42	8–18	0–0	0–0	X–11
f. *Since* the program, is the participant more inclined to be patient while training?	8–11	24–5	47–50	21–20	0–3	0–3	X–11
g. *Since* the program, while teaching an operation, is the participant asking for more questions to ensure understanding?	8–21	27–14	46–46	19–8	0–0	0–0	X–11
h. *Since* the program, is the participant better prepared to teach?	8–11	29–18	47–25	16–8	0–0	0–0	X–11
i. *Since* the program, is the participant doing more follow-ups to check the trainees' progress?	0–0	41–21	38–49	21–14	0–0	0–0	X–16

Note: An X means the question was not asked.

Figure 16-4. *Cont'd*

Appraising Employee Performance

a. Is the participant required to complete appraisal forms on his subordinates?

Yes: 62–69   No: 38–31

	Does Not Apply	Large Extent	Some Extent	Little	Don't Know
b. *Before* the program, if the participant conducted appraisal interviews, to what extent did he emphasize past performance?	48–40	10–5	40–12	2–14	X–29
c. *Before* the program, to what extent did the participant try to determine the goals and objectives of his employment?	0–0	5–15	65–52	30–30	X–3
d. *Before* the program, to what extent did the participant praise the work of his employees?	0–0	8–12	77–52	15–18	X–18

Figure 16-5.

Changes in participants' appraisal of employee performance

	Does Not Apply	Much More	Somewhat More	No Change	Somewhat Less	Much Less	Don't Know
e. *Since* the program, is the participant doing more follow-ups to see that the objectives of the appraisal interview are being carried out?	48–40	10–5	24–21	14–19	2–0	0–0	X–14
f. *Since* the program, during an appraisal interview, is the participant placing more emphasis on future performance?	48–40	24–7	17–10	10–14	0–2	0–0	X–26
g. *Since* the program, is the participant making more of an effort to determine the goals and objectives of his employees?	0–0	22–15	60–50	18–18	0–0	0–0	X–18
h. *Since* the program, how much does the participant praise his or her employees?	0–0	22–10	40–38	38–38	0–2	0–0	X–12

Note: An X means the question was not asked.

Figure 16-5. *Cont'd*

occurred in the participants' efforts to determine the employees' goals and objectives. Also, the participants were praising employees more, as well as placing more emphasis on future performance.

Sixty-nine percent of the participants supervise unionized employees. Questions *b* and *c* in Figure 16-6 show very little change in terms of the participants' role in settling grievances. Question *e* shows considerable change in favor of management's viewpoint regarding grievances and complaints.

The responses to Question *f* show very little change in the number of complaints, but *g* shows some tendency for the grievances to be less serious.

Probably the most significant behavior change appears to have occurred in the participants' success in satisfying complaints before they became formal grievances (Question *h*). This was one of the major objectives of the session on "preventing and handling grievances."

Questions *a* and *b* in Figure 16-7 reveal that 88 percent of the participants were making better decisions as the participants saw it and 80 percent as the participants' supervisors saw it. According to the responses to Question *e*, 40 percent of the participants are more involved in departmental decisions than they were prior to the institute. Question *f* indicates that most of the participants are getting their subordinates more involved in the decision-making process also.

Each of the other questions on decision making also indicates that most of the participants are applying the principles and approaches that were recommended in the institute.

Questions *a* and *b* in Figure 16-8 reveal the situation prior to the program. There is a general agreement between participants and supervisors that approximately 85 percent of the participants "sometimes" or "frequently" asked subordinates for suggestions and informed them of change and the reasons for it.

Likewise, there is agreement that a large majority of the participants are doing more of the following:

1. Follow-up on change (77%–88%)

2. Asking for ideas (42%–60%)

3. Informing subordinates of changes and reasons (55%–71%)

(text continued on page 299)

Preventing and Handling Grievances

a. Do the participant's employees belong to a union? Yes: 69–69 No: 31–31

	Participant Always	Participant Usually	Participant Sometimes	Participant Never
b. *Before* the program, if an employee had a grievance, who usually settled it?	10–12	64–38	24–43	2–5
c. *Since* the program, who usually settles employee grievances?	10–12	69–48	21–38	0–2

d. *Before* the program, to what extent did the participant defend management versus the employees in regard to grievance problems?

Always defended management: 34–17
Usually defended management: 22–39
Acted objectively in view of the facts: 44–20
Usually defended the employees: 0–10
Always defended the employees: 0–0
Don't know: 0–15

Figure 16-6.
Changes in participants' handling of grievances

	Much More	Somewhat More	No Change	Somewhat Less	Much Less	No Union	Don't Know
e. *Since* the program, is the participant more inclined to the management viewpoint regarding grievances and complaints?	19–14	31–29	48–48	10–5	0–0		X–9
f. *Since* the program, has there been a change in the number of grievances in the participants' department?	2–5	7–14	81–71	2–0	0–0		X–5
g. *Since* the program, has the degree of seriousness of grievances changed?	0–0	2–2	74–74	24–12	0–7		X–5
h. *Since* the program, has the participant been better able to satisfy employee complaints before they reach the grievance stage?	17–7	31–52	26–24	0–0	0–2	26–14	

Note: An X means the question was not asked.

Figure 16-6.
Changes in participants' handling of grievances

Decision Making

a. *Since* the program, is the participant making better decisions? (Participant only)	Yes: 88		No: 2	Don't Know: 10
b. *Since* the program, is the participant making better decisions? (Supervisors only)	Much better—12 Somewhat better—68 No change—10		Somewhat worse—0 Much worse—0 Don't know—10	
	Frequently	*Sometimes*	*Hardly Ever*	*Don't Know*
c. *Before* the program, how often did the participant's boss involve or consult him or her in the decision-making process in the participant's department?	40-65	45-30	15-5	
d. *Before* the program, to what extent did the participant involve or consult employees in the decision-making process?	24-26	57-38	19-24	X-10

Figure 16–7. *Changes in participants' decision making*

Order Giving	Much More	Somewhat More	No Change	Somewhat Less	Much Less	Don't Know
e. *Since* the program, how often does the participant's boss involve him or her in the departmental decision-making process?	13–23	25–17	60–55	3–3	0–3	X–0
f. *Since* the program, how often does the participant involve employees in the decision-making process?	26–0	38–43	33–33	3–7	0–3	X–14
g. *Since* the program, does the participant have less tendency to put off making decisions?	0–0	0–0	36–33	36–40	28–22	X–5
h. *Since* the program, is the participant holding more group meetings with employees?	12–5	26–17	62–55	0–0	0–0	X–24
i. *Since* the program, does the participant have more confidence in the decisions he makes?	29–19	60–60	12–21	0–0	0–0	X–0
j. *Since* the program, is the participant using a more planned approach to decision making (more time to define the problem and develop an answer)?	40–14	50–71	10–7	0–0	0–0	X–7
k. *Since* the program, does the participant take more time to evaluate the results of a decision?	24–3	60–62	14–12	3–0	0–0	X–24

Note: An X means the question was not asked.

Figure 16–7. *Cont'd*

Initiating Change

a. *Before* the program, when the need for change arose, how often did the participant ask his or her subordinate for suggestions or ideas regarding the change or the need for change?

Frequently: 21–21
Sometimes: 64–52
Hardly ever: 14–21

b. *Before* the program, how often did the participant inform his or her employees of the change and the reason for it?

Frequently: 50–26
Sometimes: 36–55
Hardly ever: 14–14

	Much More	Somewhat More	No Change	Somewhat Less	Much Less	Don't Know
c. *Since* the program, is the participant doing more follow-ups to the change process to make sure it is going in the right direction?	38–17	50–60	12–12	0–0	0–0	X–12
d. *Since* the program, how often has the participant involved his or her subordinates by asking them for suggestions or ideas?	17–2	43–40	40–38	0–7	0–0	X–12
e. *Since* the program, is the participant doing more in the way of informing employees of impending change and the reasons for it?	33–10	38–45	29–26	0–2	0–0	X–17

Note: An X means the question was not asked.

Figure 16-8. *Changes in participants' initiation of change on the job*

All of these behavior changes were in line with the objectives of the institute.

SUMMARY

The reactions to the institute on "Developing Supervisory Skills" were highly favorable. A tabulation of reaction sheets revealed the following (figures in percentages):

Immediate Reaction to Institute by Participants

53	Excellent
47	Very good
0	Good
0	Fair
0	Poor

The purpose of the research project was to measure changes in behavior that took place on the job because of attendance at the institute. Personal interviews were held with participants, as well as with their immediate supervisors. Each participant knew that his boss was also going to be interviewed concerning changes in behavior.

Of the original 57 participants in the institutes (two sections with 28 in one section and 29 in the other), 43 pairs of data (from the participant and boss) were complete and are included in the research report.

The research data indicate that positive changes in behavior had taken place in nearly all phases of the job that were related to the subject content of the institute. These changes were revealed by participants, as well as by their supervisors. The participants tended to indicate slightly more positive changes than did their supervisors.

In addition to the positive changes in behavior, the research also indicates significant positive results in terms of the quantity and quality of production, safety, housekeeping, and morale. Some positive results were indicated in the reduction of employee absenteeism, tardiness, and turnover.

Although the results of this research cannot be directly applied to future supervisory institutes, one can conclude that this kind of institute is probably resulting in favorable on-the-job behavior of the participants. This research, in fact, bears out the numerous unsolicited comments by participants and higher-level management that positive behavior changes have taken place. The high number of repeat enrollments from participating organizations indicate the same conclusion.[1]

---

[1]**NOTE:** The previous chapter, titled "A 10-Day Certificate Program for Supervisors," contains an update of the program described here.

17

A FRONT-LINE LEADERSHIP DEVELOPMENT PROGRAM

One organization that has consistently been a leader in the training and development field is General Electric. Following is a case study describing how the Medical Systems Division of GE developed a dynamic leadership program for its supervisors and mid-managers. This program was recognized by the American Society of Training and Development in 1991 as a National Award Winner for Management Development.

GE MEDICAL SYSTEMS,
MILWAUKEE, WISCONSIN

According to Kevin Wilde, the overall leader of this training effort, the primary objective was to improve the performance of GE's supervisors—their front-line leaders—to meet the increasing demands of the new work environment. To meet these challenges, a comprehensive training and development plan was created (see Figure 17-1).

The key challenges included:

- Greater complexity in manufacturing processes and standards
- Higher emphasis on quality, cost, and cycle times
- Expanding employee involvement and empowerment

"Our work was guided by a number of key principles," Wilde said. "First, *involvement*: We were constantly looking for ways to involve people in the creation of the program. Through the use of steering committees, task forces, training, and presentation opportunities, we involved supervisors, manufacturing management, human resources, and support-staff personnel. The training was accomplished *with* the supervisors and not *at* them.

"Second, it was *strategic*: Before we began any training, we had a hard look at what we expected from supervisors and what the workplace of the future would demand. A skills model was created that served as a foundation and guide for all training and development.

"Third, it was *comprehensive*: A series of training programs were directly aimed at the supervisors over a two-year period. In addition, we worked to develop the support system around the supervisor, including a coaching workshop for their managers, a learning resource library in each plant, and a talent-upgrade effort.

"Finally, it entailed *self-responsibility*: Once the leadership model was created, we chose to use an assessment center approach to test the current supervisors' skills. Each supervisor experienced a two-day workshop where, on the first day, they were challenged by a variety of problems and situations that would show how well they would measure up to the new leadership model.

"On the second day, they received feedback on their performance and were guided through a process where they established a self-development plan. They were asked to review these plans with their manager and

Supervisors

Objective: To improve the system and processes that impact supervisory leadership performance.

⑤ **Problem-Solving Task Force**
To improve supervisors in solving system issues affecting performance, including:
- Communication processes
- Recognition and Career Advancement

④ **In-Plant Learning Library**
To establish four in-plant leadership learning libraries, including workbooks and video tape from the Finance, Performance Management, and Business Modality courses.

③ **New Supervisor Assimilation**
To provide a disciplined process for bringing new supervisors up to speed quickly on leadership and performance expectations.

② **Talent Upgrade**
To reassign or outplace poor performing supervisors not able to adjust to the new environment and replace them with promising talent better equipped for the challenges.

① **Leadership Skills Model Application (Ongoing)**
- For new supervisors selection
- For performance appraisals

Shop Manager

Objective: To improve coaching skills and role modeling.

⑤ **Leadership Effectiveness Survey**
To assess manager leadership skills through performance feedback from supervisors and peers.

④ **Leadership Instructors Certification**
To certify a select group of managers in the Zenger-Miller Frontline Leadership Program to instruct and provide positive role models.

③ **Coaching Workshop**
To improve coaching skills, including setting performance expectations, encouraging development, and recognizing positive results.

② **Coaching Clinic Assessors**
Improve coaching skills of performance assessment and feedback.

① **Leadership Skills Model Development**
For coaching baseline.

Supervisors

Objective: To improve business knowledge (how-to's) interpersonal leadership skills.

⑥ **Leadership Effectiveness Survey**
To reassess leadership skills through performance feedback from employees and peers, creating new self-development plans.

⑤ **Business Modality Understanding Course**
To improve understanding of modality marketplace, customers, business strategy, and manufacturing operation.

④ **Performance Management Course**
To improve understanding of disciplinary practices and interpersonal skills in tough one-on-one situations such as substance abuse and sexual harassment.

③ **Financial Understanding Course**
To improve understanding of business operations/measurements and grow ownership for business strategy and changes.

② **Coaching Clinic**
To assess baseline of leadership skills and areas for personal development.

① **Leadership Skills Model Guide**
To communicate new performance expectations.

Figure 17-1. *Development steps of General Electric's Front-Line Leadership Program* establish one-on-one coaching sessions to support their ongoing development. This assessment process, called the Coaching Clinic, was a great success and provided the needed positive momentum for the training that followed."

Target Audience

The target audience was divided into two groups: the *primary audience* and the *secondary audience*.

Primary audience: GE Medical Systems (GEMS) manufacturing supervisors (60), plus service supervisors (12) for some portions of the training. Overall, 58 percent held college degrees, 70 percent had more than five years of company service, and 60 percent had two or more years on the job.

This population could be classified as follows:

- **Eager learners**: Forty percent of the supervisors generally held technical degrees, had less than two years on the job, and less than five years with the company. These supervisors were eager to learn and were very supportive of the program. Their skills and aggressiveness helped motivate the other supervisors to improve.

- **Experienced skeptics**: Sixty percent of the supervisors generally did not hold four-year college degrees, and had more than 10 years with the company and five years as a supervisor. These supervisors were cautious about training and needed motivation to develop. (The assessment center was aimed primarily at these people.) They had to be involved in the development of the course work to build ownership and relevance.

Secondary audience: Twenty manufacturing and service shop managers—the managers of the supervisors. Their backgrounds were diverse, but less than half had held the position of shop supervisor. Based on the initial data gathering and analysis of the performance appraisals they gave supervisors, they were weak in setting performance expectations and coaching skills. This group needed to be involved in the design and delivery of training, as well as the training relevant to their own jobs.

Front-Line Leadership Program

The various steps in the program were listed under two categories: *Developmental Event* and *Rationale and Results*. The 11 sections consisted of the following:

Developmental Event	*Rationale and Results*
1. Initial Data Gathering	
Interviews with manufacturing managers, shop managers, key employee relations managers, and a cross-section of supervisors; and a collection and analysis of supervisor performance appraisals.	*Objective* To determine leadership expectations and the current state of leadership training. *Findings* Little leadership training for the past five years; performance expectations higher than current level of performance; appraisals were too general and did not focus on leadership behaviors.
2. Leadership Skills Model	
Shop managers created a seven-dimension leadership skills model; an all-supervisors meeting was held to gather their input and communicate the higher performance expectations.	*Objective* To create ownership and involvement and to communicate clear leadership standards. *Results* A leadership skills model was created that served as a basis for all future course work, appraisals, and new supervisor selection.
3. Finance Course	
A business course was taught covering business economic concepts, GE Company	*Objective* To build financial understanding and business

financial measurements, GEMS measurements and concepts, manufacturing measurements, and the role of the supervisor.

ownership in the supervisory ranks (a weakness indicated from Step 1 assessment interviews).

Results
A five-week, 12-hour course for all supervisors was taught by GEMS financial managers, with follow-up meetings between plant supervisors and financial analysts; many supervisors also presented their learnings to their employees.

4. Coaching Clinic

A skills assessment center was offered involving one-on-one coaching situations, group problem-solving settings, performance feedback from assessors, and a personal leadership development plan.

Objectives
To motivate supervisors to increase their leadership skills through intensive feedback and a specific developmental action plan; to identify the collective training needs of the supervisors, per the leadership skills model; and to increase the coaching skills of shop managers.

Results
Seventy-one supervisors participated in eight coaching clinics. They received performance feedback from the assessors (shop managers) and created personal development plans. Further, the supervisors shared their plans with their managers and agreed to action items. Prior to

the clinics, 20 shop managers received eight hours of training in performance judgment and constructive feedback (the skills of coaching). The overall results of the clinic indicated that supervisors needed the most help in group leadership situations and in presentation skills.

5. Coaching Skills Training

A coaching skills course was taught concerning recognizing positive results, giving constructive feedback, and helping others learn.

Objective
To increase the coaching skills of shop managers and to ensure that the training of supervisors is supported.

Results
Two eight-hour workshops were held for a total of 20 shop managers.

6. Leadership Instructor Certification

A four-day instructor certification program was held for the front-line leadership program.

Objective
To develop the internal capacity to teach and model superior leadership skills.

Results
A select group of 12 shop managers, supervisors, and human resources managers were certified and taught leadership modules throughout the program. In fact, the group also taught leadership skills to lead technicians and hourly group leaders.

7. Performance Management Course

A leadership skills course was taught covering performance expectation setting, constructive feedback, recognizing positive results, GE work rules and practices, appraisals and coaching, the employee assistance program (EAP), substance abuse, and sexual harassment.

Objective

To increase supervisory skills in handling the most difficult one-on-one situations and to provide resources to support confrontations with low performers.

Results

Seventy-two supervisors participated in the nine-week, 36-hour program. A follow-up survey of supervisors and their managers reported that all supervisors cited personal growth in the nine key performance objectives (their managers concurred); and 70 specific situations were cited where course material was immediately applied— including EAP referrals, constructive feedback, and positive recognition.

8. Business/Modality Course

A modality-specific course, was taught covering product and market strategy, GE's modality organization and business plan, manufacturing operation today, and manufacturing values and vision.

Objectives

To increase supervisory knowledge and ownership of the business, the realities of competition, and the rationale behind business changes; and to encourage the continued transition of the supervisory role from foreman to coach by having the participants teach the material to their employees.

Results

Sixty-two supervisors participated in business courses for their modality. The courses ran an average of four sessions and 16 hours. Strong personal improvement was cited in each of the five key course objectives, with over 70 percent of the supervisors teaching the material to their employees.

9. Leadership Talent Upgrade

An ongoing effort to upgrade the supervisory talent pool, staffing the organization with new technical supervisors who had promising leadership skills.

Objective

To replace low-performing supervisors with talented new supervisors who were more able to meet leadership challenges.

Results

Higher performance standards were instituted based on the leadership skills model and potential actions tracked through the manpower review process.

10. New Supervisor Assimilation

A series of leadership tools were established to improve supervisory performance, including an assimilation process, performance management training, and an in-plant learning library.

Objective

To bring new supervisors quickly up to speed in critical leadership and performance areas; and to provide senior supervisors new growth opportunities.

Results

A detailed new supervisor training package was established covering 33 learning areas, such as safety procedures, key disciplinary practices, and performance recognition. The program was overseen by the immediate manager, and a senior supervisor provided a mentoring role. An in-plant learning library was established for new and current supervisors. Workbooks and videos were stocked for such programs as the Performance Management course, the Finance course, and the Modality/Business course.

11. Leadership Effectiveness Survey

A leadership survey was given to employees and peers of GEMS manufacturing supervisors.

Objective

To provide a new level of performance feedback to supervisors that will serve as a basis for a new personal development plan and an indication of collective training needs.

Results

The survey results showed significant improvement in a number of areas, including leadership, communication, and teamwork.

Follow-Up Procedures

Throughout the Front-Line Leadership Program, a variety of feedback tools were used to assess progress and identify needed follow-up actions. Follow-up procedures included:

1. **Participant feedback survey at the end of each course**—The survey asked supervisors to rate their skill and knowledge against specific course objectives before and after the course.

2. **Application situations**—Participants were asked to cite specific cases where they applied course material on the job. The reports from the Performance Management and the Business/Modality courses report numerous examples of applications.

3. **Shop manager feedback**—Surveys completed six weeks after the Performance Management course were used to verify the gains reported by the supervisors and the situation applications.

4. **Leadership effectiveness surveys**—These surveys indicated that the supervisors received positive reviews from their employees and peers. Specifically, the collective results reported scores of 80 percent or more on the following dimensions:

- Organizational relationships
- Decision making
- Concern for customers
- Communication
- Personal accountability
- Employee empowerment

5. **Periodic interviews, phone calls, and opinion surveys**—These were used to judge supervisory reaction to program activities.

Results

"As the program unfolded, we tried to capture supervisory performance data to determine whether we were meeting our objectives and any mid-course corrections necessary," Wilde said. "Assessing bottom-line impact of leadership development and training as an isolated variable is difficult. For example, during the last 12 months, employee unpaid absenteeism has been reduced from 3.2 percent to 2.7 percent—a 15 percent improvement, saving $220,000 in labor costs.

"One could attribute the improvement to the training supervisors received through the Coaching Clinic and the Performance Management class. The decrease, however, could also stem from a drop in product volume and overtime from one major plant. In another example, productivity in one of the plants increased from 60 percent to 82 percent. It is hard to separate the impact of improved leadership skills from productivity gains due to new products, procedures, and volume gains."

A more useful view of the results from the Front-Line Leadership Program is to look for impact indicators:

Finance Course. Over 75 percent of the supervisors cited significant knowledge gains in the following key concepts: Return on Investment (ROI), income statements and balance sheets, GE's growth strategy, GE Medical Systems productivity programs, and globalization programs.

Coaching Clinic. Over 95 percent of the supervisors voluntarily met with their managers after the clinic and created a leadership development plan. Eighty-six percent of the participants reported that the Coaching Clinic exercises enabled them to demonstrate their leadership skills and received useful feedback.

Performance Management Course. Supervisors reported a 39-percent gain in skill and knowledge in the nine key learning objectives. A separate survey of their managers concurred, citing a collective 49-percent skill and knowledge gain. Furthermore, the documented application of course material on the job included constructive feedback (16 cases), the setting of performance expectations (16), the recognition of positive employee results (15), and employee assistance program referrals (12).

Business Product Understanding Course. Supervisors reported a 42-percent gain in skill and knowledge in the 10 key learning objectives.

Overall program survey. All supervisors were asked to reflect on their growth and learning over the past year. They attributed the largest portion of their skill increase to the Performance Management Course, followed respectively by the Business and Product Understanding Course, the Coaching Clinic, and manager coaching.

"GE Medical Systems has led an intensive campaign to increase the leadership performance of its front-line supervisors," Wilde observed.

"While we have been happy with the progress so far, making a significant, sustaining improvement in an organization's leadership capability is not achieved overnight. In the long run, real success will entail multiple efforts over a sustained period of time to upgrade the overall performance of a leadership team. We are pleased with our results so far, but we need to continue and do more."

18

A LEADERSHIP DEVELOPMENT PROGRAM

A leadership development program was planned and implemented at First Indiana Bank in Indianapolis according to Dr. James Kirkpatrick, the bank's organizational effectiveness manager.

314

First Indiana Bank,
Indianapolis, Indiana

Background and Development

Cruise to Leadership, a leadership development program at First Indiana Bank, was initiated by the Chairman of the Board and the President in 1997. They were motivated by the realization that too many associates (as they call their employees) were being thrust into leadership positions without proper training. They appointed a team of internal leaders to meet with an outside consulting firm, Excelleration, Inc., to design the training program.

It was decided that leaders from the bank would be the actual facilitators of the course. The Total Quality Council of First Indiana Bank then studied the executive proposal and began to put a plan of action into motion. Specific needs were determined by a focus group led by Excelleration, Inc., made up of senior and middle-level First Indiana managers and supervisors.

While the content and delivery of Cruise to Leadership is state of the art, several foundational elements make Cruise to Leadership truly unique. This case study will focus on those elements and encourage readers to insert your own content. The first of these is its cornerstone, which is a 360-degree feedback instrument, the Leadership Effectiveness Analysis (LEA), published by Management Research Group.

Cruise to Leadership is made up of seven four-hour modules, all of which specifically address the needs of present and future First Indiana leaders. Elements of these modules correspond with targeted behaviors from the LEA, thus allowing for a research-based approach, and one whereby leadership progress can be tracked through annual LEA scores.

Secondly, a 35-question Leadership Evaluation Survey was developed by the Cruise to Leadership team. It is presented in this chapter, along with a pre- and post-assessment instrument to put into practice. This smaller survey should also be completed by the participant and by his or her direct reports. Cruise to Leadership participants are provided with a summary report in a simple format (showing both pre- and post-assessments) and meet with one or more of the Cruise to Leadership facilitators to review their results and plan action steps to improve their leadership practices.

Two additional components have contributed to the success of Cruise to Leadership. Research strongly suggests that participant involvement in course material increases understanding and use. Therefore, after each module, participants are given work time to complete "work-work" (contrasted with "homework"), which allows further personalized interaction with the material.

The "work-work" section of the course material is a specific project tied to the content of each module. Assignments are then reviewed at the beginning of the following session. This is not just a simple check on assignments, but rather a full debriefing of the participant's experience with new behaviors. It is a key expectation of the program that new behaviors are practiced and insights discussed.

Initially, participants are surprised how much attention is paid to these assignments until they understand that much of the key learning depends not only on what happens in class, but how it is applied to the actual work environment. Facilitators track each module's assignments and follow up with participants to ensure successful completion.

Finally, participants are encouraged to work with a coach or mentor, who is a past graduate of the course, in between modules. During this time, they review and discuss information they learned, and discuss relevant real-life scenarios that present opportunities to use new behaviors and procedures on the job.

By regular dialogue with a coach, participants can assess how new behaviors are working with an experienced guide, and also plan appropriate opportunities to utilize their insights from the course. The coach provides an ongoing sounding board for overall development support, and to take the initiative to try new leadership behaviors.

The actual name of the course, Cruise to Leadership, was chosen to represent the "voyage" the participants would take in order to develop effective lead management skills. Props, examples, and metaphors focus on this theme. Those who attend Cruise to Leadership are supervisors and managers below the level of department head. In addition, potential supervisors are also encouraged to take the course. Class size is limited to 15 participants, due to the participative style of the course.

Developers and User

- **Excelleration, Inc.**—Jeanne Farah, Managing Consultant; John Kirby, Senior Consultant, Indianapolis, Indiana

- **First Indiana Bank**—John Galloway, Manager of Training and Development; Jim Kirkpatrick, Organizational Effectiveness Manager

Program Objective

For supervisors and managers to understand and use effective lead management skills.

Materials

- Extensive facilitator's and participant's handbooks
- Leadership Effectiveness Analysis, Management Research Group, Portland, Maine
- Pre- and Post-Leadership Evaluation, an in-house assessment instrument

Techniques and Aids

1. Self-assessments
2. Lecturettes
3. Quotes and cartoons
4. Videos—some informational and some dramatic
5. Small-group activities
6. Guest speakers
7. One-on-one practice of techniques
8. Interactive large-group activities
9. Weekly lab assignments (work-work)
10. Suggested readings

Evaluation

1. Reaction sheets were used regularly in the project to evaluate content and facilitators.
2. A "Final Evaluation Form" was completed by all participants.
3. Behavioral changes are being measured by:

  a. Participants and their direct reports completing a 35-item Leadership Evaluation survey prior to the course (pre-test).

  b. Repeating the process six months after the course is completed (post-test).

  c. Annual completion of the Leadership Effectiveness Analysis.

Shipboard Rules for Smooth Sailing

The following points should be discussed during the module:

- Come to sessions and be prepared to participate.
- Complete your "work-work" so we can move forward.
- You are accountable for behavior changes.
- Concentrate on things you can change.
- Be "selfish"—have personal goals for each session.
- Look for the slight edge in each skill set.
- The information shared within the group stays within the group.

Course Overview

FIRST INDIANA BANK: Supervising Associates Who Own Their Processes

Overview

SESSION I: The Shift from Boss to Lead Style at First Indiana. As part of its Total Quality Initiative, First Indiana Bank began to consciously use the *lead* rather than *boss* style in 1995. The lead style of working with people and processes is participatory and promotes ownership and accountability among all associates. These concepts are the essential foundation for the supervisory series. This session enables all supervisors to understand what is expected of a lead-style supervisor so they can positively contribute to achieving a Total Quality workplace.

SESSION II: The Supervisor's Role in On-the-Job Learning. To make continuous improvement a reality, all bank associates must be given the opportunity for continuous learning. In this lab session, supervisors learn how to create associate Learning Kits. They become familiar with the principles of adult learning and experience techniques such as giving clear instructions, modeling, self-study debriefing, and coaching with performance feedback.

SESSION III: Using Recognition and Rewards to Sustain High Performance. While learning and problem-solving puts associates on the pathway to continuous improvement, their supervisors must recognize and reward exemplary performance. In this lab session, supervisors identify opportunities for exceptional performance within their lab processes and determine how to set and measure the bar for achievement, how to challenge associates, and how to use public and private rewards and recognition.

SESSION IV: The Resolution of Problems, Complaints, and Conflicts. In a Total Quality work plan, it is essential that supervisors not only use the control data to spot problems, but that they are also openly responsive when hearing the issues of associates and customers. In this lab session, supervisors practice communication techniques which enable them to separate well-founded problems from complaints and to respond to conflicts at both rational and emotional levels.

SESSION V: Positive Discipline for a Healthy Workplace. The majority of associates do achieve success when supervisors have demonstrated the lead style by providing on-the-job learning, facilitating solutions and resolutions, and by recognizing excellence. There will, however, always be situations in which individual associates need to experience the consequences of not taking ownership for the process assigned to them. In this simulated session, supervisors practice techniques to candidly confront associates and to reach agreement on immediate action steps for change. They also become familiar with the bank's human resources policy and staff who will support them when bold action is needed to maintain a productive workplace.

SESSION VI: Staffing, Scheduling, and Gatekeeping to Meet Demands. One of the major challenges to the bank as an organization is to use its human resources to the fullest with no waste, and also no burnout. All supervisors have a role in maintaining capacity utilization. In this lab session, supervisors experiment with multiple staffing and scheduling models to achieve maximum effectiveness and to experience the gatekeeper role in responding to shifting volumes. They use their process control data to determine when a staffing problem triggers the need to "unlock" for process redesign.

SESSION VII: Making a Commitment to Conscious Collegiality. While it may be "lonely at the top," it does not have to be lonely in the middle. Supervisors should not depend on their direct reports or their customers for professional support, and often their managers are removed from day-to-day issues due to their wide span of control and their project assignments. This session enables supervisors to make commitments with one another for ongoing collegial support beyond this series. They experience this using the Situation, Target, Action, and Results (STAR) method.

Boss vs. Lead Style of Management

Boss Style	*Lead Style*
1. The Boss sets the task and the standards for what the associates are to do. Bosses do not compromise; the associate has to adjust to the job as the Boss defines it or suffer any consequences the Boss determines.	1. The Lead Supervisor engages the associates in an ongoing, honest discussion of both the cost and the quality of work that is needed to meet customer expectations. They not only listen, but also encourage their associates to give input that improves quality and lowers costs.
2. The Boss usually *tells*, rather than *shows* how the work is to be done and rarely asks for the associates' input as to how it might possibly be done better	2. The Lead Supervisor shows or models the job so that the associate who is to do the job can see exactly what the supervisor expects. The Lead Supervisor works to increase the associate's sense of control over the work they do.
3. The Boss, or someone the Boss designates, inspects the work. Because the Boss does not involve the associates in the evaluation, they may do only enough to get by; they rarely even think of doing what is required by customers.	3. The Lead Supervisor eliminates most inspectors. He or she teaches associates to evaluate their own work for quality using previously established customer standards.

4. The Boss provides feedback to the associates based on his/her perception, feedback from others, complaints, and problems that arise in the course of business. Generally, the feedback is triggered by external events or the employee performance review.

4. The Lead Supervisor continually coaches the associates that by explaining the essence of quality, constant improvement will take place. To help them, he or she makes it clear that the supervisor's main job is as a facilitator, which means doing what is necessary to provide them with the best tools and a nonadversarial atmosphere in which they are paid in accordance with performance.

BOSS STYLE		*LEAD STYLE*
From:		*To:*
Directing	→	Interacting
Telling	→	Showing
Overseeing	→	Self-Monitoring
One-Way Feedback	→	Two-Way Feedback
Level Pay Increments	→	Pay for Performance

BEFORE THE NEXT LAB

The following is an example of "work-work":

- Meet with your "sounding board" to discuss the reasons for First Indiana's commitment to Total Quality. Include a brief discussion of the role of customer standards, data-based decision making, and teamwork at First Indiana Bank.

- Have associates complete the *Influencing Others Assessment for Observers*. Make a summary report and copy it.

- Complete *Influencing Others, My Personal Action Plan*.

- Select a process or task in your area that would improve if associates had more knowledge or skills. Write it on a 3 x 5 card and bring it to Lab 2.

CRUISE TO LEADERSHIP EVALUATION FORM

The following is an example of a weekly evaluation:

Series Number: _____   Date: _____

Session: _____   Training Location: _____

Overall:

1. Did this session meet your expectations?   ☐ Yes   ☐ No
If no, why not?

_____

_____

_____

Instruction/Facilitation:

Please give your frank and honest reactions. Insert the appropriate number. **For any score of 3 or less, please provide feedback as to why and specific recommendations for how to improve.** Thank you.

5=Excellent   4 = Very good   3 = Good   2 = Fair   1 = Poor
NA = Not applicable

Facilitator	Knowledge of subject	Presentation skills: Clarity of presentation	Facilitation skills: Guiding group interaction and learning	Pace
_____	_____	_____	_____	_____

Feel free to write any additional comments below or on the back. Thank you for taking time to give constructive feedback on this course. Your responses will be used to improve future courses.

_____

_____

_____

_____

_____

CRUISE TO LEADERSHIP FINAL EVALUATION FORM

Series Number: _____

Date: _____

Training Location: _____

Participant Information:

Please check the appropriate box. I am a:

☐ Banking Center Manager or Assistant Manager

☐ Other

How many associates do you supervise? _____

How long have you been a supervisor? _____ (Please include the number of years you have been a supervisor at First Indiana Bank and those years before you were employed by First Indiana.)

Overall:

1. What value was the overall series?

_____

_____

_____

2. What did you gain overall as a leader?

_____

_____

_____

3. Did the course meet your expectations?   ☐ Yes   ☐ No
   If no, why not?

_____

_____

_____

Class Content:

1. Circle which session was *least* useful or effective. 1 2 3 4 5 6 7
Why?

_____

_____

_____

2. Circle which session was *most* useful or effective. 1 2 3 4 5 6 7
Why?

_____

_____

_____

3. What specific content would you *add* to Cruise to Leadership?

_____

_____

_____

4. What specific content would you *delete* from Cruise to Leadership?

_____

_____

_____

5. Where (specifically) should we spend less time?

_____

_____

_____

6. More class time should be spent on what topics?

_____

_____

_____

For the next seven statements, please use the following scale:

5 = Strongly agree
4 = Agree somewhat
3 = Neutral
2 = Disagree somewhat
1 = Disagree strongly
NA = Not applicable

Because of the Cruise to Leadership class, I...

1. Understand and practice lead management.	5 4 3 2 1 NA
2. Can develop learning kits for my unit.	5 4 3 2 1 NA
3. Can define and identify when to use feedback, praise, redirection, and positive reinforcement.	5 4 3 2 1 NA
4. Can better draw out and respond to conflicts and complaints from associates.	5 4 3 2 1 NA
5. Can use positive discipline to influence associates to take ownership for their performance.	5 4 3 2 1 NA
6. Am able to play the roles of matchmaker, gatekeeper, and work designer to target capacity concerns, analyze situations, and identify what resources need to be adjusted or added.	5 4 3 2 1 NA
7. Am able to use the STAR method to coach my peers.	5 4 3 2 1 NA

Learning Activities Between Sessions:

To evaluate the following learning activities, when you respond to the statement "The value to me was," please insert the appropriate number as follows:

5 = Excellent   4 = Very good   3 = Good   2 = Fair   1 = Poor

Did you do the learning activity?	The value to me was:	Assignments:
☐ Yes ☐ No	_____	1. Meet with your "sounding board" to discuss the reasons for First Indiana's commitment to Total Quality.

☐ Yes ☐ No   _____   2. Have associates complete the "Influencing Others Assessment for Observers."

☐ Yes ☐ No   _____   3. Complete the "Influencing Others, My Personal Action Plan."

☐ Yes ☐ No   _____   4. Create a learning kit.

☐ Yes ☐ No   _____   5. Mark down every day the amount of time you invest in coaching your staff.

☐ Yes ☐ No   _____   6. Tally up how many times you use the four coaching tools in a week—both at work and at home.

☐ Yes ☐ No   _____   7. Read the article "25 Do's and Don'ts Every New Supervisor Should Know."

☐ Yes ☐ No   _____   8. Count how many complaints or problems are brought to you each day.

☐ Yes ☐ No   _____   9. Read the "Supervisor's Troubleshooting Guide for Dealing with Associate Complaints."

☐ Yes ☐ No   _____ 10. Read the articles "Managing Baby Boomers" and "Figuring Out Generation X."

☐ Yes ☐ No   _____ 11. Read the articles "Discipline Without Punishment—at Last," "Common Causes for Disciplinary Actions," and the "Supervisor's Troubleshooting Guide for Using Positive Discipline."

☐ Yes ☐ No   _____ 12. Read the "Supervisor's Troubleshooting Guide for Using Positive Discipline."

☐ Yes ☐ No   _____ 13. Apply the "Checklist for Taking Disciplinary Action" to the sample warning.

☐ Yes   ☐ No   _____ 14. Review the "Termination
                                Checklist."

☐ Yes   ☐ No   _____ 15. Complete the Self-Assessment
                                using the last discipline action
                                you supervised as your case study.

☐ Yes   ☐ No   _____ 16. Read the articles "Developing
                                Skilled and Flexible People,"
                                "Cross-Training Programs—Help
                                Employees Retool and Learn
                                New Systems," and "Cross-
                                Training: A Matter of
                                Commitment."

☐ Yes   ☐ No   _____ 17. Review the "Overtime
                                Regulations."

☐ Yes   ☐ No   _____ 18. Select one process or job that
                                needs a capacity study, name it on
                                a file card, and explain the trigger
                                for the study.

If you did not do some of the learning activities, why not?

_____

_____

_____

Please comment on how you felt about the learning activities.

_____

_____

_____

Schedule:

How do you feel about the schedule?

Four hours in length: ☐ Just right   ☐ Too long   ☐ Too short
One class per week: ☐ Just right   ☐ Too many   ☐ Too few
Morning classes: ☐ Okay   ☐ Prefer afternoon classes
Start time: ☐ Just right   ☐ Too early   ☐ Too late
Seven sessions: ☐ Just right   ☐ Too many   ☐ Too few

Other comments about scheduling:

_____

_____

_____

Instruction/Facilitation:

Please give your frank and honest reactions. Insert the appropriate number.

5 = Excellent   4 = Very good   3 = Good   2 = Fair   1 = Poor
NA = Not applicable

Facilitator	Knowledge of subject	Presentation skills: Clarity of presentation	Facilitation skills: Guiding group interaction and learning	Pace
_____	_____	_____	_____	_____
_____	_____	_____	_____	_____
_____	_____	_____	_____	_____
_____	_____	_____	_____	_____
_____	_____	_____	_____	_____

Module 7 Lunch:

Insert the appropriate number:

5 = Excellent   4 = Very good   3 = Good   2 = Fair   1 = Poor

Quality	Quantity	Hot/Cold	Presentation
_____	_____	_____	_____

Additional comments:

_____

_____

_____

Whom do you recommend we invite to future Cruise to Leadership classes?

_____

_____

_____

Feel free to write any additional comments on the back. Thank you for taking time to give constructive feedback on this course. Your responses will be used to improve future courses.

Pre- and Post-Leadership Evaluation

☐ Self   ☐ Direct Report

Please check "Self" if you are the leader and "Direct Report" if you work for the leader.

Leader's Name _____ Date _____

Department _____

This evaluation will be used to determine if the Cruise to Leadership supervision training series is influencing positive behavior changes in leadership. Your participation will remain confidential because your individual responses will not be shared with your leader. Therefore, please be totally candid with your answers.

Please circle the appropriate response after reading each statement:

3 = My supervisor regularly demonstrates this behavior.
2 = My supervisor sometimes demonstrates this behavior.
1 = My supervisor rarely demonstrates this behavior.
0 = My supervisor does not practice this type of leadership behavior.

Quality

3 2 1 0   1. My leader confirms that I meet customer standards for each process, project, or product I produce.

3 2 1 0   2. My leader teaches me how to measure my own work.

3 2 1 0   3. My leader collects relevant data from our team.

3 2 1 0   4. My leader uses our work data to complete my performance evaluations.

3 2 1 0   5. We are making continuous improvement in my area by revising our processes and systems.

On-the-Job Learning and Coaching

3 2 1 0   6. My leader correctly identifies any gaps that I may have in knowledge or skills that block effective performance of my job.

3 2 1 0   7. My leader makes sure that I know how things should be done.

3 2 1 0   8. My leader makes himself/herself available for training and for questions from me about how to do things better.

3 2 1 0   9. My leader arranges for me to get the new skills and training that I need.

3 2 1 0   10. My leader follows up with me after I attend training classes to be sure that I have applied what was instructed.

Using Feedback, Redirection, Praise, and Positive Reinforcement

3 2 1 0   11. My leader gives me feedback that clearly helps me understand what went right or wrong.

3 2 1 0   12. My leader encourages me to offer feedback, insights, and comments to make positive changes.

3 2 1 0   13. When my leader needs to correct situations, he or she redirects my behavior with a focus toward future outcomes rather than focusing on blame.

3 2 1 0   14. When my leader comments on a job well done, she or he gives specific examples of what was done well.

3 2 1 0   15. My leader creates a positive environment that motivates us to work as a team.

Handling Complaints

3 2 1 0   16. My leader encourages me to share my complaints, business problems, and conflicts with him or her.

3 2 1 0   17. My leader gets an agreement on the root cause of the complaint or problem.

3 2 1 0   18. My leader encourages me to analyze information and solve problems on my own.

3 2 1 0   19. My leader asks me for suggested solutions to problems and complaints.

3 2 1 0   20. After investigating, my leader makes an action plan to solve complaints or problems.

Positive Discipline

3 2 1 0   21. My leader steps up to performance problems early, before they become discipline problems.

3 2 1 0   22. My leader encourages candor and complaints.

3 2 1 0   23. My leader gives serious attention to both the complaint and its resolution.

3 2 1 0   24. In discipline situations, my leader focuses on the behavior and does not make it personal.

3 2 1 0   25. My leader models proper work performance, ethics, and professional behavior.

Capacity Planning

3 2 1 0   26. My leader has analyzed the work load within his or her area of responsibility.

3 2 1 0   27. My leader helps me balance my work load.

3 2 1 0   28. My leader designs effective work patterns to make work flow quickly.

3 2 1 0   29. My leader looks for duties, reports, or tasks that can be eliminated to gain capacity for newer responsibilities.

3 2 1 0   30. My leader is effective at getting the resources and equipment needed to maximize the department's productivity.

Environment

3 2 1 0   31. My leader creates an environment that fosters teamwork.

3 2 1 0   32. My leader makes difficult decisions when he or she has to.

3 2 1 0   33. My leader is well respected in our department.

3 2 1 0   34. I feel supported and respected by my leader.

3 2 1 0   35. There is an atmosphere of trust in the area in which I work.

19

AN INTERNAL
TRAINING
PROGRAM

One of the most popular courses in the 1990s was, and will continue to be, Managing Change. Professional trainers in more and more organizations realize that supervisors need training in how to make decisions and get them accepted and implemented by their subordinates. The following case study describes the approach used by Dana Corporation, a manufacturer of various parts for the automobile industry.

DANA CORPORATION, TOLEDO, OHIO

Following is an abbreviated lesson plan provided by Larry Lottier, the dean of Dana University's Business School, of their approach to training their supervisors on how to manage change:

1. Lecturette: Do people resist change? A poll of the group results in a usual overwhelming "yes." Then we develop the concept that people do resist *some* changes, but, more important (especially for supervisors and managers to realize), people resist *being* changed.

2. The "valley of despair" concept:

   a. Begins with the status quo.

   b. Shows a dip of performance into a "valley" when changes are planned such as new people, tools, processes, materials, etc.

   c. Shows an improvement in performance when the new things become more familiar and are accepted.

3. Discuss the following five steps to successful behavior change:

   a. Desire

   b. Knowledge

   c. Visualization

   d. Planning

   e. Action

4. Discuss William James' following suggestions for getting people to change their habits:

   a. Launch a new behavior as strongly as possible. First, you must define exactly what that behavior is to be. Then think of ways to practice the new behavior with gusto. Public announcement is a good technique.

   b. Seize the first opportunity to act on the new behavior. Remember, your new actions will not be comfortable, so you will have to be extremely conscious of what you are doing.

   c. Never let an exception occur until the new behavior is firmly rooted. Once you make an exception, your resolve is broken, and it is more difficult to begin again.

5. Discuss and list on flipcharts the changes each person is going to make back on the job.

   a. Focus on changes in you

   b. Focus on changes in your department to improve the work situation

   c. Be specific and write changes in the present tense beginning with "I now . . . "

6. Have each team present its flipchart report.

7. Each individual completes the form called "A Contract With Myself," which contains the following sentence fragments to finish:

   a. "What I learned in the workshop was . . . "

   b. "Goals I plan to achieve as a result of what I learned are . . . "

   c. "The evidence I have accomplished these goals will be . . . "
   The name and address are written on the bottom of the form. One copy of the completed form is kept by the supervisor and one copy is given to the class instructor.

Several handouts are given to the supervisor for future study. One of them contains the following suggestions from Gordon Lippitt on how to turn resistance into acceptance:[1]

Involve employees in planning the change. Resistance to change will be less intense when those to be affected, or those who believe they might be affected, know why a change is being made and what the advantages are. This can be done effectively by letting them participate in the actual planning. Besides helping them to understand the when, what, where, and why of a change, participation eases any fears that management is hiding something from them.

In addition, participation can stimulate many good ideas from those who probably are best acquainted with the problem that necessitates the change. It also alerts a supervisor to potential problems that might arise when the change is implemented.

Provide accurate and complete information. When workers are kept in the dark or get incomplete information, alarms and rumors start to circulate. This creates an atmosphere of mistrust. Even when the news

---

[1]Gordon Lippitt, *The Change Resistors* (Englewood Cliffs, N.J.: Prentice-Hall, 1981).

is bad, employees would rather get it straight and fast than receive no news at all. A lack of information makes them feel helpless, while the whole story—even if it's unpleasant—lets them know where they stand.

Give employees a chance to air their objections. Change is more easily assimilated when a supervisor provides an opportunity for employees to blow off steam. A gripe session also gives supervisors useful feedback that may reveal unsuspected reasons for opposition. For example, a man may balk at using another machine only because he will have to move away from a window.

Always take group norms and habits into account. When change is contemplated, a supervisor should ask himself if it will:

- Break up congenial work groups.
- Disrupt commuting schedules or car pools.
- Split up long-standing luncheon partners.
- Unfavorably affect anticipated vacations, priorities, and preferences.
- Require temperamentally incompatible employees to work together.

Make only essential changes. Most employees can tolerate only so much change. When they are confronted with any trivial or unnecessary changes, their reaction will be irritation and resentment. Even more important, they will be less receptive to major changes.

Learn to use problem-solving techniques. Research in behavioral science furnishes some useful guidelines in solving problems that arise from implementing change. First, identify the real problem. A supervisor may think, "If I could only get Mary to retire, the morale of the group would improve." Deep-seated problems, however, are rarely caused by a single individual in a group. Second, be aware of timing. It is much easier to influence people favorably toward data processing equipment before it's installed than afterward. Third, help people solve problems to their own satisfaction. They will react negatively to such advice as, " You shouldn't take that attitude," or attempts at persuasion like, "I'm sure that when you have all the facts, you'll see it my way."

Adjusting to change is difficult enough under the best of conditions. The supervisor can make it far easier for his subordinates—and for himself—by taking positive steps to forestall potential resistance.

The supervisors are encouraged to discuss with their bosses the program and the contract they have completed. In addition, the instructor sends a follow-up letter about four weeks after the program. The letter reminds them of the program and the form they completed, asks for feedback on what they have done, and encourages continued application of what they learned. Additional reading related to the program and a follow-up survey is enclosed with the letter. (See Figures 19-1 and 19-2 for samples.)

WOULD YOU TELL US...

Now that you have been "back on the job" for a month or so, we'd like some information from you. OK? Thanks.

You recently completed "How to Develop Your Personal Strengths for Effective Managing" at Dana University. We'd like to know if you learned and benefitted as a result of the four days you invested and how you're applying what you learned. With that in mind, please respond to the following questions:

1. Since you graduated, have you been involved in a listening situation in which you used your Stop, Think and Listen skills?

        _____ Yes   _____ No

If "Yes," would you briefly describe the situation:

_____

_____

_____

_____

2. Have you been involved in a situation where you were able to set a "motivational climate" for your people to motivate themselves?

        _____ Yes   _____ No

Describe briefly:

_____

_____

_____

_____

Figure 19-1. *Follow-up Sample No. 1*

3. Have you had the opportunity to put into practice your knowledge of understanding yourself and others (the Personal Profile and Values Profile)?

Describe the outcome:

_____

_____

_____

_____

4. Have you been involved in a situation where you were able to communicate the "Dana Style of Management" to help your people understand our company and its values and philosophies?

_____ Yes   _____ No

Please describe:

_____

_____

_____

_____

5. What have you done for yourself in terms of self-development since your return?

_____

_____

_____

_____

Thanks for taking the time to help us.

Please return this form to Dean, Business School, Dana University, Toledo.

Figure 19-1. *Cont'd*

COURSE EFFECTIVENESS SURVEY
30-Day Follow-up

Course: _____

Date: _____

Now that you have been back on the job for a while after participation in a Dana University Course, could you take a few minutes and answer these questions for us?

1. How applicable was the course material for you in improving your job performance? (Circle one.)

1	2	3	4
Not Very	Somewhat	Useful	Very Useful

Comments:

_____

_____

2. The tools and ideas that I received in the course have allowed me to improve my quality and productivity on the job.

1	2	3	4
Not Very	Somewhat	Useful	Very Useful

Comments:

_____

_____

3. To what extent have you used the materials/knowledge learned in the course?

1	2	3	4
Not Very	Somewhat	Useful	Very Useful

Comments:

_____

_____

Figure 19-2. *Follow-up Sample No. 2*

4. How confident are you in using the skills learned in the program?

1	2	3	4
Not Very	Somewhat	Useful	Very Useful

Comments:

_____

_____

5. The one thing I remember most about this course is...

Name _____ Location _____

Please return by FAX to:
DANANET 8-555-0000
or
(419) 555-000

Figure 19-2. *Cont'd*

20

A PROGRAM ON EFFECTIVE WRITING

Crucial for the office supervisor and middle-level manager today is the ability to write effective business letters, memos, and informal reports. Crucial, yes, but rarely do management education programs provide writing instructions that get results. Courses typically place too much emphasis on principles of writing rather than on practice. They spend too little time reviewing and criticizing correspondence and discussing broad principles, instead of building specific writing skills needed by the organization. One program that has broken this mold was developed for Warman International, a manufacturer of slurry pumps for the mining and utility industries.

WARMAN INTERNATIONAL, INC., MADISON, WISCONSIN

Warman International, Inc., a small but growing manufacturer, produces slurry pumps for the mining and utility industries—pumps that are referred to as the "Cadillacs" of the field. Young, growing, and confident of their ability to produce a high-quality product, Warman's managers wanted their business letters and memoranda to reflect their professionalism and get better results. Their technical sales engineers, project engineers, technical sales assistants, and administrative assistants were competent professionals. The quality of their correspondence, however, was unsatisfactory. They were especially in need of learning how to:

- Plan correspondence with a stronger results orientation.
- Create a more positive tone in their writing.
- Develop a deeper and broader understanding of the needs of their audiences and techniques of addressing those needs.
- Create technical but clear and readable work.
- Write more persuasive sales letters.

To meet these needs, the following program was developed and implemented by Buck Joseph, an associate professor of management for the University of Wisconsin's School of Business.

Program Planning

To assess writing needs, several techniques were used:

1. Interviews were conducted with the personnel manager and utility sales supervisor to learn their perceptions of the current writing strengths and weaknesses of the target clientele group.
2. Three unedited samples of correspondence from each program participant were analyzed.
3. A discussion was held with administrative assistants, middle-level managers, and the general manager to determine the desired results from the writing program.

Armed with this information—an inventory of the existing situation and what Warman wanted—I created a course.

Writing Effective Business Letters and Memos

Session 1

1. Orientation
   - Climate setting
   - Program goals, methods, focus

2. Planning for Results
   - Understanding the importance of clarity of purpose in written communication
   - Clarifying the results we wish to accomplish through the communication
   - Understanding audience needs

Session 2

Organizing for Impact

- Keys to structure: purpose statements, lead sentences, heading and subheadings
- Organizing the middle: strategic paragraphing
- Sequencing for readability and emphasis

Session 3

Developing a Positive Tone in the Letter or Memo

- The "you" attitude
- Building in empathy
- Saying "no" tactfully

Session 4

1. Keys to Readability

    ■ Assessing readability
    ■ Reducing sentence length
    ■ Reducing wordiness

2. Summary, evaluation

In planning the specific schedule, I considered the following principles:

■ The timing and duration of a writing program are critical to its success.

■ The intensity of instruction over a short period of time (two to three months) seems to work best.

■ Sessions should be spaced just far enough apart to allow for practice, review, and critiquing by the instructor, but not so far apart as to destroy group climate and program continuity.

Thus, Warman personnel and I scheduled sessions to run for three hours a day every two weeks. We agreed that the group size and program objectives would require four group sessions. Following the second and fourth sessions would be a unique feature: time for one-on-one consultation with the instructor. These 30-minute sessions were designed to help the trainee receive straightforward, objective feedback from the trainer on writing strengths and areas needing improvement.

Climate Setting

Creating a positive learning climate was critical to the success of the program. To remove anxiety, fear of criticism, and defensiveness, I used the following approach:

■ Introduced myself and my role in a personal way and asked for their help in understanding the slurry pump industry in exchange for my help in improving their writing abilities.

■ Created the understanding that the goal of the program was to help them improve their writing by small degrees, not to perfect their abilities.

- Indicated that except for grammar, punctuation, and spelling conventions, no clear, concrete rules for effective writing exist. Our objective was to discuss and learn what will work for Warman.

- Pointed out that open, honest discussion is essential to program success.

- Memorized participants' names during their self-introductions and used first names throughout the program.

- Informed participants that my criticism of their writing would be balanced—strengths as well as areas needing improvement would be noted.

- Assured them that my comments on their writing should not be interpreted as evaluations of their total beings, but only of their current skill level in writing.

Methods

In order to make the session interesting as well as effective, we used the following methods:

- Analysis of samples of letters and memos by small teams (three to four members) for strengths and weaknesses.

- Small group identification of "must-know" factors of our audiences.

- Individual and small group work on the revising of samples, building in the "you" attitude, and creating sensitivity to reader needs.

- Listening teams, reporting on key information communicated in the film *Writing Letters That Get Results*.

- Reviewing examples of positive models (memos and sales letters) through passouts and overhead transparencies.

- Sharing and critiquing participants' original drafts and revisions.

- Reviewing overhead transparencies made of participants' revised work, followed by a group discussion of their strengths.

- Individual work on revisions for conciseness and clarity.

- Using hypothetical case studies, such as The Case of the Fledgling District Supervisor (see Figure 20-1).

The Case of the Fledging District Supervisor

You are the General Accounting Supervisor of Flexnor Corporation, responsible for the work of six district supervisors. Four field accountants report to your newest supervisor, Jack Adams.

Recently, several complaints from the field have landed on your desk. Customers are dissatisfied with the services of the four accountants in the Southeastern District, Jack Adams's territory. Inaccuracies, delays in getting the jobs finished, and, above all, rudeness, comprise the complaints.

In addition, each complaint mentioned previous unsuccessful contacts with Jack Adams about these problems. You have heard nothing from Jack about these difficulties. In fact, you have had little face-to-face contact with him during the first six months on the job because of the 2,000 miles separating you. You do have a performance appraisal scheduled with him, but you feel that this problem cannot wait until that date, which is three months away. Unfortunately, you cannot meet with him now and have decided that telephoning him would be inappropriate.

During the next 45 minutes:

1. Write a memo to Jack Adams, seeking to:

_____

_____

2. Prepare a letter directed to the distinguished customers for the purpose of:

_____

_____

_____

Figure 20-1.
A case study used in the writing program at Warman International

Consultation Sessions

A one-on-one consultation day was interspersed between Sessions 2 and 3 and also followed Session 4. During these days, I met with each participant to answer any questions and to provide feedback on his writing. Balanced criticism and honest, objective evaluation marked the sessions.

Evaluating the Program

The best measure of the success or failure of a writing program is the degree of change in the participants' writing. For Warman, I conducted three types of postprogram assessments:

- I compared participant samples written *before* the program with those written *following* the instruction, using a checklist as a basis of evaluation (see Figure 20-2).
- Participants analyzed their before and after samples for improvements and reported their judgments to me.
- Participants' superiors did the same.

All assessments indicated that the level of writing skills was improved significantly because of this program.

Introduction

1. Does the letter or memo contain a subject line?   _____ Yes   _____ No
2. Does it *clearly* indicate the work's subject matter?   _____ Yes   _____ No
3. Does the introduction convey clearly the work's purpose?   _____ Yes   _____ No
4. Does it clearly forecast the content *and* organization of the body of the letter or memo?   _____ Yes   _____ No
5. Does it convey the "you" attitude?   _____ Yes   _____ No
6. Does it convey enough background information or context?   _____ Yes   _____ No

---

Figure 20-2. *Writing assessment checklist, Warman International*

Body

7. Does the overall design move from the general to the particular? _____ Yes _____ No

8. Are headings, subheadings, numbers, or bullets used effectively to divide the body? _____ Yes _____ No

9. Do the individual sections and paragraphs fit the purpose and organization forecasted by the introduction? _____ Yes _____ No

10. Is enough information included in each section, subsection, and paragraph? _____ Yes _____ No

11. Do the paragraphs' opening sentences clearly organize and forecast their contents? _____ Yes _____ No

12. Are clear transitional markers present between paragraphs? _____ Yes _____ No

13. Do the paragraphs contain extraneous information? _____ Yes _____ No

14. Are the paragraphs kept short for readability? _____ Yes _____ No

Closing

15. Does the letter or memo contain a closing paragraph? _____ Yes _____ No

16. Does it indicate clearly what the reader should do, say, or think as a result of the letter or memo? _____ Yes _____ No

17. Does it relate directly to the purpose of the work? _____ Yes _____ No

Language and Tone

18. Does the work convey a positive, courteous, friendly, but professional tone? _____ Yes _____ No

19. Is the language level appropriate to the audience and purpose? _____ Yes _____ No

20. Are simple, familiar words used? _____ Yes _____ No

21. Do any words require definition? _____ Yes _____ No

22. Does the letter or memo convey a negative message about the author and organization? _____ Yes _____ No

Figure 20-2. *Cont'd*

Sentences

23. Are the sentences concise?   _____ Yes   _____ No
24. Do they clearly communicate their meaning?   _____ Yes   _____ No
25. Are they arranged in a coherent, logical order?   _____ Yes   _____ No
26. Do they vary in length?   _____ Yes   _____ No
27. Are their ideas properly subordinated?   _____ Yes   _____ No

Mechanics

28. Does the memo or letter contain distraction-free mechanics?

  • Grammar   _____ Yes   _____ No
  • Spelling   _____ Yes   _____ No
  • Punctuation   _____ Yes   _____ No

Overall Assessment:

_____

Figure 20-2. *Cont'd*

21

A COMPREHENSIVE IN-HOUSE PROGRAM

St. Joseph's Hospital in Milwaukee implemented a well-planned and comprehensive training and development program for supervisors and those recommended for supervision. It began with Prevision, a program that provides an introduction to management for nonsupervisory employees who had been approved for the course by their boss. For those who were already supervisors, a Management Institute of numerous courses was developed. Finally, as refresher courses, one-hour classes were offered on various hospital and supervisory subjects.

St. Joseph's Hospital, Milwaukee, Wisconsin

A coordinated training and development program was implemented at St. Joseph's Hospital to fill the needs of staff at all levels of the organization. According to the hospital's manager of Human Resources Development, George J. Koleas, the following beliefs and practices met our organization philosophy of Human Community Development:

Human: Respecting the sacredness of life and the dignity and worth of every person.

Community: Creating caring communities in which the needs of those serving and of those being served are being met.

Development: Providing opportunities for personal and professional growth.

Mission Statement for the Department of Human Resources Development

To assure that there are educational opportunities internally and externally for the personal as well as professional growth and development of staff to assist them in the continuous improvement in the quality of patient care.

This mission statement is supported through a variety of training initiatives including the following:

- *Prevision*—An introduction to management. It contains basic concepts of management for nonsupervisory personnel who aspire to become supervisors.

- *Management Institute*—Provides ongoing educational opportunities for supervisors, managers, and other individuals with high potential. The objective of these programs is to provide insights into the science and art of management.

- *The Continuing Education Program*—Contains a wide variety of courses available to all employees to upgrade skills and advance their knowledge.

- *Ad Hoc Training*—Designed and provided to meet specific needs identified by supervisors and managers in collaboration with the human resources development staff.

Prevision: Introduction to Management

Following are details on course titles and teaching staff:

- All classes are held on Mondays for five consecutive weeks.
- All classes will be held from 12:00 – 1:00 p.m. in Room M105.
- Class limit is 25.
- Must have managerial/supervisory approval to be registered for the program.
- Must attend all five classes and pass a computer simulation which is due within three (3) weeks of completion of session.
- Functions as a prerequisite to the Management Institute.

Class Title	Instructor
Management Overview	Mary Poehls, human resources generalist/training specialist
Planning, Organizing, and Staffing	Nancy Christensen, human resources generalist
Leadership and Motivation	Jeff Mehring, supervisor, safety/security
Communication	Katie Graceffa, human resources generalist
Controlling and Decision Making	Mary Poehls, human resources Generalist/training specialist

The Management Institute

I. Orientation

   A. Mission

   B. Upgrade current management skills

   C. Mentor employees to fill management/supervisory roles

   D. Facilitate communication and understanding of roles between management and staff levels

II. Requirements to Enter Program

   A. Completion of prevision or waiver

   B. Permission and signature of current manager or supervisor

   C. Hired as a manager/supervisor with previously related education and/or experience

   D. Must attend mandatory orientation offered in June/January and Module 1, the Principles of Management, before being allowed to enroll in future modules

III. The Management Institute Program

   A. Scheduled by fiscal year – July/June

   B. Twenty-two classes offered

   C. Approximately one and a half years to complete

   D. Eight National Continuing Education Credits

   E. Certificate in Management

   F. Must complete 15 classes

      1. Thirteen required – noted by number only

      2. Five electives – noted by number and letters

   G. All classes held in Room M105

IV. Module Design

   A. Typically, three to four hours of classroom training and a one-hour presentation worth .4 or .5 continuing education units (CEU)

   B. Integrate theory to application on the job

   C. Class size 12 to 15 participants; limit 25

   D. Contents of courses

      1. Lecture

      2. Learning activities/discussions

      3. Action plans/assignments/tests

   E. Requirements to pass a module

      1. Attend all classes

         a. Automatically dropped if you miss first class

         b. If unable to attend a class, contact instructor either prior to the start of the class or within two days after the class

      2. Complete required assignments

Following are the course offerings in the Management Institute.

Course	CEUs Accredited	Instructor
Mandatory Orientation		Mary Poehls, training specialist
Introduction to the Principles of Management	.4	George Koleas, manager of training and human resources development
Organizing and Delegating	.4	George Koleas, manager of human resources development
Time Management	.4	Mary Moat, director of nursing/medicine
Managing Employees with Special Problems	.5	Tom Vanden Heuvel, manager of employee assistance programs
Management Planning, Monitoring, and Evaluation	.5	Marjorie Wilbur, director of planning WFSI-Milwaukee, and Kathleen Murray, business development manager
Selecting New Employees	.4	Sherri DuCharme, human resources generalist
Improving Your Listening Skills	.4	Marge Roth, supervisor of infection control
Managerial Communication Presentation Skills	.4	Mary Poehls, training specialist
Managing Financial Services	.5	Susan Pitta, controller
Decision Making: Problem Solving and Problem-Solving Tools	.5	George Koleas, manager of human resources development

Course	CEUs Accredited	Instructor
The Future of Management: Participation and Team Building	.4	Mary Poehls, training specialist
The Human Resources Legal Environment in Health Care	.4	Bob Weiss, vice-president of human resources
Statistics	.5	Brian Kay, budget manager
Managing Conflict	.4	George Koleas, manager of human resources development
Establishing a Climate for Motivation	.4	Bob Weiss, vice-president of human resources
Managing Stress	.4	Mary Poehls, training specialist
Coaching, Counseling, and Appraising Employee Performance	.5	George Koleas, manager of human resources development
Managing Change	.4	George Koleas, manager of human resources development
Managerial Communication: Writing Skills	.4	Rick Romano, director of public affairs
Discipline and Appeal Handling	.5	George Koleas, manager of human resources development
Using St. Joseph's Data for Decision Making	.4	Gene Markiewicz, director systems and data processing
Managing in a Multicultural Environment	.4	George Koleas, manager of human resources development

The Continuing Education Program

- All Continuing Education course offerings are one hour and are held on Thursdays, with the exception of the Self-Paced Skill Development sessions, which are scheduled on Mondays, Tuesdays, and Thursdays from 1:30 – 2:30 p.m. or 3:30 – 4:30 p.m.
- Must have manager/supervisory approval for each class registered.
- Class limit is 25.

Course	Instructor(s)
Self-Paced Skill Development: Practical Reading and Writing	Community and hospital employee volunteers
Change	George Koleas, manager of human resources development
Icebreakers: Gaining Your Audience's Attention	Mary Poehls, training specialist
Stress Management	Mary Poehls, training specialist
Personal and Career Development	George Koleas, manager of human resources development
Marketing Yourself: In Writing and in Person	Mary Poehls, training specialist
Franklin Time Management[1]	George Koleas, manager of human resources development
Coaching and Counseling	George Koleas, manager of human resources development
Guest Relations: Dealing with Difficult People	Don Green, director of safety and security
Franklin Time Management User Group[2]	George Koleas, manager of human resources development

[1]Requires five or more students enrolled—$90.00 materials cost. You must register six weeks prior to the course in order to receive Franklin Planner. Alternative dates may be scheduled.

[2]Must have completed Franklin Time Management Group.

Guest Relations: Telephone Courtesy and First Impressions Coordinator	Cathie Callen, media/guest relations
Developing Positive Assertiveness	Mary Poehls, training specialist
Developing Self-Esteem	Mary Poehls, training specialist
Deming's 14 Points	George Koleas, manager of human resources development
Team Development	George Koleas, manager of human resources development
Team Development Workshop[3]	George Koleas, manager of human resources development
Business Writing	Public affairs staff
Special Event Planning	Public affairs staff
Two-Way Communications	Mary Poehls, training specialist
Active Listening	George Koleas, manager of human resources development
PC Hardware and Disk Operating System	Joe Orlando, DP Electronics Tech, and Pam Bruening, decision support specialist
Microcomputer Applications	Pam Bruening, decision support specialist
St. Joseph's Computer Systems	Larry Noldan, software systems supervisor, and Joan Kurszewski, supervisor systems development
Constructive Criticism	George Koleas, manager of human resources development
Balancing Work and Family	Jeanne Faupl, sick bay coordinator
Constructive Feedback	George Koleas, manager of human resources development
Holding Effective Meetings	Mary Poehls, training specialist
Time Management	Mary Poehls, training specialist

---

[3]Must have completed Team Development course.

To ensure that needs are being met, we conduct an annual Employee Climate Survey and periodic needs assessments. The purpose of these surveys is to ensure that programs are being provided that fulfill the organizational philosophy as well as the mission of the human resources department.

SELECTED REFERENCES (BIBLIOGRAPHY)

ORGANIZATIONS OFFERING RESOURCE MATERIALS

American Society for Training and Development, 1640 King St., Alexandria, VA 22313. *The Books Catalog*, December 1999, provides a description of the many resources that ASTD offers. This includes software as well as toolkits and books.

The Center for Effective Performance, 2300 Peachford Rd., Suite 2000, Atlanta, GA 30338. All of Robert Mager's books, workshops, and other resources are described in their catalog.

HRDQ, Inc., 2002 Renaissance Blvd. #100, King of Prussia, PA 19406. This organization publishes an extensive number of products, including assessments, games, books, and other resources.

TALICO, Inc., 4375-4 Southside Blvd., Suite 157, Jacksonville, FL 32216. Their pamphlet, Training Ideas for the Third Millennium, describes: Team-Building Exercises; Assessment and Survey Instruments; Training Activities; Packaged Training Programs on Management and Leadership Development; and Training Videos.

Books

Berry, Donna, Charles Cadwell, and Joe Fehman. *Coaching for Results.* Amherst, PA: HRD Press, 1996.

Craig, Robert L., ed. *Training and Development Handbook, 4th ed.* New York: McGraw-Hill, 1996. This book includes chapters by leaders in all areas of training and development.

Crane, Thomas. *The Heart of Coaching.* San Diego: FTA Press, 1998.

Doyle, James S. *The Business Coach.* New York: John Wiley & Sons, 1999.

Fisk, Catherine N., *Evaluation Instruments.* Alexandria, VA: American Society for Training and Development, 1991. This tool kit contains several articles and instruments used by various organizations to evaluate their training programs.

Humphrey, Brad, and Jeff Stokes. *The 21st Century Supervisor.* San Francisco: Jossey-Bass, 2000. This book describes nine essential skills for frontline supervisors and is accompanied by a Facilitator's Guide and a Participant's Workbook.

Kirkpatrick, Donald L., ed. *Another Look at Evaluating Training Programs.* Alexandria, VA: American Society for Training and Development, 1998. Contains all the articles on evaluation that appeared in the *Training and Development Journal* from 1987 to 1998. Many of the articles dealt with technical training.

Kirkpatrick, Donald L., ed. *Evaluating Training Programs.* Alexandria, VA: American Society for Training and Development, 1975. Contains all the articles on evaluation that appeared in *Training and Development Journal* from 1965 to 1975.

Kirkpatrick, Donald L. *Evaluating Training Programs: The Four Levels, 2nd ed.* San Francisco: Berrett-Koehler, 1998. This book has become the "standard" in the field of evaluation. It is used throughout the world as a model for evaluating training programs by such organizations as Motorola and Intel. It provides guidelines, forms, examples, and 15 case studies describing how organizations applied the four levels. Their forms and procedures can be adapted to other organizations.

Kirkpatrick, Donald L. *How to Improve Performance Through Appraisal and Coaching.* New York: AMACOM, 1983. The contents of this practical book are included in Chapter 10 of this book.

Kirkpatrick, Donald L. *Management Inventory on Performance Appraisal and Coaching.* Elm Grove, Wis.: 1987. This inventory was developed as a tool to use in a training program. A complementary review set (test, answer booklet, and instructor manual) will be sent on request of Dr. Jim Kirkpatrick, 3137 Citadel, Indianapolis, IN 46268.

Kirkpatrick, Donald L., ed. *More Evaluating Training Programs*. Alexandria, VA: American Society for Training and Development, 1987. Contains all the articles on evaluation that appeared in *Training and Development Journal* from 1976 to 1986. "Judging From the Feds" by Ruth Salinger is of special interest; it describes a number of evaluation studies conducted by federal agencies.

Kirkpatrick, James. *Supervisory/Management Inventories*. 3137 Citadel, Indianapolis, IN 46268.

Mitchell, Gary. *The Trainer's Handbook: The AMA Guide to Effective Training, 3rd ed*. New York: AMACOM, 1998. A brush-up guide for experienced trainers and a look-up reference for novices.

Peters, Tom, and Nancy Austin. *Passion for Excellence*. New York: Random House, 1985.

Phillips, Jack J. *Handbook of Training Evaluation and Measurement Methods, 3rd ed*. Houston, TX: Gulf Publishing, 1997, Chapter 14, pp. 237-254.

Phillips, Jack J. *Return on Investment in Training and Performance Improvement Programs*. Houston, TX: Gulf Publishing, 1997. This book guides you through a proven, results-based approach to calculating the return on investment. It provides user-friendly ROI calculations, post-program data collection methods, strategies for determining the amount of improvement that is directly linked to training programs, techniques for converting both hard and soft data to monetary values, and more.

Phillips, Jack J., Patricia Pulliam Phillips, and Ron D. Stone. *The Human Resources Scorecard: Measuring the Return on Investment*. Houston, Tex.: Gulf Publishing, 2000.

Shula, Don, and Ken Blanchard. *Everyone's a Coach*. Grand Rapids, MI: Zondervan Publishing House, 1995.

Tracey, William R., ed. *Human Resources Management and Development Handbook, 2nd ed*. New York: AMACOM, 1994. Many different authors have provided principles and techniques. Of particular interest will be the section relating to supervisory training and development.

INDEX